Loyalists & Malcontents

Loyalists & Malcontents

Freemasonry & Revolution in South Carolina and Georgia

Ric Berman

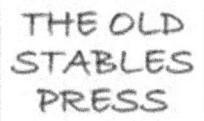

• Oxfordshire •

Copyright © 2015, 2017, Ric Berman
The right of Richard Berman to be identified as the author of this work has been asserted in accordance with the Copyright, Designs and Patents Act, 1988.

First published in 2015; reprinted in a revised second edition 2017.
The Old Stables Press, Goring Heath, Oxfordshire RG8 7RT
theoldstablespress@gmail.com

All rights reserved. Except for the quotation of short passages for the purposes of criticism and review, no part of this publication may be reproduced, stored in a retrieval system, or transmitted in any form or by any means without the prior permission of the author.

Unless stated otherwise, images and illustrations are copyright © UGLE Library & Museum of Freemasonry and used with their kind permission.

British Library Cataloguing in Publication Data
A CIP catalogue record for this book is available from the British Library

Library of Congress Cataloguing-in-Publication Data
Berman, Ric
Loyalists & Malcontents: Freemasonry & Revolution in South Carolina and Georgia/Ric Berman
p. cm.
Includes biographical references.

ISBN: 0995756821
ISBN 13: 9780995756823 (The Old Stables Press)

1.   Freemasonry - America – History – 18th century.
2.   Freemasonry – Great Britain and Ireland– History – 18th century.
I. Title

In Memory of Michael Fitch
1931-1999

Other titles by Ric Berman

*The Foundations of Modern Freemasonry –
The Grand Architects: Political Change and the
Scientific Enlightenment, 1714-1740*

Schism: the Battle that Forged Freemasonry

*Foundations - new light on the formation and early years of
The Grand Lodge of England*

*Espionage, Diplomacy & the Lodge -
Charles Delafaye and The Secret Department of the Post Office*

*From Roanoke to Raleigh:
Freemasonry in North Carolina, 1730-1800*
- To be published in 2018 -

Contents

Acknowledgments · x
Abbreviations · xi
Introduction · 1
Chapter One · 11
   John Hammerton – the first Provincial Grand Master of South Carolina · · · 11
Chapter Two · 32
   Craft Connections · 32
Chapter Three · 55
   'Calling On' – Peter Leigh · 55
Chapter Four · 68
   'Calling Off' · 68
Chapter Five · 77
   A Merchant Prince · 77
Chapter Six · 108
   The Georgia Project · 108
Chapter Seven · 132
   A Schism in Georgia · 132
Chapter Eight · 157
   Slavery in the Colonial South and Prince Hall Freemasonry · · · · · · · · · 157
Reflections · 190
Appendices · 193
Appendix One · 194
   The Colonization and Commerce of South Carolina · · · · · · · · · · · · · 194
Appendix Two · 222
   Moderns and Antients – An Irish Legacy · · · · · · · · · · · · · · · · · · 222
Appendix Three · 251
   Selected Lodge Membership Data · 251
Appendix Four · 253
   Georgia's Grand Officers (1780), Antients and Moderns · · · · · · · · · · 253
Selected Bibliography · 255
   Manuscripts · 255
   Other Selected Primary Sources · 257
   Selected Secondary Sources · 260
   Journal Articles · 263

Acknowledgments

This second edition of *Loyalists & Malcontents* is a revised and re-edited version of that published in 2015. Although many of South Carolina and Georgia's masonic records were destroyed or lost in the eighteenth and nineteenth centuries, correspondence and other records held in Britain remain intact and these form part of the foundations for this work.

I would like to express my thanks to the Department of History, Philosophy and Religion at Oxford Brookes University; the British Library, London; the Bodleian Libraries at the University of Oxford; the University Library at the University of Cambridge; and the Library and Museum of Freemasonry at the United Grand Lodge of England, Great Queen Street, London. Thank you for your assistance.

I am grateful to those who gave their time to read and comment on drafts of the first edition of this work and to others who have added insights. Any idiosyncrasies and all errors are entirely my own.

Dates are given in the Gregorian calendar which was adopted by Britain and its then American colonies in 1752.

Richard Berman
Oxfordshire
December, 2017

Abbreviations

1723 *Constitutions*	James Anderson, *The Constitutions of the Freemasons* (London: John Senex & John Hooke, 1723).
1738 *Constitutions*	James Anderson, *The New Book of Constitutions of the Antient and Honourable Fraternity of Free and Accepted Masons* (London: Cæsar Ward and Richard Chandler, 1738)
AQC	*Ars Quatuor Coronatorum*, the *Transactions* of Quatuor Coronati Lodge, No. 2076, London
BL	British Library
Burney	Burney Collection of 17th and 18th century newspapers at the British Library
CUL	Cambridge University Library
CUP	Cambridge University Press
Foundations	Ric Berman, *The Foundations of Modern Freemasonry. The Grand Architects: Political Change and the Scientific Enlightenment, 1714–1740* (Brighton: Sussex Academic Press, 2012 & 2014)
Fn./fn.	footnote
Fo./fo.	folio
FRS	Fellow of the Royal Society
GM/DGM	Grand Master/Deputy Grand Master
Grand Lodge *Minutes I*	*The Minutes of the Grand Lodge of Freemasons of England, 1723-1739*, QCA (London, 1913), Volume X
Grand Lodge *Minutes II*	*The Minutes of the Grand Lodge of Freemasons of England, 1740-1758*, QCA (London, 1960), Volume XII

	In each case page references are to *AQC Masonic Reprints*, volumes *X* and *XII*, published in 1913 and 1960, respectively
HSP	Historical Society of Pennsylvania
HMSO	His/Her Majesty's Stationery Office
IHR	Institute of Historical Research
Lane's *Masonic Records*	John Lane, *Masonic Records, 1717–1894*, version 1.0 www.hrionline.ac.uk/lane
LL	*London Lives 1690-1800*: www.londonlives.org
LMA	London Metropolitan Archives
Loyalists & Malcontents	Ric Berman, *Loyalists & Malcontents: Freemasonry and Revolution in the Deep South* (Goring Heath: The Old Stables Press, 2015).
MP	Member of Parliament
MS[S]	Manuscript[s]
NA	National Archives
n.s.	new series
ODNB	*Oxford Dictionary of National Biography* (Oxford: OUP, 2004) online edition October 2009, unless stated otherwise
o.s.	old series
OUP	Oxford University Press
PC	Privy Councillor
PGM	Provincial Grand Master
QC	Quatuor Coronati Lodge, No. 2076, London
QCA	*Quatuor Coronatorum Antigrapha*
Schism	Ric Berman, *Schism: The Battle that Forged Freemasonry* (Brighton: Sussex Academic Press, 2013)
SP	State Papers
UGLE	United Grand Lodge of England

UNC	University of North Carolina
USC	University of South Carolina
YUP	Yale University Press

1723 Constitutions: Cover Plate
Engraved by John Pine

Introduction

When Harland-Jacobs commented on freemasonry's role in cementing Britain's global empire in the nineteenth century she described it as a social, cultural and political matrix that bound the old world to the new.[1] For Harland-Jacobs, freemasonry was part of an international structure that played a pivotal role in building, consolidating and perpetuating Britain's Empire, providing an 'ideological network, a set of emotional and mental connections that fostered ... an *imperialist identity* among its members'. Her viewpoint has been criticised as too generalised but whether or not that is correct, her work provides a valuable insight into Britain's empire building, most clearly in the case of Imperial India. But in an eighteenth-century context and with respect to Britain's American colonies, Harland-Jacobs' analysis may be less useful. Indeed, this book argues that freemasonry's influence on colonial America was more nuanced and - from Britain's standpoint - arguably detrimental.

English freemasonry had been re-moulded in the second and third decades of the eighteenth century into a pro-Hanoverian organisation, and under the self-interested auspices of the Grand Lodge of London and Westminster, later the Grand Lodge of England, it emerged as one of the most vibrant and influential of England's many fraternal societies. The new grand lodge was fronted by malleable young aristocrats who provided freemasonry with celebrity appeal, financial resources and political security. The last was an essential feature given the continuing Jacobite threat and the government's fear of secret societies. A procession of noble grand masters and the initiation of 'men of quality' and 'persons of distinction' garnered positive press coverage which created a widespread interest in freemasonry and gave the press a hook on which to hang their reporting of masonic events.

---

[1] Jessica Harland-Jacobs, 'Hands Across the Sea: The Masonic Network, British Imperialism, and the North Atlantic World', *Geographical Review* (89.2), 1999, 237-53; and Harland-Jacobs *Builders of Empire: Freemasonry and British Imperialism, 1717-1927* (Chapel Hill, NC: UNC Press, 2007).

Freemasonry's actual leadership was at the level of the deputy grand master and grand officers, and the masters and senior members of an elite group of masonic lodges in London, the Horn Tavern, Rummer, Bedford Head, Bear & Harrow and King's Arms among them. The members of this inner circle included parliamentarians, professional men, senior crown servants and military officers, and clubbable intellectuals, a mixture that gave freemasonry a compelling imprimatur and the frisson of an elite club.

By the late 1720s, freemasonry commanded Britain and Ireland's social heights, allying fraternal dining and drinking with 'ancient' masonic ritual. Enlightenment concepts were also promoted, including religious toleration and constitutional rather than absolutist government, and property rights and the rule of law, the latter championed by a raft of senior members, many of whom were government-appointed magistrates on the Middlesex and Westminster benches. Its values, establishment credibility and promotion of Newtonian natural science and education underpinned its evolution to a national and then international organisation.

English freemasonry was essentially pro-Hanoverian, a political stance whose roots were embedded in the profound religious and political insecurities that had preceded and followed the accession of George I in 1714. The Glorious Revolution of 1688 had swept William and Mary to the throne and secured Queen Anne as their successor, but it failed to void the threat posed by James Francis Edward Stuart - 'the king over the water' – the 'Pretender', whose claim to rule as James III of England and James VIII of Scotland was considered by many to be valid.

James's political allies and constitutional apologists were not limited to Catholic France, Spain and the Papal States. Many in England and Scotland, Protestant and Catholic, held the Hanoverian succession to be illegitimate. Indeed, even after the 1715 Jacobite rising had been crushed and attempts at invasion thwarted in 1717, 1719 and again in 1721, the Stuarts' claims were pushed forward in the 1730s and 1740s, not least by Charles Stuart, James's charismatic son. The danger posed to Whig political supremacy and the survival of the Hanoverian line, both genuine and imagined, did not dissipate until the Jacobite threat was dismembered after the 1745 uprising. Until then, European and British support for the Stuarts remained a political undercurrent. The issue was a thread in an ongoing battle for religious and political supremacy in Europe that dated from the mid-sixteenth century, a conflict voiced in more than a century of genocidal persecution by Catholic France of its Protestant Huguenots from the St Bartholomew's Day massacre in 1572 through to the 1680s and Louis XIV's Dragonnades[2] and revocation of Henry IV, his grandfather's Edict of Nantes.[3] It was a chain of events that fashioned the mould in which English freemasonry's leaders were cast.

John, 2nd Duke of Montagu, freemasonry's first noble grand master, the son-in-law of the iconic Duke of Marlborough and one of the wealthiest men in Britain, and Charles, 2nd Duke of Richmond & Lennox, whose lodge at the Horn Tavern was central to the creation of the new grand lodge, were avid supporters of the Hanoverian line.[4] Thomas Holles, Duke of Newcastle,[5] Sir Robert Walpole's[6] parliamentary manager, described Richmond as 'the most solid support of the Whig interest in Chichester', and Richmond himself noted that he had been 'bred up from a child in the Whig principles'.[7]

---

[2] Louis XIV's intimidatory policy of billeting French dragoons on Huguenot households with implicit authority to abuse the family and steal or destroy their possessions. Introduced in 1681/2, it was another means of forcing Protestant Huguenots to convert to Catholicism.

[3] Henry IV's Edict of Nantes in 1598 had granted French Huguenots limited religious freedoms. Louis XIV's revocation of the edict in 1685 was accompanied by the destruction of Protestant churches and ramped up Huguenot persecution.

[4] Cf. *Foundations of Modern Freemasonry*, esp. chapters two and five.

[5] Thomas Pelham-Holles ((1693-1768), 1st Duke of Newcastle, secretary of state at the Southern Department with responsibility for the American colonies from 1724-48.

[6] Robert Walpole (1676-1745), 1st Earl of Orford, known before 1742 as Sir Robert Walpole, the de facto first prime minister of Britain.

[7] BL, Add. MS 32700, fol. 264.

John, 2nd Duke of Montagu (1690-1749)
Sir Godfrey Kneller, 1723

Loyalists & Malcontents

Charles Lennox, 2nd Duke of Richmond and Lennox (1701-1750)
Jonathan Richardson the Elder, *c.*1725

Members of Richmond's Horn Tavern lodge included a raft of prominent figures among whom were Charles Delafaye, a senior under-secretary of state and the government's anti-Jacobite spymaster; William Cowper, the Clerk to the Parliaments, the highest-ranked administrator at the House of Commons and House of Lords; and the Rev. Dr John Theophilus Desaguliers, a Huguenot émigré, FRS and Newtonian scientist, one of the most influential figures at the new grand lodge and the principal author of its new *Regulations* and *Charges*.[8]

By the late 1730s freemasonry had grown to become the largest of England's many fraternal societies. Its reputation was such that it was emulated elsewhere, and not only in the home nations. In addition to Ireland, Wales and Scotland, lodges and grand lodges were established in France and the Low Countries, and freemasonry gained a presence in Austria, the German states and Russia; in Italy, Spain, Portugal and Sweden; and above all in Britain's North American colonies.

But in England circumstances were changing. As English freemasonry's original grand officers aged and died, administrative control passed into other hands. The resulting changes led to grand lodge becoming disconnected from its membership in the 1740s and within three decades of Montagu installation as its first noble figurehead, the Grand Lodge of England stumbled into bureaucracy and incompetence. Disaffection grew so great that by the end of the 1740s between a fifth and a quarter of London's lodges had been erased from the grand register following their failure to contribute to the grand charity and attend the quarterly communications.[9] Others seceded by choice.

Lacking effective leadership and characterised by condescension towards those in society's lower ranks, especially the Irish, English freemasonry became factionalised and in the 1750s a rival grand lodge emerged: 'the Grand

---

[8] *Foundations of Modern Freemasonry*, esp. pp. 38-63.
[9] Some estimates are higher. Cf. *Schism*, esp. pp. 118-32.

Lodge of England according to the Old Institutions'.[10] Formed in 1751, the Antients Grand Lodge was shaped and led by the expatriate London Irish. Within a decade it began to transform freemasonry, cleverly and derogatively describing the original Grand Lodge of England as 'Moderns', a term that drew attention to the changes that had been introduced to masonic ritual in the 1720s and 1730s.[11] The tag awarded the more recently constituted Antients with greater masonic legitimacy and positioned it as a promoter and defender of masonic tradition.[12]

The grand lodges of Ireland and Scotland compounded England's masonic schism, allying themselves to the Antients in successive mutual alliances which recognised the Antients as the only legitimate representative of English freemasonry.

Ireland moved first. The Earl of Blessington, a former grand master of Ireland, bestowed his patronage in 1756, becoming the Antients' first noble grand master, and two years later the Grand Lodge of Ireland followed suit, ceasing fraternal correspondence with the Moderns.

Scotland split with the Moderns a decade later. The grand master of the Grand Lodge of England in 1762, Lord Aberdour, had been a past grand master of Scotland, continuing an association that had linked London to Edinburgh since 1736. The following year the relationship ended. From 1763-65, Thomas Erskine, 6th Earl of Kellie, was grand master of the Grand Lodge of Scotland and simultaneously grand master of the Antients Grand Lodge. His successors maintained the same connection, not least when the wealthy and influential 3rd and 4th Dukes of Atholl, were grand masters of Scotland in 1773-74 and 1778-80 respectively, and grand masters of the Antients Grand Lodge in 1771-74 and 1775-81, and 1791-1813.

---

[10] Later warrants gave the organization the title of 'The Grand Lodge of the Most Ancient and Honourable Fraternity of Free and Accepted Masons (according to the Old Constitutions granted by His Royal Highness Prince Edwin, at York...'

[11] Berman, Schism, pp. 15-7.

[12] Ibid., esp. chapter one.

Scotland's break with the Moderns was solemnised under the 3rd duke in in 1773 when the Grand Lodge of Scotland entered into tri-partite pact with the Antients and Irish grand lodges. His prestige was such that the Antients' lodges later became known colloquially as Atholl lodges.

Ireland and Scotland's support underwrote the growth of Antients freemasonry both in Britain and overseas, especially in America, a process that began in the mid-1750s when Pennsylvania's lodge No. 4 petitioned the Antients to request a charter. The Antients' grand master's lodge, Lodge No. 1, accepted the petition and issued a warrant for 'the Brethren at Philadelphia', creating the Antients' first provincial grand lodge in America.[13]

In the second half of the eighteenth century the dispute between London's rival grand lodges became loudly adversarial. The animosity was expressed by the Moderns' grand secretary, Samuel Spencer, in *A Defence of Freemasonry*.[14] The pamphlet ratcheted up the rhetoric and led to a retaliation in kind from the Antients grand secretary, Laurence Dermott's cleverly-worded 2nd and 3rd editions of *Ahiman Rezon*, the constitutional basis of Antients freemasonry on both sides of the Atlantic. The battle was also fought in the press, where Dermott ensured that it was known widely that 'Modern Masons are acting entirely inconsistently with the antient customs and principles of the craft'.[15]

The schism between Moderns and Antients undermines the idea that freemasonry can be treated as a single integrated entity in the second half of the eighteenth century. The opposite was the case. And in America the schism between the factions was bound up with other divisions, including

---

[13] Cf., Berman, 'The London Irish and Antients Grand Lodge', *Eighteenth Century Life*, 39.1 (2015), 103-30, esp. 127. Dashwood, *Early Records*, has suggested that the warrant was held back until it could be signed by a member of the nobility (*QCA* 11: ix).

[14] Anonymous [Samuel Spencer], *A Defence of Freemasonry* (London: published privately, 1765).

[15] *Middlesex Journal or Chronicle of Liberty*, 9-11 April 1772.

loyalty to Britain versus American patriotism, and social exclusivity versus inclusivity.

Given the number of books written about American freemasonry, an obvious question would be 'why this book'. One answer is that research has in the past focused mainly on America's northern colonies, in particular, Pennsylvania, Massachusetts and New York. *Loyalists & Malcontents* centres on what has been under-researched and perhaps misunderstood: the genesis of freemasonry in South Carolina and Georgia. It offers a new perspective on the growing division between Britain and America and on the issues that fractured eighteenth-century freemasonry. *Loyalists & Malcontents* tells the story of freemasonry in the Deep South from the 1730s through to Independence, and includes essays on the colonization of South Carolina and Southern slavery, the latter the key to the wealth that sustained the South's masonic lodges and Southern Society more broadly. Indeed, it was the legalisation of slavery in Georgia that transformed the lodge at Savannah from a mere 'tippling society' into an expression of affluence and prestige on a par with Charleston's elite lodges.

John Pine's *Engraved List of Lodges*
London, 1725

CHAPTER ONE

JOHN HAMMERTON – THE FIRST PROVINCIAL GRAND MASTER OF SOUTH CAROLINA

The deputation[1] from the Grand Lodge of England that chartered Solomon's Lodge was brought to Charleston in 1736 by John Hammerton (d.1762).[2] The lodge had already been working for at least a year since its establishment in conjunction with Boston freemasons, possibly under a warrant from Massachusetts.[3] Hammerton was South Carolina's secretary and register and a member of the royal council. He had been appointed the colony's provincial grand master a few months earlier.

Mackey's *History of South Carolina Freemasonry* describes Hammerton as 'a man of talent and considerable social distinction in the colony' and his offices as evidence of the 'high esteem in which he was held by the parent government'.[4] But although he held positions of 'great honour and trust', as Mackey put it, and ranked third in precedence after the governor and lieutenant-governor, Hammerton's standing fell short of Mackey's over-vaulting description. He

---

[1] Lodge warrants and charters were not issued by the Grand Lodge of England until the 1750s. Instead 'deputations' were granted. Regardless, the terms 'warrant' and 'charter' are used throughout this book since the effect of a deputation was in all important respects identical.

[2] Solomon's Lodge was not in the grand lodge lists until 1760 and in 1762 was placed at the number 74, a place vacated by Bristol Lodge. Cf., www.hrionline. ac.uk/lane/record.php?ID=235, accessed 12 October 2017. The lodge made no payments after 1781 but was retained on the roll until 1813.

[3] 27 December 5735 [1735]: 'About this time sundry Brethren going to South Carolina met with some Masons in Charleston who thereupon went to work, from which sprung Masonry in those parts': *Proceedings in Masonry. St John's Grand Lodge 1733-1792. Massachusetts Grand Lodge 1769-1792. With an appendix, containing copies of many ancient documents, and a table of lodges* (Boston, MA: Grand Lodge of Massachusetts, 1895), p. 5. I am grateful to Dr Hans Schwartz for the reference.

[4] Albert G. Mackey, *History of Freemasonry in South Carolina* (Columbia, SC: South Carolinian Steam Press, 1861), pp. 6-7.

would be accused of fraud and misfeasance and dismissed, and in 1755 confined to the Fleet, one of London's most notorious debtors' prisons.

Matters had started rather differently. To many Carolinians Hammerton was simply another British placeman. But although he lived in London for the majority of his life and spent only ten years in South Carolina, Hammerton had family connections to South Carolina and his path to office had begun a decade before he was appointed secretary and register. His brother, William, was the naval officer for Charleston, a position obtained through Lord Carteret's patronage.[5] And family members who had migrated to Jamaica in the seventeenth century and become successful planters had ties to South Carolina. It was through these relationships that Hammerton was made aware that Charles Hart, the incumbent secretary and register, was nearing retirement and of the opportunity to acquire his positions. Indeed, Hammerton's family did more than merely pass on the information. They also interceded with Robert Walpole to advance his case.[6] Hammerton's correspondence with Walpole and the Duke of Newcastle supports this thesis, as does Walpole's direct involvement.

Hammerton sailed for Charleston in around 1722. He reached an agreement with Hart to acquire his offices and subsequently served a brief apprenticeship. The position of colonial secretary would provide a mid-level stipend and a reasonable social status, and that of register a more lucrative income stream. Legal documents, including land grants, required registration in order to be valid, something achieved through the register's office, with part of the fee being retained by the register personally.

---

[5] He was commissioned by the Lords Proprietors on 10 May 1716. Cf., also, Cecil Headlam (ed.), *Calendar of State Papers Colonial, America and West Indies, Volume 32, 1720-1721* (London: HMSO, 1933), pp. 212-28: 24 December 1720, William Hammerton to Lord Carteret. '*Prays* for his protection and support in the Commission he holds, against the intrigues of Mr Trott, who is making interest with the Lords Proprietors for a young fellow of this place *etc. Signed*, William Hammerton.'

[6] Alan D. Watson, 'Placemen in South Carolina: The Receiver Generals of the Quitrents', *South Carolina Historical Magazine*, 74.1 (1973), 18-30.

Public office in the eighteenth century was considered the property of the incumbent. The transfer of office nonetheless required approval and in the case of 1720s South Carolina this was problematic. Although the colonists' petition for crown rule had been accepted and the Lords Proprietors' governor had vacated his office, the colony's formal legal status and the Proprietors' compensation had yet to be settled. In the interim there was a lack of clarity over who had authority to make and confirm appointments. Given the context, the administrative default position was to defer decisions. But this was not Hammerton's only problem. In 1725, shortly after Hammerton had secured his agreement with Hart, the Lords Proprietors put forward an alternative candidate. This was Edward Bertie, the son of the Hon. James Bertie, MP for Middlesex, himself the second son of the 2nd Earl of Abingdon,[7] a man with political influence.[8]

Faced with a combination of bureaucratic gridlock and a credible rival, Hammerton pressed his case in a flurry of letters to government officials. In a missive to Walpole he argued that South Carolina's incoming royal governor would be incapable of doing his job without the support of a secretary, register and attorney general,[9] each of which appointments had been frozen. But despite the accuracy of Hammerton's argument, the administrative impasse persisted.

Hammerton had no choice but to defer travelling to Charleston and his connections to London freemasonry appear to date from this time when he became a member of the Duke of Richmond's Horn Tavern lodge, London's most influential and best-connected masonic lodge.[10]

---

[7] *London Gazette*, 16-19 January 1731; *Country Journal or The Craftsman*, 23 January 1731, et al.

[8] Several were also freemasons, including Lord Vere Bertie, the brother of the 1st Duke of Ancaster; Peregrine Bertie (Rainbow Coffee House, York Buildings); and Thomas Bertie (Queen's Arms, Newgate Street).

[9] CUL, Department of Manuscripts and University Archives: Cholmondeley (Houghton), Correspondence, 1, 2757 *c*.21 February 1730.

[10] Hammerton was not named in the Horn's membership list dated 27 November 1725; he may have joined in 1726 or earlier, since membership lists generally recorded those present in lodge on the day of census.

The Horn Tavern Lodge

The Horn was the driving force behind English freemasonry from 1717 until the late 1730s. Four lodge members were the grandsons of Charles II, and a fifth the grandson of James II.[11] Others sat in parliament or could influence those who did. A few financed their own military regiments, including Earl Delorraine, colonel of the 2nd troop of horse guards and of a regiment of foot, and the Duke of Montagu, who had his own regiments of horse and foot and was colonel of His Majesty's Own Troop of Horse Guards, later the Life Guards, the army's premier cavalry regiment. Others had senior roles within the administration and were among the twenty or so members who sat as magistrates on the Westminster and Middlesex benches[12]

The Horn's masonic standing was also considerable. The lodge provided five grand masters between 1719 and 1726; a deputy grand master in every year bar two from 1720 until 1735;[13] and members held the pivotal positions of grand secretary, occupied by Cowper from 1723-26, and Edward Wilson the following year, and grand treasurer, held by Nathaniel Blackerby from 1730-38. With such colleagues it was no coincidence that Hammerton achieved grand rank. He was appointed acting junior grand warden in December 1729, his temporary elevation being orchestrated by two fellow members of the Horn: Blackerby, the sitting deputy grand master; and

---

[11] The four grandsons of Charles II were Charles Lennox, 2nd Duke of Richmond (1701-1750); Charles FitzRoy, 2nd Duke of Grafton (1683-1757); Henry Scott, Earl Delorraine (1676-1730); and Francis Scott, Earl of Dalkeith, 2nd Duke of Buccleuch (1705-1751). James Waldegrave was the grandson of James II; he was created Earl Waldegrave by George II in 1729.

[12] Berman, *Foundations*, esp. chapter three.

[13] The Horn's deputy grand masters were George Payne, 1720; John Desaguliers, 1722-3, 1725; William Cowper, 1726; Andrew Chocke, 1727; Nathaniel Blackerby, 1728-9; Thomas Batson, 1730-4; and George Payne (again) 1735. John Beale (Crown & Anchor) was deputy grand master in 1721; and Martin Folkes (Bedford Head), a great friend of the Duke of Richmond, in 1724.

George Payne, a former grand master and deputy grand master, then acting senior grand warden.[14]

Despite losing money in the South Sea Bubble crisis,[15] Hammerton's financial position appears to have been relatively sound. The grand lodge minutes for 21 April 1730 record his donation of £15 to the grand charity on behalf of the Horn, with payment made by Hammerton personally via a promissory note.[16] And in December the same year, Hammerton was one of five who volunteered to act as a grand steward to organise and underwrite the forthcoming grand feast.[17]

LOBBYING IN LONDON

With his position as South Carolina's secretary and register unconfirmed, Hammerton continued lobbying, writing letters to Delafaye, Newcastle's undersecretary, and Walpole,[18] and contacting Sir Francis Nicholson,[19] South Carolina's

---

[14] William J. Songhurst (ed.), *The Minutes of the Grand Lodge of the Freemasons of England, 1723-1739* (London: Quatuor Coronati Lodge, No. 2076, 1913), 27 December 1729. Henceforth: 'Grand Lodge *Minutes I*'.

[15] Cf., Watson, 'Placemen in South Carolina', 19.

[16] Grand Lodge *Minutes I*, 21 April 1730, p. 122. It is however equally possible to read this in the opposite way, with Hammerton having taken the Horn's cash donation and issued a promissory note in its place.

[17] Grand Lodge *Minutes I*, 15 December 1731, p. 137. Given the small number of volunteers, grand lodge was nervous of proceeding and instead 'proposed and agreed that the six junior stewards who served last year should be desired to attend the Deputy Grand Master at the Horn Tavern ... who is desired to fix this affair in such manner as he shall think fit'. In the event, Hammerton was not selected to serve.

[18] Headlam (ed.), *Calendar of State Papers Colonial, America and West Indies* (London: IHR, 1936), volume 34, 1724-5, pp. 490-4, Hammerton to Newcastle; Hammerton to Delafaye; Hammerton to Walpole, et al, 1725.

[19] Kevin R. Hardwick, 'Nicholson, Sir Francis (1655-1728)', *ODNB*.

royal governor,[20] to ask that he intercede.[21] Nicholson had taken medical leave from Charleston in 1725 and his agreement to become involved was probably due to Delafaye's influence. The two were friends as well as colleagues.[22]

Nicholson's support added to the cumulative weight in Hammerton's favour and an indication that progress was being made is evident in the text of a letter from the Lords Proprietors to Lord Carteret complaining that 'Mr Hart formerly our Secretary hath taken upon him to treat for the sale of his office, and Mr Hammerton who was to be the purchaser has applied to the crown for a grant of it, against which we thought proper to enter a caveat'.[23] The Proprietors' disquiet was directed less at Hammerton taking office than what they saw as an undermining of their authority before the formal transfer of their interests to the crown had been finalised. The 'caveat' reflected this:

> *Richard Shelton to the Duke of Kingston, Lord Privy Seal.* Enters Caveat that no grant may pass of any office, employment or land in South Carolina without notice being given to him. Memorandum: the above caveat was upon the account of John Hammerton having HM warrant to be Secretary of the province according to the agreement with Charles Hart.[24]

Hammerton responded by writing to Newcastle, underlining that Shelton's 'caveat in the Signet Office against the said patent passing the Seals dispute' was at variance with 'his Majesty's royal power in the government of that province'.

---

[20] Sir Francis Nicholson took office in May 1721 but returned to England four years later. He was not replaced formally until Robert Johnson succeeded him as governor in 1729. Between May 1725 and December 1730, Arthur Middleton, a wealthy Carolinian planter, served as acting governor.

[21] Headlam, *Calendar of State Papers Colonial, America and West Indies* (London: IHR, 1936), volume 35, 7 January 1726.

[22] The *Sackler Archives* of the Royal Society. Cf., also, Berman, *Foundations*, p. 79.

[23] Headlam, *Calendar of State Papers Colonial, America and West Indies* (London: IHR, 1936), volume 35, pp. 188-204, 16-31 December 1726.

[24] Headlam, *Calendar of State Papers Colonial, America and West Indies*, volume 35, pp. 161-80, November 1726.

He argued that the caveat should be considered meritless since it was contrary to 'his Majesty's Order [and] your Grace's and the rest of the Lords Justices' warrant for a patent for the Secretary's place of South Carolina'.

Hammerton's appeal fell on fertile ground and he followed up with a second letter to make certain that the forthcoming warrant would also cover the position of register: 'the Duke of Newcastle has ordered my business to be done, but the warrant for the patent drawn by Mr Delafaye is for 'Secretary, Clerk of the Council, and Clerk of the Enrolments', but the chief appendance belonging thereto is not inserted, viz. Register of the Records. All the records of the province, and the public transactions of both Council and Assembly have always been Registered and filled in the Secretary's office (and it is a considerable perquisite), there being no salary, and the whole income of that office, with all the perquisites does not exceed £300'.[25]

HAMMERTON'S APPOINTMENTS ARE CONFIRMED

There nonetheless remained the matter of Edward Bertie, Hammerton's rival. In the event a compromise was agreed and Hammerton received patents for secretary and register on the basis that these would be shared basis with Bertie.[26] Hammerton accepted the result with good grace.[27] The joint appointment was granted on both their lives such that when one of them died the survivor would succeed to both offices in his sole name until his own death. As recompense for concurring with the arrangement, Walpole granted Hammerton a further warrant, that of Receiver General of the Quit Rents in North and South Carolina, and the prestige of a seat on the royal council.[28]

---

[25] Ibid., Hammerton to Walpole, undated.

[26] Headlam, *Calendar of State Papers Colonial, America and West Indies* (London: IHR, 1936), volume 36, pp. 565-78, 23 December 1729.

[27] This point is made explicitly in Ch (H), Corr., 1, 2757 *c*.21 February 1730.

[28] *British Journal*, 10 October 1730 et al. Cf., also, *London Evening Post*, 15-17 December 1730 for a full list of appointments to the colony; and *Read's Weekly Journal Or British Gazetteer*, 19 December 1730.

The position of receiver-general brought with it an annual salary of £100 and the right to receive 'the usual fees': a levy of up to 10% on the monies collected.[29] The over-ride was shared with the Auditor and Surveyor General of his Majesty's Revenues in America, a sinecure held by Horatio Walpole, Walpole's younger brother. An indication of the importance of the office was that it required a financial guarantee to be lodged with the Treasury to ensure the incumbent's probity. This was procured in October 1731 with George Rooke, a merchant and masonic colleague, acting as a surety for Hammerton.[30]

AND DENIED

Bertie and Hammerton arrived in South Carolina in 1732[31] but immediately ran into political difficulties. Hart had stepped down but the South Carolina Assembly had determined that it, rather than London, had the right to appoint the colony's register and Robert Johnson, now the royal governor, had nominated his son. Hammerton's position as receiver-general was also compromised by Johnson. Hammerton was furious and wrote to the Board of Trade protesting that this was the first time a colonial assembly had presumed 'to take to [itself] an employment previously given as a freehold by the king'.[32] He also wrote to Delafaye, carping that the assembly had acted improperly when it decided 'to dispose of what his Majesty has granted': 'I was so troublesome to you when in England that I should not repeat it again at this time but on this particular occasion. The Assembly in making their

---

[29] The levy may have been as high as 10 per cent: Cf. Shaw, *Treasury Books and Papers, 1742-5* (London: IHR, 1903), volume 5, p. 211, 9 February 1742, ref. *King's Warrant Book, XXXIV*, pp. 485-6.

[30] William A. Shaw (ed.), *Calendar of Treasury Books and Papers, 1731-4* (London: IHR, 1898), volume 2, p. 145, *Warrants, Letters etc.* 1731.

[31] Hammerton's brother, William, accompanied the pair to Charleston but died at sea before they reached port. Cf., *South Carolina Gazette*, Death Notices, 29 April 1732.

[32] Headlam, *America and the West Indies, November 1732, Calendar of State Papers Colonial, America and West Indies* (London: IHR, 1939), volume 39, 12 November 1732.

Quit Rent Act have taken upon them to provide and dispose of what HM has granted in the patent to Mr. Bertie and myself, the place of Register. By the patent the king has been pleased to grant for our lives or the longer liver the employments of secretary and Register of this HM Province. The patent bears date 11 February, eight months before the act was made and I imagine they might as well have provided for the surcharges as that we having the same right to one as the other; the Registry is worth sixty pounds per annum sterling; and the Secretary does not exceed £200 a year, out of which I am obliged to pay Mr Bertie £80 a year and a clerk here £40.'[33]

Hammerton continued, asking Delafaye to ensure that Newcastle 'take notice in council when the said act is debated' and complaining that 'the people here are in great confusion about their lands and quit-rents, which they don't care to pay; they are very obstinate and very opinionated and [unless] parliament settles the laws here, nothing will be done with them. In the Northern Provinces it is the same, they all believe themselves men of greater capacities than all the Council and Senate of England.'[34]

Johnson ignored Hammerton's protests and refused to allow him to assume his position as clerk to the royal council. Hammerton was impotent. Johnson was popular in the colony and Hammerton an outsider and four thousand miles from London. Barred from the more lucrative of his offices Hammerton's financial position became precarious. He had paid to succeed Hart, expended funds petitioning in London, financed the cost of travel to Charleston and, following his arrival, funded his own upkeep and that of his staff. Prevented by Johnson from assuming office, his only income was from his post as secretary - and that was shared with Bertie. The position remained unchanged until September 1733 when Bertie contracted a fever and died. But although Hammerton now held both offices in his sole name, Johnson continued to bar him from his offices as register and receiver-general.[35]

---

[33] Ibid., John Hammerton to Charles Delafaye, 10 November 1732.
[34] Ibid.
[35] *London Evening Post*, 20-22 September 1733.

In 1735 Hammerton was allowed to return to England, ostensibly to attend to his personal affairs and recover his health.[36] It gave him an opportunity to lobby in person for compensation and for the restitution of the offices he possessed in name only. The catalyst had been Johnson's death in May:

> As it is my duty so I take this first opportunity to acquaint your Grace that our Governor, Mr Johnson, died last Saturday the third instant. Mr Broughton who H.M. was pleased to commission as Lieutenant Governor and President of the Council, is sworn into the administration of the Government... The Lords of the Treasury having been pleased to give me leave to go to England... I hope I shall have the honour to kiss your Grace's hand.
> Being with the greatest regard and deference *etc.*
> *John Hammerton*, Secretary.[37]

Hammerton's relationship with Johnson had been dysfunctional and although it is not evident from the content of his note, he viewed Johnson's death as providential. Unfortunately, Hammerton had an equally poor relationship with Gabriel Johnston, the governor of North Carolina. Johnston had also excluded Hammerton from office and appointed Eleazer Allen as receiver-general.[38] He explained his reasons in a note to the Board of Trade in which he argued that with 'the Receiver General's living out of this province ... there is a considerable arrearage of Quit Rents', and since [Hammerton] is Secretary and Receiver General of the province of

---

[36] Shaw, *Calendar of Treasury Books and Papers, 1731-34* (London: IHR, 1898), volume 2, p. 587, 31 December 1734.
[37] *Calendar of State Papers Colonial, America and West Indies* (London: IHR, 1953), volume 41, *Hammerton to Newcastle*, 8 May 1735.
[38] Eleazer Allen (1692-1750), a SC merchant who had settled at Cape Fear. Cf., *From Roanoke to Raleigh*.

South Carolina, he is by virtue of his said offices obliged to reside within the said province, by which means the receipt of his Majesty's rent is here neglected'.[39]

Back in London, Hammerton worked his connections to recover his losses. The administrative wheels moved slowly and his case against Robert Johnson was not resolved until December 1738 when the Council for Plantation Affairs concluded that 'this is one of the plainest cases ever drawn into question: Mr Hammerton is well entitled and has an undoubted right to the office of Register as well as Secretary'.[40] But that decision was three years away.

In the meantime, Hammerton attended the Horn and grand lodge. And although the minutes are silent on the exact date of grant, whether in late 1735 or early 1736, when he returned to Charleston Hammerton carried with him the charter for Solomon's lodge. The warrant had been issued in the name of the grand master, the twenty-five year old Thomas Thynne, 2nd viscount Weymouth. However Weymouth did not attend grand lodge other than at his installation and the charter was probably issued in Thynne's name by George Payne, the deputy grand master, a fellow member of the Horn, who at the same time appointed Hammerton provincial grand master of South Carolina.

CONSTITUTING SOLOMON'S LODGE

On 28 October 1736, shortly after Hammerton's return, the *South Carolina Gazette* reported that 'last night a Lodge of the Ancient and Honorable Society of Free and Accepted Masons was held for the first time at Mr

---

[39] Shaw, *Treasury Books and Papers*, October 1735, *Calendar of Treasury Books and Papers, 1735-8* (London: IHR, 1900), volume 3, pp. 53-4, 8 October 1735.

[40] Davies, *Calendar of State Papers Colonial, America and West Indies, 1738* (London: IHR, 1969), volume 44, pp. 256-76, 8 December 1738.

Charles Shepheard's [tavern] in Broad Street when John Hammerton Esq., Secretary and Receiver General for this Province, was unanimously chosen Master'.[41] Hammerton's first slate of officers may have been relative unknowns but this changed rapidly and within less than a year the lodge was patronised by the colony's plantocracy. Masonically-themed concerts, theatrical evenings and public processions were introduced to Charleston as they had been to London, Dublin and elsewhere. And although Solomon's Lodge may have had less than forty members,[42] they were among the colony's most socially and financially eminent:

> Thursday night last, *The Recruiting Officer* was acted for the entertainment of the Honourable and Ancient Society of Free and Accepted Masons, who came to the play house about 7 o'clock in the usual manner and made a very decent and solemn appearance ... A proper prologue and epilogue were spoke and the Entered Apprentice's and Master's song sung upon the stage which were joined in chorus by the Masons in the Pit to the satisfaction and entertainment of the whole audience. After the play the Masons returned to the lodge at Mr Shepheard's in the same order observed in coming to the playhouse.[43]

A masonic procession was an advertisement for the Craft and validated its status. Accompanied by musicians, a masonic procession usually featured a sword-bearer, a symbol of the gentlemanly nature of freemasonry, and a formation of lodge stewards carrying white-painted wooden rods

---

[41] Shepherd's Tavern, one of Charles Town's principal buildings, was constructed c.1720. and located at the town's centre at the junction of Broad Street and Church Street. Its 'long room' hosted plays, concerts and public celebrations; it was also the location of the Court of Session.
[42] *South Carolina Gazette*, 23 July 1737: 'the whole society ... were 30 in number'.
[43] *South Carolina Gazette*, 28 May 1737.

as a symbol of their authority. The master would be at the centre in a carriage, followed by other members of the lodge in pairs in sedan chairs or carriages. They would be dressed in 'the proper clothing' - aprons, white gloves and white stockings - with lodge officers wearing the jewels of their offices. The event was a form of street theatre that identified freemasonry with the colony's elites: justices of the peace and law officers; merchants and planters; and senior officials. It was comparable to a mayoral progress, a display of power in which the public's role was to observe.

A RETURN TO ENGLAND

Hammerton remained master of Solomon's Lodge only briefly and in July 1737 the *South Carolina Gazette* reported that he was returning once more to England: 'last Thursday, John Hammerton Esq., Receiver General of his Majesty's Quit Rents, Secretary and one of his Majesty's Honourable Council, who has been the first Master of the Lodge of the Ancient and Honourable Society of Freemasons in this place ... intending to embark on board the ship *Molly*, John Caruthers, Master, for London, at a lodge held that evening, resigned his office. James Graeme Esq., was then unanimously chosen Master ... and having been duly installed into that office with the usual ceremonies was pleased to choose and appoint James Wright Esq., who was Junior Warden, to be Senior Warden, and Maurice Lewis Esq., Junior Warden'.[44]

The lodge officers were representative of Charleston's freemasons. James Graeme (d.1752), the Barbados-born attorney who succeeded Hammerton as master and provincial grand master, had migrated to South Carolina in the late 1720s. He built a law practice in Charleston and in 1731

---

[44] *South Carolina Gazette*, 23 July 1737.

was elected to the Commons House of Assembly.⁴⁵ In 1740 he was appointed sole judge of the Court of Vice Admiralty and in 1749 South Carolina's chief justice; he was appointed to the royal council in 1750.

Graeme is first recorded as a freemason in 1737 but would have been initiated before that date. He was re-elected provincial grand master in 1737 and again in 1739, and sat as provincial junior grand warden in 1738-9 and again in 1740-2. There is no indication that his role as provincial grand master was approved by the Grand Lodge of England. At the time, London had its own more pressing concerns.⁴⁶

Graeme's senior warden, James Wight (1716-1785) was his brother-in-law. Wright's father, Robert Wright, had been the former chief justice in the colony.⁴⁷ James Wright had previously served as junior warden of Solomon's

---

⁴⁵ South Carolina's Commons House of Assembly had thirty-six members in the 1720s, a number that rose to forty-eight over the next half century as the colony's population and territory expanded. Although prestigious, the position was not a sinecure. Assemblymen were unpaid and could be in session over an extended period, sometimes for several days per week for up to eight months of the year. It was unsurprising that up to a quarter of those elected declined to serve and those that did were usually Charleston-based and affluent, able to employ overseers and managers at their estates. Planters dominated the Assembly as they did polite South Carolina society more generally, holding two-thirds of seats. Merchants were the second most common group, making up a fifth of assemblymen, with lawyers next. But almost all assemblymen, whether merchant, lawyer, banker or affluent artisan, would have owned, co-owned or aspired to own a plantation. Land, especially that in the Low Country, was considered to be (and was, once developed) a secure and rapid route to wealth creation with one's capital investment capable of doubling in value within five years. What drove the process was Britain and Europe's demand for South Carolina's agricultural products and the economics of slave production itself. Cf., Walter B. Edgar & N. Louise Bailey, *Biographical Directory of the South Carolina House of Representatives* (Columbia, SC: USC Press, 1977), volume II, pp. 3-6.

⁴⁶ Cf., *Schism*, 118-58.

⁴⁷ A 'Robert Wright', perhaps the same person, had been a member of the Bull's Head lodge in Southwark, and a 'Mr Wright' a member of the King's Arms Tavern, St Paul's Churchyard.

Lodge and succeeded Graeme as its master and then as provincial grand master. He was appointed acting attorney general for the province the same year, 1738, at the age of 22, a position made permanent in 1742 when he returned from London after studying at Gray's Inn.[48]

Wright was highly competent and widely respected and in 1757 was persuaded to return to England as the colony's agent. His skill impressed the government and in 1760 Wright was offered the role of lieutenant-governor of Georgia; he became governor the following year. Wright's landholdings in Georgia and his ownership of more than 500 slaves reflected his South Carolina heritage and set an example that helped to institutionalise slavery in Georgia.

Graeme's junior warden, Maurice Lewis (d.1739), was another recent migrant and lawyer. He was appointed master of the Court of Chancery in 1736 and shortly afterwards sole judge of the Court of Vice Admiralty. He held both appointments until his death from fever. Lewis represented Prince Frederick Parish in the Commons in the eleventh and twelfth assemblies and was the author of a resolution that argued that only the assembly had the right to originate money bills, an argument based on the prerogatives of the English House of Commons. His approach had much in common with that of the opposition in the Anglo-Irish money bills dispute some two decades later.[49] Lewis served as provincial grand master in 1738-9.[50]

HAMMERTON'S FINANCIAL DECLINE

Hammerton arrived in England in September 1737. He pursued his ongoing case before the Board of Trade and his claim for the 'fees due to him as Secretary and Register of South Carolina [and] the refusal [of] the late Governor ... to admit the Petitioner to the Office of Register of that

---

[48] Edward J. Cashin, 'Wright, Sir James, first baronet (1716-1785)', *ODNB* (online edn., Jan 2008).

[49] Cf., *Schism*, pp. 159-80.

[50] Edgar & Bailey, *Biographical Directory of the South Carolina House of Representatives*, pp. 404-5.

province'.[51] The Board's delay in adjudicating on the matter compounded Hammerton's financial problems and sparked a petition from George Rooke for permission to withdraw as Hammerton's guarantor. Hammerton's failure to release financial information made matters worse and Rooke argued that the Treasury should order Hammerton to make disclosure: 'now he is arrived in England he may be ordered to pass his accounts'.[52]

Rooke's social status is indicated by his membership of Viscount Montagu, the grand master's lodge at the Bear & Harrow Tavern in Butcher Row, Temple Bar, and his personal friendship with Montagu. Rooke had been a grand steward in 1731 and was appointed senior grand warden by Montagu the following year. Rooke and Montagu were also fellow members of the lodge at the Golden Spikes Tavern in Hampstead, where Montagu succeeded Rooke as master in 1731. The installation ceremony and celebration had been lavish and the attendance of Lord Lovell, then grand master, and a contingent of grand officers and guests of 'quality and distinction' was reported widely by the press.[53]

Hammerton's modest revenues from his offices in South Carolina and the scale of his outgoings, including payments to clerks and deputies, was known. Hammerton's other guarantor, Filmer Southouse,[54] was as concerned as Rooke regarding the assets he had posted as security for Hammerton and, like Rooke, petitioned the Treasury, complaining that his surety was 'very inconvenient' and that 'he hath long since given notice to [Hammerton] to make up his accounts and propose some other security, which not having been complied with, prays their Lordships to compel

---

[51] Ledward, *Journal of the Board of Trade and Plantations, 1735-41* (London: IHR, 1930), volume 7, pp. 252-6, October 1738.

[52] Shaw, *Calendar of Treasury Books and Papers, 1735-8* (London: IHR, 1900), volume 3, p. 388, *Reference Book X*, 28 September 1737.

[53] *London Evening Post*, 12-15 June 1731; *Daily Post*, 14 June 1731.

[54] Filmer Southouse, an antiquarian and a friend of Martin Folkes, was the second son of Thomas Southouse, a bencher at Gray's Inn. He was probably but not conclusively a freemason.

him'. Given Hammerton's circumstances, the Board of Trade was reluctant to acquiesce. However it was willing to note the petitioners' concerns and refer the matter back to Hammerton with a request that alternative arrangements be proposed.[55] There is no record of any response.

Hammerton's reputation was threatened further by an accusation of malpractice. An anonymous letter from Charleston to Walpole listed 'irregularities'[56] and referred to Hammerton's refusal to register land held in trust for two orphans whose father had died in the colony. It alleged a conspiracy within the royal council and stated that an investigation had determined that of 16,000 acres supposedly in trust for the children, 6,000 acres had been granted to each of the governor and lieutenant-governor with Hammerton taking 4,000 acres personally. The accusation was probably valid. Land fraud was common practice, especially among those with political influence. The irony was that Hammerton had insufficient capital to develop the land and put it to use.

Although the Board eventually ruled in Hammerton's favour and settled a part of his outstanding fees at the end of 1738,[57] he was not made whole and delayed his return to Charleston for another three years while he sought redress.[58] His finances were now in disarray and shortly before sailing for South Carolina Hammerton approached the Georgia Trustees for a short term loan of £200. Although Hammerton was rebuffed, the trustees were pressed to reconsider and eventually agreed, justifying the loan in the belief that it would be advantageous to have a highly placed 'friend of the colony' in South Carolina. Hammerton's masonic connections may have lent weight

---

[55] Shaw, *Calendar of Treasury Books and Papers* (London: IHR, 1901), volume 4, p. 91, *11 April 1739*.

[56] Anonymous to Walpole, undated, 1730s: CUL, Department of Manuscripts and Archives: Ch (H), Political Papers, 84, 79.

[57] K.G. Davies (ed.), *America and West Indies, August 1739, Calendar of State Papers Colonial, America and West Indies, 1739* (London: IHR, 1994), volume 45, pp. 153-74.

[58] Davies, *Calendar of State Papers Colonial, America and West Indies, 1738* (London: IHR, 1969), volume 44, pp. 256-76, 8 December 1738.

to his appeal. The trustees included several prominent freemasons and the colony had been part-financed by lodge collections.[59] Hammerton is noted as having attended grand lodge in April 1738 and again in January 1739, described in the minutes as 'PGM of S Carolina'.[60] There is no information on his activities at the Horn; the lodge minutes are no longer extant.

And Fall

Following his return to Charleston, Hammerton ordered that Georgia's loan be repaid from the quit-rent account. The loan could have been reimbursed by Hammerton from his share of the quit-rents but doing so from the quit-rent account itself was unlawful. George Saxby, Hammerton's deputy and receiver-general in his absence, refused to advance the monies fearing he would become complicit in a fraud. Disbursements from the account were allowed only with the sanction of the Treasury or the formal approval of the auditor general. The matter became known publicly and a diary entry by the Earl of Egmont, chair of the Georgia Trustees, noted the regrettable 'protest and return of Mr Hammerton's bill of exchange for 200*l*. on Mr George Saxby, his deputy receiver in South Carolina'.[61] With no prospect of immediate repayment, William Stephens, Georgia's president from 1741-50, was instructed to sue Hammerton in South Carolina's courts. Hammerton stymied the action by legal manoeuvrings and two years later with the case unresolved, Stephens settled for a second charge over Hammerton's fees as secretary and register to remain in place until Georgia's claim was satisfied.

Worse was to follow as Hammerton's stewardship of the quit-rents came under the scrutiny of Henry McCulloh, a land speculator appointed

---

[59] Berman, *Foundations*, pp. 85-6.
[60] Hammerton's final appearance in English Grand Lodge may have been on 24 October 1751'; he was acting senior grand warden to Fotherley Baker's acting grand master.
[61] John Perceval, Lord Egmont, *Diary of the First Earl of Egmont* (London: HMSO, 1923) volume 3, p. 131.

Commissioner for Supervising, Inspecting and Controlling His Majesty's Revenues and Grants of Land in North and South Carolina, and charged with examining land grants in the Carolinas and improving quit-rent collection.[62]

Many settlers had landholdings that were unrecorded in the rent rolls and avoided quit-rents through blank land patents.[63] McCulloh responded by asking Hammerton to provide a statement of rent arrears, a copy of his receipts, and a list of the land grants that had been issued since 1730. Hammerton refused, arguing that his clerks did not have the time. The snub was unwise. McCulloh's report was delivered to the Treasury on 8 November 1741 and began by noting that his work had been obstructed. He set out a copy of his order to Hammerton and stated that Hammerton had not complied and was not expected to 'feeling sure that he is in arrears with the Crown at least £1,500 and, from his books, indebted to the Crown up to the 1738 March quarter date as to over £1,280'. These were huge sums.

McCulloh continued, asserting that he suspected Hammerton of fraud: crediting himself with 'several sums paid as he alleges but for which vouchers are not forthcoming'.[64] He concluded his report with the observation that the crown's outstanding receivables could be collected but *only* if Hammerton were removed from office. The account was received in London in August 1742. McCulloh's charges stuck and despite Hammerton's protests he was dismissed from office.

While the investigation had been continuing, Hammerton had resumed his place at the helm of South Carolina freemasonry with John Houghton, the incumbent PGM, stepping aside. As in past years however Hammerton remained in Charleston only briefly before leaving for London in 1744. Although he may have intended otherwise, Hammerton would not return.

---

[62] Cf. Alan D. Watson, 'Henry McCulloh: Royal Commissioner in South Carolina', *South Carolina Historical Magazine*, 75.1 (1974), 33-48.

[63] Davies, *Calendar of State Papers Colonial, America and West Indies, 1739* (London: IHR, 1969), volume 45, pp. 90-111, 16 May 1739.

[64] Shaw, *Calendar of Treasury Books and Papers* (London: IHR, 1901), 8 November 1741.

A month into the voyage his vessel was seized by the French navy and Hammerton was captured and imprisoned by at Brest. His release on parole was eventually secured by the Duke of Newcastle.

Hammerton's extended absence from the colony had allowed the governor to nominate William Bull Jr. to take his place on the council. Hammerton petitioned Newcastle and the Duke of Bedford, his successor, asking to be reinstated. He also wrote to the Board of Trade to request an extension to his leave of absence. But McCulloh's evidence coupled with Hammerton's failure to repay his debt to the Georgia trustees had alienated former supporters, including masonic colleagues. The Board was not willing to indulge Hammerton. In October 1748 it ruled that 'Mr Hammerton … having been absent from his seat in the said Council for several years without applying for his Majesty's licence' would be replaced by Bull - 'to be of the said Council in his room'.

IMPRISONMENT

No longer a council member or receiver-general, and secretary and register in name only, Hammerton's salaries were eaten away by the salaries of clerks and deputies and loan repayments. With his credibility compromised, Hammerton sank under the weight of his financial obligations. In 1755 he was arrested and imprisoned for debt, confined to a bailiff's house for three months and then sent to the debtors' prison at the Fleet.

Hammerton did not recover. A petition from a Thomas Currant of Beach Street in St James's states that by an indenture dated 2 July 1755 he had been bound for five years as an apprentice to Hammerton 'then of Beak Street' to learn the business of writer or clerk in his office at Charleston.[65] Currant's petition contested that Hammerton had agreed to instruct and 'find him in clothes, meat, drink, washing and lodging', and that the arrangement

---

[65] Westminster Justices' Working Papers, January 1755: LL ref: LM WJPS 654600008.

had ceased in June following Hammerton's arrest and his incarceration at the Fleet 'where he now continues'. Currant was thus 'destitute of employment and in great danger of being incapable of getting his own living'. Not only had Hammerton 'in no wise performed his ... agreement' but he now threatened to sue anyone who employed Currant despite not being 'able to employ your petitioner'. Currant asked that the magistrates discharge him from his indenture, allow him to take up alternative work, and grant 'such relief ... as to your Worships shall seem meet'.

Little is known of Hammerton after the mid-1750s but an address in Beak Street would reinforce the sense of a man whose life was ruined. Strype's *Survey* notes that 'Beak Street butts against Warwick Street, cometh out of Swallow Street and falleth into Silver Street, another small street.[66] '[Its] houses were single-fronted and four storeys high with roof garrets ... the construction was cheap ... and the finishings ... simple, befitting houses intended for tradesmen and lower middle-class occupation'.[67]

Hammerton may not have been the 'rascal' of Alan Watson's description but his decline was now close to complete.[68] At his death in 1762,[69] Hammerton 'was unable to meet his financial obligations, spending time in Fleet Prison for non-payment of debts [and] was virtually penniless, a luckless man who failed his government and himself'.[70] There is no record of an obituary nor does it appear that Hammerton's estate was sufficiently valuable to justify probate.

---

[66] John Strype, *Survey of London* (London, 1720), II, book 6, chapter 6.

[67] F.H.W. Sheppard (ed.), *Survey of London* (London: English Heritage, 1963), vols 31 & 32, pt 2, pp. 173-5.

[68] Alan D. Watson, 'Placemen in South Carolina: The Receiver Generals of the Quitrents', *South Carolina Historical Magazine*, 74.1 (1973), 8-30.

[69] Ibid., 22; other sources give 1766.

[70] Watson, 'Placemen in South Carolina'.

Chapter Two

Craft Connections

Within two years of receiving a charter from the Grand Lodge of England, Solomon's Lodge had become the preserve of the colony's elites and freemasonry an expression of status. The names of lodge officers are detailed in the *South Carolina Gazette*:

> On Tuesday last being St John's Day, all the members of the Ancient and Honourable Society of Free and Accepted Masons in this place met at Mr Seaman's, Master of Solomon's Lodge, from where they proceeded, all properly clothed, under the sound of French horns, to wait on James Graeme Esq., PGM, at his house in Broad Street, where they were received by all the members of the grand lodge. After a short stay there, they went in procession and with the ensigns of their order into the Court Room at Mr Charles Shepheard's house, making a very grand show. Here, to a numerous audience of ladies and gentlemen who were admitted by tickets, the Grand Master made a very elegant speech in praise of Masonry, which we hear was universally applauded. Then the Grand Lodge withdrew in order to proceed to the election of a Grand Master for the ensuing year, when James Graeme, Esq., was unanimously rechosen Grand Master, who appointed James Wright, Esq., Deputy Grand Master; Maurice Lewis, Esq., Senior Grand Warden; John Crookshanks, Esq., Junior Grand Warden; James Michie, Esq., Grand Treasurer; and James Gordon, Esq., Grand Secretary. The same day Mr James Crokatt was unanimously chosen Master of Solomon's Lodge.[1]

---

[1] *South Carolina Gazette*, 29 December 1737. South Carolina's masonic archives were destroyed in fires that razed much of Charleston in 1838 and Columbia in 1865. Newspaper reports, pamphlets and private correspondence provide an alternative record.

George Seaman

George Seaman (1705-1769), the outgoing master of the lodge, was one of Charleston's wealthiest merchants. Born in Leith, Scotland, close to Edinburgh, he had migrated to South Carolina in the early 1730s and in 1736 combined with John Crokatt to establish *Crokatt & Seaman*, a trading partnership. Seaman opened his own merchant house two years later. Highly successful, his profits were invested in plantations, including the 700-acre *Walnut Hill* estate, development land at Goose Creek, property lots in Charleston, and sole ownership of the *Mary Ann*, a 120-ton schooner, defying the convention that merchants pool their risk by sharing ownership.

Seaman's losses of over £5,300 sterling in Charleston's Great Fire of November 1740 make his later achievements even more were remarkable. The fire, described as 'one of the worst in any city during the colonial period',[2] destroyed a large swathe of the city, including Seaman's premises. London's *Weekly Miscellany* described the event by printing a report from the colony.

> A most terrible fire has happened here, which began on Tuesday the 18th at about 2 o'clock in the afternoon in a saddler's house opposite to Mr James Crokatt's in the Broad Street and, in four hours, by a strong north-west wind, all the houses on the south side of the street, also all the houses on every street from the river to Church Street, including both sides of it in a line south to Granville's Bastion, were in flame, and burnt all the wharves and store houses on them in that part of the town which was the chief for

---

[2] Matthew Mulcahy, 'The "Great Fire" of 1740 and the Politics of Disaster Relief in Colonial Charleston', *South Carolina Historical Magazine*, 99.2 (1998), 135-57. Hurricanes and fires were a fact of life and treated as a manageable risk with past losses of buildings measured in single or low double figures and financial losses in the low thousands. The fire of 1740 was on a different scale.

trade. In short, except the north end of the Bay, the whole of the trading part of the town is entirely destroyed, not one house left standing. Wood, stone or brick, all are now in ruins. The number great and small must be at least 300 and includes most of the best houses in the town…

In short, from one of the most flourishing towns in America, Charles Town is at once, in five hours' time, reduced to ashes. The loss of the houses may be valued at £100,000 sterling and of the goods twice as much, if not more, but at present none can tell what the losses are, being all in confusion…[3]

Charleston recovered. Relief funds were raised from private and public sources within the province, and monies remitted from other American colonies. Much of the support came from the city's wealthier residents and was directed to help the burned out artisans and storekeepers, and to relieve the homeless. Britain's Parliament provided assistance in the form of a £20,000 grant, the only occasion on which disaster aid was made available to colonial America. The funds were pledged to those who had suffered the greatest losses and to aid the city's reconstruction. As intended, they went mainly to Charleston's merchants. British support was necessary. The fire had endangered the colony's military effectiveness and its commercial capacity and posed a threat to British interests in the region. There was also a risk of social disorder.

Seaman married in 1751 and withdrew from trade to become a full-time planter. His wife, Mary Allen, a widow, owned *Thorogood*, a 3,000-acre rice plantation worked by around 140 slaves, one of the first estates in Berkeley County.[4] It became Seaman's main home. He eventually owned more than 250 slaves, including over thirty at his townhouse in

---

[3] *Weekly Miscellany*, 10 January 1741.
[4] Michael James Heizler, *Goose Creek, South Carolina: A Definitive History 1670-2003* (Charleston, SC: History Press, 2005), volume 1, p. 257.

Charleston, described as 'probably the most elegantly furnished mansion in the city'.[5]

Provincial politics failed to attract Seaman and although he was elected to the assembly in 1751, he declined to serve the following year. Seaman nonetheless held a clutch of local offices in St Philip's Parish, including vestryman[6] and churchwarden, and became a commissioner of the Charleston work house and city markets, taking responsibility for both bodies from 1749 until 1752. In South Carolina as in England, the parish office was the basic unit of local government and the parish officers had both ecclesiastical and civil responsibilities.[7]

Within freemasonry Seaman became provincial senior grand warden in 1739 and deputy provincial grand master in 1740 and 1741; he was also a member of the St Andrew's Society and the Charleston Library Society. Seaman had no children and the main part of his estate was left to his stepdaughter, Elizabeth.[8] She had married John Deas, master of Charleston's

---

[5] Edgar & Bailey, *Biographical Directory of the South Carolina House of Representatives*, p. 606.

[6] Seaman was elected vestryman of St Philip on eighteen occasions between 1741 and 1768.

[7] Walter B. Edgar, *South Carolina: A History* (Columbia, SC: USC Press, 1998), p. 125. Each parish elected two churchwardens and seven vestrymen who were responsible for the church's estates and for the tax assessment that funded parish poor relief and education. Charleston's vestrymen also administered municipal works, as did commissioners who oversaw individual projects. The latter were either appointed by the assembly or elected; a minority selected their successors.

[8] Seaman's will was proved at the Prerogative Court of Canterbury on 24 July 1769.

Union Kilwinning Lodge,[9] later PGM, and a partner with his brother in the slave trading house of *David & John Deas*.

JAMES CROKATT

James Crokatt (1701-1777), the cousin of Seaman's former business partner, succeeded Seaman as master of Solomon's Lodge.[10] The family was from Edinburgh[11] and Dobson argues that they were Jacobites, drawing an analogy with other members of the St Andrew's Society where James Crokatt had been a founder member and treasurer.[12] Although some members had Jacobite sympathies, Crokatt's concerns were commercial and his membership of the society, like that of Solomon's Lodge, reinforced his business and social connections rather than his political views.

The Crokatts had settled in the early 1730s and established a succession of trading houses including *James Crokatt, John Crokatt, Crokatt & Seaman,*

---

[9] Union Kilwinning Lodge, No. 4, was chartered in May 1755. Among the founders were Samuel Bowman, D. Campbell, John Cooper, Robert Wells, William Michie, John Bassnet and John Stewart. Other Scottish surnames on the membership roll in the 1750s included a Gordon, Rowand, Macaulay and Bailie. Cf., *The Free Masons Pocket Companion* (Edinburgh: Auld & Smellie, 1765), p. 265. It is recorded as No. 98 on the register of the Grand Lodge of Scotland.

[10] For an excellent overview, cf. Huw David, 'James Crokatt's "Exceedingly Good Counting House": Ascendancy and Influence in the Transatlantic Carolina Trade', *South Carolina Historical Magazine*, 3.3-4 (2010), 151-74.

[11] *South Carolina Historical and Genealogical Magazine* (Charleston, SC: South Carolina Historical Society, 1923), p. 18.

[12] David Dobson, *Scottish Emigration to Colonial America, 1607-1785* (Athens, GA: University of Georgia Press, 2004), p. 107.

Crokatt & Michie, and *Simmons, Smith & Crokatt*. They also owned an extensive property portfolio and equity interests in several ocean-going vessels.[13]

James Crokatt married in the early 1730s. His wife, Esther, was the daughter of John Gaillard, head of one of South Carolina's oldest and wealthiest Huguenot families. They had migrated to South Carolina in the 1680s and now owned plantations in St James Santee Parish. Crokatt's own estate was similarly extensive with around 1,000 acres in Craven County and 1,200 acres in Granville County, each adjacent to new settlements and acquired for capital growth in anticipation of selling plots for housing. Crokatt also owned properties in Charleston, including three large houses on a prime riverside lot and at least five tenement buildings, as well as warehouses and a dock extending from Bay Street into the Cooper River. This was 'Crokatt's bridge', one of only eight wharfs in Charleston.[14]

Crokatt's first fortune was built on trading with the first nations. He became one of the colony's main deerskin exporters, responsible for thirty-one shiploads between 1735 and 1740.[15] He made a second fortune in the reciprocal import of manufactured and dry goods,[16] and a third from rice exports. Crokatt's empire was run from a large building on Broad Street that contained offices, a counting house and a retail store. It was one of the

---

[13] Family members were masters of the *James Goodwill* and *Johnson Galley*, respectively, and involved in the transatlantic trade. Each featured regularly in the London press. Cf., among many examples, *Daily Journal*, 23 June 1729 and 17 July 1732.

[14] Other properties were acquired in lieu of debts.

[15] W.O. Moore, Jr., 'The Largest Exporters of Deerskins from Charles Town, 1735-1775', *South Carolina Historical Magazine*, 74.3 (1973), 144-150, esp. 147.

[16] Stuart O. Stumpf, 'South Carolina Importers of General Merchandise, 1735-1765', *South Carolina Historical Magazine*, 84.1 (1983), 1-10.

city's prime commercial addresses and so well-known that it was used as a reference point by other merchants and in classified advertisements.[17]

Crokatt has been described as embodying South Carolina's entrepreneurial spirit - a man who shaped the colony's culture and used his influence shrewdly.[18] In David's words, 'Crokatt demonstrated the traits of an elite Hanoverian merchant, cultivating an array of associative, affective and ethnic ties to enhance his commercial and personal status'.[19] Crokatt was undoubtedly astute and drove himself hard; and in the late 1730s he concluded that South Carolina was too small a pond to accommodate his ambitions.

Despite having been appointed to the royal council in 1738, Crokatt left for London the following year. He nonetheless retained links to South Carolina, including plantations, a commercial property portfolio, and a one third equity interest in a new partnership with two former employees, Ebenezer Simmons and Benjamin Smith.

Simmons, Smith & Crokatt operated from Crokatt's Broad Street premises and serviced *Crokatt & Co.*'s former clients, providing commercial continuity and unchanged trading terms: two years' credit and the ability to exchange agricultural produce directly for imported goods. The firm was established to run for a seven-year term, giving Crokatt preferential access to South Carolina's commodity exports through a reliable agency in which he had an equity stake, and a route to market for imported manufactured and other goods. Simmons and Smith gained an astute counterpart in London and a ready-made business in Charleston.

For a period after his arrival in London, Crokatt was condescended to and nicknamed the 'Scotch Jew', a comment on his supposedly sharp trading practices and willingness to litigate. But *James Crokatt & Co.* thrived. Crokatt

---

[17] David, 'James Crokatt's "Exceedingly Good Counting House": Ascendancy and Influence in the Transatlantic Carolina Trade', *South Carolina Historical Magazine*, 3.3-4 (2010), 151-74.

[18] Ibid.

[19] Ibid., esp. 153.

surpassed his rivals to become the dominant player in the Carolina trade, supplanting Samuel and Joseph Wragg who had been the foremost Carolina merchants in the 1720s and 1730s.

Crokatt took offices in Coleman Street in the City of London but moved in the mid-1740s to larger premises in Cloak Lane. Over the following years the area attracted a cluster of other Carolina merchants eager to associate and be associated with him. By the 1750s, in large part through Crokatt's efforts, London's trade with the Carolinas had expanded to the extent that it had its own walk in the south west corner of the Royal Exchange and was comparable in terms of value to the trade with New England and Virginia. Crokatt was by then acknowledged as one of London's foremost merchants whose wealth, reputation and political lobbying skills had secured a parliamentary bounty to encourage South Carolina's indigo exports. In the wake of his success, Crokatt was pressed to become South Carolina's London agent.[20] He was also in demand as a mentor for aspiring young Carolinians despatched to London for training, including Henry Laurens.

Crokatt followed the practice of many other London merchants who dealt with South Carolina and chose not to become involved directly with the colony's slave trade. Crokatt had owned slaves when in South Carolina and the colony's staple exports of rice and indigo were possible only because of slavery. But the 1740s marked a quiet period in the South Carolina slave trade as a result of punitive import duties introduced after the 1730 Stono Rebellion in an attempt to rebalance the population in favour of white settlers. Fewer than 10 slave ships carrying some 2,000 slaves disembarked during the decade to 1749, a figure that stands in contrast to the previous decade in which over 90 vessels shipped over 22,000 slaves to the colony. However, even after the slave trade reopened in 1749 Crokatt chose not to

---

[20] Crokatt asked to be relieved as London agent in 1753. He cited conflicts of interest but may simply have become frustrated at the distraction. Charleston's failure to agree who should replace him obliged Crokatt to remain in post for a further three years.

participate. When Henry Laurens proposed a slaving joint venture, Crokatt's responded that he was 'fully employed' and preferred 'to be confined in that way'.

The potential profits from the slave trade were vast but so were the financial risks. Perhaps this lay behind Crokatt's emphasis on importing rice, indigo and deerskins, and exporting manufactured and luxury goods. In comparison with slaving the trade was low risk and predictable. Crokatt had made his fortune and saw no need to jeopardise it as his focus swung to building his social position in England. He bought *Chigwell Manor*, a Palladian mansion and estate at Luxborough in Essex, for £19,500 and spent another £10,000 on furnishings. And the marriage of his eldest son, Charles, to Anna, daughter of Henry Muilman, an Anglo-Dutch Russia merchant, further reduced his wealth. The ceremony was held at St George's in Mayfair and Crokatt matched Muilman's £10,000 dowry with his own gift of the same amount.

Crokatt's status and commercial success in the 1730s had been matched and enhanced by his position within South Carolina freemasonry. There is no information on whether he was active in London freemasonry but this means little since few lodge records remain extant from the 1740s and 1750s. Nonetheless, on balance, it is probable that freemasonry remained a key business network.

THE PROVINCIAL GRAND LODGE OF SOUTH CAROLINA

James Michie (d.1760), another Scottish migrant, provincial grand treasurer from 1737-40 and deputy provincial grand master in 1742-43, 1754-56 and 1757-58, had been associated with John Hammerton professionally as South Carolina's deputy secretary from 1737-39. Michie was an attorney and assemblyman, representing St Philip's Parish[21] in 1742-46 and again from

---

[21] Among numerous parish offices, Michie was a vestryman for St Philip's with commissions that included oversight of trade with the Creek Indians.

1752-55, speaker of the house from 1752-54, and appointed to the royal council in 1755.[22] He was made sole judge of the Court of Vice Admiralty in 1752 and capped his career with appointment as chief justice in 1759. Michie used his position to amass a large estate valued at around £11,600 sterling at his death. It included three plantations and almost 120 slaves, and around 10,000 acres of undeveloped frontier land.[23] A small part, an 827-acre estate on Charleston Neck,[24] was inherited from his brother, Kenneth (*d*.1749), a member of Solomon's Lodge.

The only non-Carolinian named in the *South Carolina Gazette* is John Crookshanks (1708-1795), the provincial junior grand warden, an officer in the naval detachment stationed at Charleston. Crookshanks had been commissioned in 1732 and in December 1734 was appointed to a lieutenancy on the *Rose*, the guard ship at Charleston from 1735-39. His naval career ended with his court martial and dismissal from the service in 1747.[25]

In December 1738, the *South Carolina Gazette* reported James Wright's election as provincial grand master and named the officers of Solomon's Lodge:

> Yesterday being the festival of St John the Evangelist, the day was ushered in with firing of guns at sunrise from several ships in the harbour with all their colours flying. At 9 o'clock all the members of Solomon's Lodge belonging to the Ancient and Honourable Society of Free and Accepted Masons met at the house of the Honourable James Crokatt Esq., Master

---

[22] Edgar & Bailey. Also Henry A. M. Smith, 'Charleston and Charleston Neck: The Original Grantees and the Settlements along the Ashley and Cooper Rivers', *South Carolina Historical and Genealogical Magazine*, 19.1 (1918), 19.

[23] M. Eugene Sirmans, 'The South Carolina Royal Council, 1720-1763', *William and Mary Quarterly*, 3rd Series, 18.3 (1961), 373-392, esp. 376.

[24] Smith, 'Charleston and Charleston Neck: The Original Grantees and the Settlements along the Ashley and Cooper Rivers', 3-76.

[25] J.K. Laughton, 'Crookshanks, John (1708-1795)', rev. Richard Harding, *ODNB* (online edn., Jan 2008).

of the said lodge, and at 10, proceeded from thence properly clothed with ensigns of their order and with music before them to the house of the Provincial Grand Master, James Graeme Esq., where a Grand Lodge was held and James Wright, Esq., elected Provincial Grand Master for the ensuing year...

At 11 o'clock, both lodges went in procession to church to attend divine services and in the same order returned to the house of Mr Charles Shepheard where, in the Court Room, to a numerous assembly of ladies and gentlemen, the newly elected Provincial Grand Master made a very eloquent speech of the usefulness of societies and the benefits thereof arising therefrom to mankind. The assembly being dismissed, Solomon's Lodge proceeded to the election of their officers for the ensuing year, when Mr John Houghton was chosen Master; Dr John Lining, Senior Warden; Mr David McCellan, junior warden; Mr Arthur Strahan, secretary; and Mr Alexander Murray, Treasurer. After an elegant dinner, all the brethren were invited by Captain Thomas White on board the *Hope*; there several loyal toasts were drank and at their coming on board and returning on shore, they were saluted by the discharge of 39 guns, being the same number observed in different salutes of this day so that in all there were about 250 guns fired. The evening was concluded with a ball and entertainment for the ladies and the whole was performed with much grandeur and decorum.[26]

The naval salute confirms freemasonry's establishment credentials and the prominence of those involved. Charleston was now emulating the processions, dinners and balls that had become a staple of London Society. Masonic processions dated from 1721 and the installation of the Duke of Montagu as the first aristocratic grand master of grand lodge, an event that was preceded by a relatively short procession from St Paul's to the nearby Stationers' Hall

---

[26] *South Carolina Gazette*, 28 December 1738.

comprising the past grand master, George Payne, and his grand wardens, other former grand officers, and the master and wardens of twelve lodges.[27]

The processions that accompanied the installation of subsequent grand masters were substantially more elaborate. It became a tradition for them to begin at the incoming grand master's townhouse in Mayfair or St James's with a lavish breakfast followed by a procession east to the City where a formal reception - the grand feast – would be held at a livery hall. The installation of the Earl of Dalkeith in 1723 was a spectacle of 'many Brothers duly clothed [proceeding] in coaches from the West to the East'. That of the Duke of Norfolk in 1729 saw Lord Kingston, the former grand master, 'met by a vast number of Brothers duly clothed' at Norfolk's mansion in St James's from where they rode in carriages and walked on foot to the Merchant Taylors' Hall: 'Brother Johnson to clear the way, six Stewards ... clothed proper with their Badges and White Rods, two in each Chariot [containing] noble and eminent Brethren ... former Grand Officers ... former noble Grand Officers ... the Secretary alone with his Badge and Bag ... the two Grand Wardens ... the Deputy Grand Master ... and in the final coach, Kingston, Grand Master, and Norfolk, Grand Master Elect, clothed only as a Mason'.

Lord Crawford's parade two years later boasted 'trumpets, hautboys, kettle drums and French-horns, to lead the van and play at the gate till all arrive'. The Earl of Loudon in 1736 was carried 'in a Chariot richly carved and gilt drawn by six beautiful grey horses' with three groups of musicians comprising 'a pair of kettle drums, four trumpets and four French horns, the others of a pair of kettle drums, two trumpets and two French horns'. And the procession the following year involved 'upwards of a hundred coaches ... closed by the Great Officers and the Earl of Darnley [GM-elect] in a fine,

---

[27] James Anderson, *The new book of constitutions of the antient and honourable fraternity of free and accepted masons* (London: Caesar Ward and Richard Chandler for Anderson, 1738).

rich, gilt chariot, drawn by six long tail grey horses, with fine morocco harness and green silk reins, and several servants in rich liveries'.[28]

Other more modest ceremonies took place in towns across provincial England and Ireland.[29] At Loughrea, in Co. Galway, 'yesterday being St John's Day, the Patron Saint of the Most Antient and Honourable Fraternity of Free and Accepted Masons, the Free Masons of this Town, of lodge No. 248, met at some distance from the town from whence they marched in procession preceded by a band of music to the Fountain Tavern where they dined and after dinner drank all the toasts peculiar to Masonry, the Royal Family, the Glorious Pious and Immortal Memory of King William and other loyal toasts. At six in the evening they marched to the Assembly Rooms where they gave an elegant Ball to the Ladies and Gentlemen. The Ball was opened by the Master, the first set consisted of twenty couple, the Men all Masons, and the Ladies (to do honour to the Fraternity), wore blue ribbons and … a blue rose on each of their left breasts'.[30]

The celebration in Charleston in December 1739 was not dissimilar:

> Saturday last being the festival of St John the Evangelist, the day was ushered in with the firing of guns at sunrise from several ships in the harbour with all their colours flying. At 9 o'clock all the members of Solomon's Lodge belonging to the Ancient and Honorable Society of Free and Accepted Masons, met at the house of Benjamin Smith, Master of the said lodge, and at 10 proceeded from thence, properly clothed, with the ensigns of their Order, to the house of the Provincial Grand Master, James Graeme, where a Grand Lodge was held, and Mr John Houghton was elected Provincial Grand Master…

---

[28] *The Daily Advertiser*, 29 April 1737.
[29] *The Dublin Weekly Journal*, 26 June 1725.
[30] *Dublin Gazette*, 24-28 June 1755. Cf., also, *Faulkner's Dublin Journal*, 28 June - 2 July 1757.

At 11 o'clock both Lodges went in procession to church to attend divine service and in the same order returned to the house of Mr Charles Shepheard, where Solomon's Lodge proceeded to the election of officers for the ensuing year...

After an elegant dinner, all the brethren being invited, went on board the *Lydia*, Captain Allen, and from thence on board the *John* and *William*, Captain Fishbourne, where several loyal healths were drunk under the discharge of many guns. The above ships were on this occasion decked out with many great colours and illuminated at night with a great number of lights regularly disposed on the yards both of which made a very agreeable appearance. In the evening the brethren returned to Mr Shepheard's again where they concluded the day suitable to the occasion. The whole was conducted with the utmost order and decency.[31]

The day would have been marked with masonic iconography. Glasses, jugs, dinnerware and cutlery were available in masonic versions, marked with the square and compasses, the 'all-seeing' eye, and other masonic symbols, as were watches and clocks, and even domestic furniture, including tables, chairs and sideboards. Freemasonry was popular and masonic membership celebrated proudly.

Lodges on both sides of the Atlantic lay at the centre of formidable social networks. This was especially true of South Carolina, where family, business and political connections overlapped.[32] John Lining (c. 1708-1760), one of Charleston's less prominent figures, provides a good example.

The 'ingenious Dr John Lining of Charles Town', senior warden of Solomon's Lodge in 1738, had opened a medical and pharmaceutical practice in Charleston and forged a scientific reputation based on 'papers and experiments in philosophy'[33] and a string of correspondents stretching from

---

[31] *South Carolina Gazette*, 1 January 1740.
[32] Edgar, *South Carolina: A History*, p. 123.
[33] *Public Advertiser*, 7 September 1753.

Benjamin Franklin in Philadelphia to Fellows of the Royal Society in London. Lining married in 1739. His wife, Sarah, was the daughter of Charles Hill, a planter and a former chief justice, owner of the *Hillsborough* estate, a plantation on the Ashley River. Two of Lining's brothers-in-law were also members of the lodge: Richard Hill (*d*.1746), Charles's son; and Maurice Lewis, married to another daughter. John Guerard (1706-1774), another brother-in-law, was Richard Hill's partner in *Hill & Guerard* (1736-46), one of the leading Indian and slave-trading houses in the colony. He had also married one of Charles Hill's daughters.

BENJAMIN SMITH

The pattern of masonic progression in South Carolina was for the officers of Solomon's Lodge to be promoted to provincial grand lodge where they would join the grand line. There were however exceptions and in 1744 Benjamin Smith (1717-1770) vaulted over George Seaman to become provincial grand master. Smith was born in South Carolina, the eldest son of Thomas Smith (1691-1724), a mid-scale planter, and Sabina Smith, whose family owned over 24,000 acres. Smith himself inherited a 2,000-acre plantation in St James Goose Creek and later acquired *Accabee* on the Ashley River. But despite his planter background, Smith was set on a career as a merchant trader and in the early 1730s obtained a clerkship, an apprenticeship, with James Crokatt. He was a founding principal in *Simmons, Smith & Crokatt* and then established his own trading house. He continued to cooperate with Crokatt, jointly owning several vessels, including the 200-ton *Flamborough's Prize* and the 100-ton brigantine *Charming Nancy*.[34] Among Smith's other vessels – he invested in around twelve – was the *Charles Town*, a privateer. His co-owners included Robert Pringle, a merchant, planter

---

[34] R. Nicholas Olsberg, 'Ship Registers in the South Carolina Archives 1734-1780', *South Carolina Historical Magazine*, 74.4 (1973), 189-299.

and privateer investor,[35] as well as Edmund Cossens, John Palmer, George Inglis and Jacob Motte (1729-1780), the public treasurer of the colony from 1743-70. The yield from captured merchantmen was immense and once the Court of Vice Admiralty had ruled that a vessel was a prize, its cargo could be sold and the ship claimed or auctioned. Contemporary opinion was that few other activities were 'near so profitable as a proper vessel or two well-fitted out for privateering'.[36]

After two years as a sole trader, Smith entered into a partnership with John Palmer. *Smith & Palmer* operated from 1747-52, after which he established *Benjamin Smith & Co.* with Miles Brewton (1731-1775),[37] and John Jones (1752-57), and then *Smith & Brewton* with Brewton alone. The firm was renamed *Smith, Brewton & Smith* when Smith's son, Thomas Loughton Smith (c.1740-1773), joined in 1761. Smith retired the following year. He was 45 and one of South Carolina's pre-eminent figures. Described as 'in the first rank of company in Carolina and … the head of a house of very extensive trade',[38] Smith was regarded as possessing an 'extensive acquain-

---

[35] Cf., Theodore Corbett, *St Augustine Pirates and Privateers* (Charleston, SC: History Press, 2012), esp. p. 110. Also, Walter B. Edgar (ed.), *Letter Book of Robert Pringle 1737-1745* (Columbia, SC: USC Press, 1972).

[36] Carl E. Swanson, 'American Privateering and Imperial Warfare, 1739-1748', *William and Mary Quarterly*, 3rd series, 42.3 (1985), 357-82; quote from 366. There were of course exceptions, including that of thirty-five Charleston merchants who subscribed £50 each to commission a privateer, *Recovery*, that in 1744 sank in the English Channel on its second voyage. Charleston's role in privateering was modest compared with other American ports with most merchants focused on the profits to be made from trade.

[37] Brewton, a merchant and planter, had married Mary Izzard. His brothers-in-law included William Mathewes, a planter in Colleton County; Jacob Motte; Charles Pinckney (1732-1782); and Benjamin Smith. Brewton was one of South Carolina's largest slave dealers alongside George Austin, Henry Laurens, Thomas Middleton and Samuel Brailsford.

[38] Laurens, *Papers of Henry Laurens*, pp. 500-1, letter to William Fisher, 16 July 1763.

tance and ability in dispatch of business as well as influence with the planters at least equal to those of any other man in the province'.[39] At his peak his income was at least £10,000 annually, the equivalent of around US$ 15 million today.[40]

Smith had engaged in every aspect of the colony's import and export trade during a career that spanned almost thirty years, shipping agricultural products and animal pelts to Britain and Europe, and importing manufactured and luxury goods. In the deerskin trade *Simmons, Smith & Crokatt* was responsible for twenty-three cargoes, *Smith & Brewton* and *Smith & Palmer* for a further twenty-eight, and *Benjamin Smith & Co.* for six.[41] All four firms were similarly active in rice and indigo. In general merchandise and luxury goods, *Smith & Brewton* ranked one of the top five import houses.[42] And in the slave trade, *Smith & Brewton* and *Benjamin Smith & Co.* arranged fourteen cargoes.[43] Although it is not possible to determine the extent to which his trading business was assisted by freemasonry, his prominence makes it reasonable to assume an association.

Smith was as successful politically as he was financially. His career in public office began as a vestryman in St Philip's Parish and then churchwarden, roles he held virtually continuously from 1740-70. He was elected Charleston's Firemaster, and was appointed to numerous commissions ranging from supervising the workhouse and town markets, to overseeing trade with the first nations. In the assembly, Smith represented St Philip's Parish

---

[39] Quoted in Kenneth Morgan, 'Slave Sales in Colonial Charleston', *English Historical Review*, 113.453 (1998), 905-27; quote from 910.

[40] Based on an average earnings inflator.

[41] Moore, Jr., 'The Largest Exporters of Deerskins from Charles Town, 1735-1775', 144-50.

[42] Stumpf, 'South Carolina Importers of General Merchandise, 1735-1765', 1-10.

[43] W. Robert Higgins, 'Charles Town Merchants and Factors Dealing in the External Negro Trade 1735-1775', *South Carolina Historical Magazine*, 65.4 (1964), 205-17.

from 1746,[44] and was speaker from 1755-63. He declined the offer of a seat on the royal council in 1760. Generally a political moderate, Smith adopted a patriotic stance in the mid-1760s following the introduction of the Stamp Act.

Smith's connection with freemasonry dates from his apprenticeship with James Crokatt. Crokatt's influence explains why Smith was elected master of Solomon's Lodge aged 22 and provincial grand master at 25. Following Peter Leigh's selection by London as South Carolina's new provincial grand master in 1754, Smith was appointed provincial senior grand warden and in 1760 following Leigh's death, he was deputed by London as PGM for North and South Carolina.

Information on South Carolina freemasonry from the mid-1740s to the early 1750s is sparse. Following a ruling by Fotherley Baker, the deputy grand master of the Grand Lodge of England,[45] masonic processions celebrating St John's Day were suspended in the late 1740s and resumed only in the mid-1750s. From that point the *South Carolina Gazette* recorded the event annually with the exception of 1759, when the event was cancelled as a result of the Anglo-French war.[46]

Smith was speaker of the assembly and one of the leading merchants in the colony when he took the chair as provincial grand master in 1760. His slate of provincial grand officers was led by the late Peter Leigh's son, Egerton, and included several prominent figures. William Henderson, Smith's provincial senior grand warden, was master of Charleston's Free

---

[44] Aside from St Philip's Parish, Smith represented St George Dorchester 1749-51, St James Goose Creek 1766-68, and Sir John Colleton Parish in 1770. He did not serve in the eighteenth and twenty-eighth assemblies.

[45] Cf., *Schism*, esp. chapter five. One of the most important freemasons in the 1740s, Fotherley Baker (*d*.1754) held a succession of grand offices: JGW, 1744; SGW, 1745-6; DGM, 1747-52. A City-based lawyer and later clerk to the Worshipful Company of Haberdashers, he was a member of the St Paul's Head lodge in Ludgate Street.

[46] *South Carolina Gazette*, 22 December 1759.

School, a high status positon, and librarian of the Charleston Library Society in 1755.[47] The comment that 'no man in the settlement was more honoured nor more honourable' offers a contemporary assessment,[48] as does his portrayal as 'a man of talent and education [and] a poet'.[49] He returned to England in 1763.[50]

William Burrows, the provincial junior grand warden, a lawyer and magistrate, had settled in South Carolina in around 1741 and married the daughter of John Ward, a planter and assemblyman. Burrows co-founded the Charleston Library Society and was president of the South Carolina Society and St George's Society. A successful merchant, he invested in property and by the 1760s had land holdings that exceeded 10,000 acres across Craven, Berkeley and Colleton counties. He was considered one of the colony's leading citizens and owned one of the largest mansions on Broad Street.[51]

Robert Wells, the provincial grand secretary, settled in Charleston in 1752 and opened *Well's Stationery and Book Store* two years later; it would become the pre-eminent book shop and stationery outlet in the Carolinas.[52] He diversified into printing and publishing and with British government backing founded the loyalist *South Carolina and American General Gazette* (1764-74). Unlike many contemporaries but in common with Egerton Leigh and other members of

---

[47] A decision to fund education in the province had been taken by the assembly in the 1710s.

[48] Cf. Virginia B. Bartels (ed.), *The History of South Carolina Schools* (Center for Educator Recruitment, Retention, and Advancement – SC), p. 3. at www.teacher-cadets.com/media/documents/2010/8/History_of_South_Carolina_Schools.pdf, accessed 31 January 2014.

[49] Mackey, *History of Freemasonry*, p. 30.

[50] Henry Laurens, *Papers of Henry Laurens: 10 October 1771 – 19 April 1773*, p. 130.

[51] Cf. Harriett P. and Albert Simons, 'The William Burrows House of Charleston', *South Carolina Historical and Genealogical Magazine*, 70 (1969), 155-76.

[52] Cf. Christopher Gould, 'Scottish Printers and Booksellers in Colonial Charleston, S.C.', *Studies in Scottish Literature*, 15 (1980): scholarcommons.sc.edu/ssl/vol15/iss1/15, accessed 22 September 2014.

Union Kilwinning Lodge, Wells took a royalist line. He fled Charleston when news of the battles of Concord and Lexington reached the city.[53]

Smith gave notice of his intention to resign as provincial grand master on 28 December 1767 citing declining health.[54] Egerton Leigh took over on an acting basis and in 1769 was appointed formally by deputation from the Grand Lodge of England. Smith died in 1770 at Newport, Rhode Island; his body was brought back to be reinterred in Charleston.[55]

SOLOMON'S LODGE

Smith's masonic contemporaries in the 1740s and 1750s were largely public officials, planters, merchants and ship owners. John Gwyn, the master of the lodge, was a partner in the firm of *Houghton, Webb and Gwyn* based on the Bay,[56] which exported deerskins, rice and naval stores, and imported dry goods.[57] The principal partner, John Houghton (d.1751), had been master of Solomon's Lodge in 1738 and provincial grand master the year after.[58]

---

[53] Cf. David Moltke-Hansen, 'Wells, Robert (1727/8–1794)', *ODNB* (online edn., Jan 2008).

[54] *South Carolina Gazette*, 1 January 1768.

[55] Smith married twice, first in 1740 to Anne Loughton, one of Carolina's oldest families having settled in the 1680s. Anne died of smallpox in February 1760 and Smith married again in October of the same year. His second wife, Mary, was Joseph Wragg's daughter. The marriage combined two of the colony's foremost merchant dynasties.

[56] Henry Laurens, *Papers of Henry Laurens* (Columbia, SC: USC Press, 1968), p. 17, letter to Rogers & Dyson, 8 July 1747; also, Henry Laurens and Joseph W. Barnwell, *South Carolina Historical and Genealogical Magazine*, 28.3 (1927), 165-6, letter to Smith & Clifton; and Jeanne A. Calhoun, Martha A. Zierden and Elizabeth A. Paysinger, 'The Geographic Spread of Charleston's Mercantile Community, 1732-1767', *South Carolina Historical Magazine*, 86.3 (1985), 182-220.

[57] Moore, 'The Largest Exporters of Deerskins from Charles Town, 1735-1775'; also Stumpf, 'South Carolina Importers of General Merchandise, 1735-1765', 1-10.

[58] *South Carolina Gazette*, 27 December 1739.

John Mackenzie,[59] the senior warden, had premises on the Bay and a Broad Street, and traded mainly as an importer of dry goods and general merchandise. He co-owned eight vessels, several with members of the lodge, including Kenneth Michie (d.1749), lodge secretary, and his brother, Benjamin. The Michies had migrated to Charleston in the 1730s and founded *Kenneth & Benjamin Michie*. Described as 'eminent merchants' by the *South Carolina Gazette*, they exported deerskins and imported luxury and general goods.[60] Michie invested his profits in *Oak Grove*, a 684-acre plantation on the Charleston Neck,[61] and in shipping. Five of his nine vessels were co-owned with Mackenzie and one with John Crokatt.

Kenneth Michie married in 1746. His wife, Mary, 'a young lady of great fortune',[62] was the daughter of Gillson Clapp (d.1737), a planter and merchant whose main business was in Dorchester, eighteen miles inland from Charleston on the Ashley River. Clapp was also linked to North Carolina through Eleazer Allen and William Rhett. Mary remarried after Michie's death. Her second husband, David Deas, was a loyalist and member of the royal council,[63] a partner in *Lennox & Deas* (1746-55),[64] and subsequently

---

[59] Also written as 'McKenzie'.

[60] A.S. Salley, Jr., *Death Notices in the South Carolina Gazette, 1732-1775* (Columbia, SC: Historical Commission of South Carolina, 1917), p. 22.

[61] Henry A.M. Smith, 'Charleston and Charleston Neck: The Original Grantees and the Settlements along the Ashley and Cooper Rivers', *South Carolina Historical and Genealogical Magazine*, 19.1 (1918), 3-76, esp. 60-2.

[62] Clapp's Dorchester-based business supplied Berkeley County; it was a partnership with four merchants: Thomas Satur of Dorchester and Jacob Satur of London, both Huguenots; and Eleazer Allen and William Rhett Jr., brothers-in-law, of Charleston and later Brunswick, NC.

[63] K.H. Ledward (ed.), *Journals of the Board of Trade and Plantations, Volume 13: January 1768 - December 1775* (London: IHR, 1937), pp. 241-245: 'April 1771, fo. 85', www.british-history.ac.uk/report.aspx?compid=77700&strquery=David Date, accessed 6 October 2014.

[64] George C. Rogers Jr., et al (eds.), *Papers of Henry Laurens, volume 5, 1 September 1765 – 31 July 1768* (Columbia, SC: USC Press, 1976), p. 612, fn. 4.

David & John Deas, a leading slave-trading house. His brother, John, became provincial grand master.

Thomas Smith, the treasurer, was probably Benjamin Smith's brother (1720-90), who traded from Broad Street, rather than the unrelated Thomas Smith (1695-1769), located on the Bay.[65] Both had extensive connections in Charleston's merchant community and co-owned numerous vessels.[66] Smith 'at Broad Street' was a junior partner in *Hopton & Smith* before trading on his own account, financing five slave cargoes in 1753-4 but specialising mainly in manufactured goods, with twenty-one cargoes between 1754-60. Smith 'on the Bay' was in partnership with Edward Cossens, a Bristol merchant, until 1747, after which he traded independently, handling seventy-five cargoes between 1741-65.

Smith 'at Broad Street' owned the 840-acre *Broom Hall* estate, a plantation used as a country retreat. He was commissioned a captain, then adjutant, of the Berkeley County Regiment of Foot, served in the assembly (1769-73) and was elected to the first provincial congress in 1775.[67] Smith 'on the Bay' was a justice of the peace for Berkeley County (1734) and from 1747-9 a commissioner of the workhouse, markets and poor. He served in the assembly from 1751-55.[68]

John Oyston, the junior warden, a former lodge secretary and treasurer, operated from Simmons Wharf and traded mainly with counterparts in Philadelphia.[69] He co-owned the *Speedwell*, a 15-ton schooner, with John Barksdale and James Howell.[70] Henry Harramond, one of two stewards, a

---

[65] Each was known by the address of the premises he occupied.

[66] The South Carolina Ship Registry does not differentiate between the various Thomas Smiths.

[67] He was also a member of the South Carolina Society and Charleston Library Society.

[68] He was also president (1756) of the Charleston Library Society.

[69] Calhoun et al, 'The Geographic Spread of Charleston's Mercantile Community, 1732-1767', 200.

[70] Olsberg, 'Ship Registers in the South Carolina Archives 1734-1780', 267.

master mariner, owned three vessels outright and co-owned a fourth, *Molly*, a 25-ton schooner, with Thomas Johnson.

Among the handful of members who were not merchants were Robert Blythe, the second steward, who owned 'Mr Blythe's Tavern' in Broad Street;[71] Alexander Murray (d.1746), a naval officer, a former master of the lodge and later provincial senior grand warden and provincial grand secretary, 'a gentleman of a universal good character';[72] and Hugh Anderson (d.1748), a provincial junior grand warden (1742) and the master of Charleston's Free School.

---

[71] Edward McCrady, *The History of South Carolina under the Royal Government 1719-1766* (London: Macmillan, 1899), p. 493.

[72] Salley, Jr., *Death Notices in the South Carolina Gazette, 1732-1775*, p. 21.

Chapter Three

'Calling On' – Peter Leigh

Charleston was one of the leading commercial and social centres in America, ranking in importance alongside New York, Philadelphia and Boston. It was also an important hub for freemasonry. Although the Grand Lodge of England had selected John Hammerton as South Carolina's first provincial grand master, they had no involvement in the choice of Hammerton's successors until 1754, when Peter Leigh, was granted a deputation as provincial grand master by the Marquis of Carnarvon, later the 2nd Duke of Chandos.[1]

Mackey interprets Leigh's appointment as marking the rebirth of South Carolina's provincial grand lodge but offers no explanation as to why this was necessary or that it was the case. Whether freemasonry had 'languished', as Mackey suggests, or operated without publicity following an over-zealous interpretation of Fotherley Baker's new grand lodge regulations is unclear.

Lord Byron's departure as grand master of the Grand Lodge of England in 1752 ended a five-year hiatus in English freemasonry.[2] His successor, Lord Carysfort, appointed Thomas Manningham as deputy grand master and the Hon. James Carmichael and Sir Richard Wrottesley as grand wardens. Wrottesley, MP for Tavistock in the Duke of Bedford's interest,[3] was a member of the King's Arms in the Strand, one of London's more influential lodges

---

[1] Leigh was initiated into the Black Lion lodge at Jockey's Fields, Gray's Inn, London, in or around 1731.

[2] Following his installation, Byron was present in grand lodge only once: on 16 March 1752 when he proposed that Lord Carysfort be installed as his successor; in the intervening years Baker acted as DGM with 'full authority and right'.

[3] Sir Richard Wrottesley, 7th Bt., (1721-1769), was related to the Earls of Stamford through his mother. His wife, Lady Mary, was the daughter of the 1st Earl of Gower. He was a Tory and allied himself to the Leveson-Gowers in Parliament. Wrottesley gave up politics in 1754 to take holy orders, becoming chaplain to George III (1763) and Dean of Worcester (1765).

with strong ties to grand lodge, many of whose officers were members,[4] and of the Queen's Head at Bath, where court favourites the Duke of St Alban,[5] Viscount Cobham[6] and Lord Hervey were members.[7] Wrottesley had been a grand steward and nominated Leigh as his successor in 1752. Leigh's appointment as South Carolina's chief justice was announced the following year and Wrottesley, now senior grand warden, used his influence to make certain that Leigh was appointed South Carolina's provincial grand master before departing for Charleston.

PETER LEIGH

Peter Leigh (1711-1759), the youngest son of Cheshire minor gentry, entered the Middle Temple in 1732 and was called to the Bar in November 1734. He was an effective barrister and a decade later acquired the position of High Bailiff of Westminster.[8] This included the roles of sheriff and electoral returning officer for Westminster, one of the country's most important constituencies.

Leigh presided as High Bailiff at the election of 1747. The successful candidates for the constituency's two seats standing in the Duke of Bedford's interest[9] were the duke's brother-in-law, Granville Leveson-Gower,[10] and Sir

---

[4] Cf. Berman, *Schism*; also Colin Dyer, *The Grand Stewards and their Lodge* (London: privately published, 1985), p. 257.

[5] Charles Beauclerk, 2nd Duke of St Albans (1696-1751), grandson of Charles II.

[6] Richard Temple (1675-1749), 1st Viscount Cobham, 4th Baronet of Stowe.

[7] John Hervey, 2nd Baron Hervey (1696-1743). The eldest son of John Hervey, 1st Earl of Bristol, he pre-deceased his father.

[8] *Daily Advertiser*, 12 March 1744 et al; and *Daily Gazetteer*, 29 March 1744. Although the preserve of the dean and chapter of Westminster, the office of High Bailiff was in practice sold by each incumbent as his personal property.

[9] Leigh was second cousin to the Duchess of Bedford and, through marriage, Leveson-Gower's second cousin.

[10] Granville Leveson-Gower, 1st Marquess of Stafford (1721 - 1803), known as Viscount Trentham (1746-54) and as Earl Gower from 1754-86.

Peter Warren, a prominent naval officer.[11] The duke was First Lord of the Admiralty and his patronage enabled Leveson-Gower to be appointed alongside him. It was a requirement that any MP accepting government office should resign and offer himself for re-election, and in 1749 Leveson-Gower did so. His opponent at the by-election was Sir George Vandeput, standing for the borough's independent voters in association with the Prince of Wales's opposition Leicester House faction.

The by-election was aggressively and expensively contested and at the count Leveson-Gower claimed victory by a margin of 4,811 to 4,654. Vandeput's supporters demanded a recount and confirmation that each elector had been eligible to vote. As returning officer, Leigh granted the request, albeit at a fee of paid at £4 guineas per day.[12] The recount and his scrutiny of the electoral roll continued for three months before the exercise was curtailed, at which point around 700 ineligible votes were found to have been cast for each side. The result was upheld and Leveson-Gower returned with a majority of 170.[13]

The opposition accused Leigh of bias and complained that the government had interfered with due electoral process. Parliament was petitioned in favour of an annulment and agreed that a debate should be held. But rather than enquire into the merits of the argument, the Commons passed a motion requiring that Leigh be brought to the Bar of the House to explain why his scrutiny had lasted three months. Leigh's supporters had arranged that he would be available in the lobby in order to respond and when Leigh went before the House he defended himself and launched a counter-attack, accusing Vandeput's supporters of obstruction and disrespect of parliamentary

---

[11] Peter Warren (1703-1752) commanded British naval forces in the attack on the French position at Louisburg in Nova Scotia in 1745. He was later promoted Admiral of the Red.

[12] A guinea was £1 1s, equivalent to £1.05 post-decimalisation. Professional services and luxury goods were traditionally priced in guineas. The value would be around £5,000 per day in current money.

[13] *London Evening Post*, 12-15 May 1750.

process. The House found in his favour and Vandeput's attorney and two of his supporters were arraigned, interrogated and found guilty of contempt.

The by-election had undoubtedly been corrupt but almost all contested elections followed the same pattern: mobs would be hired by both sides to intimidate their opponents, and alcohol and cash dispensed to encourage their own. But this was Westminster and the government did not welcome opposition at the heart of the establishment, not even with the backing of the Prince of Wales. There was additionally no evidence that Leigh had ruled arbitrarily; indeed, the *Gentleman's Magazine* in December 1749 noted that he had 'acted with great impartiality',[14] and prior to declaring the result, Leigh had faced counter accusations that he favoured the borough's independent voters, prompting one diarist to write that he had 'never [seen] an accusation worse supported by anything but numbers'.[15]

No charges against Leigh were pursued and, despite reports to the contrary, he was not forced from office but instead chose to accept the more remunerative and prestigious position of South Carolina's chief justice. The prospect had been trailed in the press for weeks,[16] and the description of his move to Charleston as 'one of the famous political deals of the period'[17] and of Leigh being 'under suspicion of improper conduct in a former office'[18] were disingenuous.

Peter Manigault's judgment expressed in a letter to his father offers a more accurate analysis: 'as I have had occasion to hear great prejudices have arisen in Carolina against Mr Leigh, the worthy gentleman who has been appointed our Chief Justice, I think it will not be improper to let you into the

---

[14] *Gentleman's Magazine*, December 1749.

[15] H.P. Wyndham (ed.), *Diary of the late George Bubb Dodington, Baron of Melcombe Regis* (London: G. & T. Wilkie, 1785), 3rd edn., p. 88.

[16] *London Evening Post*, 13-15 February 1753.

[17] H.L. Osgood, *The American Colonies in the Eighteenth Century* (New York, 1924), volume 4, p. 274.

[18] McCrady, *The History of South Carolina under the Royal Government 1719-1766*, esp. pp. 279-81.

source of those prejudices & the slight foundation upon which they are built; that you may by your influence, recover as much as possible the character of this gentleman, thus grossly aspersed. He was at the Bar for twenty years and in all that time had never anything objected to his conduct, except now and then a little imprudence. It was his misfortune some time ago to be appointed High Bailiff of Westminster by virtue of which office he is the person that returns the members to serve in parliament for that borough. About three years ago there was an election much controverted ... the losers in this election ... finding that the number of votes were superior on the other side ... without any more consideration grasped at all opportunities to destroy his good character. But they did not stop here. They were so hardy as to present a petition. I happened to be in the House when this petition was presented and it appearing that most of the suggestions in it were false, it was almost unanimously rejected, and what was very remarkable, a letter was produced from the very member that brought in the petition, to Mr Leigh, in which he passed many encomiums upon his candour in the affair. This, Sir, is the shortest state I could give you of the abuse offered this worthy gentleman'.[19]

Leigh established himself in Charleston as 'a man of family and fashion'.[20] His seniority as chief justice, ranking fourth behind the governor, lieutenant-governor and secretary, and his seat on the royal council, gave him status, as did his position as the colony's new provincial grand master. Even Edward McCrady who accused him of being a 'discredited English barrister' considered Leigh's time in South Carolina a period when there was not 'the least cause of suspicion as to his integrity' and described him as 'a man of ability, a good lawyer' and 'a gentleman'.[21]

---

[19] H. Hale Bellot, 'The Leighs in South Carolina', *Transactions of the Royal Historical Society*, 5th series, volume 6 (1956), 161-87, esp. 173-4.

[20] Harriott H. Ravenal, *Eliza Pinckney* (New York: C. Scribener's Sons, 1896), p. 135.

[21] McCrady, *The History of South Carolina under the Royal Government, 1719-1776*, pp. 36, 280-1, 465.

Provincial Grand Master for South Carolina

Carrying a deputation from the Marquis of Carnarvon dated 30 March 1754 signed by the deputy grand master, Thomas Manningham, and witnessed by John Revis, the grand secretary, Leigh's masonic standing in South Carolina was impeccable. Hammerton had been absent from Charleston for years and Leigh saw his appointment as an opportunity to remould South Carolina freemasonry in London's image. It explains the classified advertisements for the annual grand feast and general communication printed in the *South Carolina Gazette* in December 1754 issued *By Order of the Grand Master* which in keeping with London practice was signed by Leigh's newly appointed grand stewards.

The advertisements announced that the event was to be held in Charleston on Friday 27 December, St John the Evangelist's day, and that 'all brothers are desired to provide themselves with tickets … and to meet that day by eight o'clock in the morning at the house of brother John Gordon in order to attend the Grand Master and his officers to St Philip's Church where a sermon is to be preached by a Rev brother whence they are to return in procession to the Lodge room where a decent and suitable entertainment will be provided'.[22]

Attendance would have been enhanced by the appointment of a number of leading merchants and planters to serve as grand officers.

Hon. Peter Leigh	Provincial Grand Master
Hon. James Michie	Deputy PGM
Hon. Benjamin Smith	Provincial Senior Grand Warden
William Henderson	Provincial Junior Grand Warden
William Burrows	Provincial Grand Treasurer
Samuel Perkins	Provincial Grand Secretary

---

[22] *South Carolina Gazette*, 5 December 1754.

Samuel Carne	Provincial Grand Sword Bearer
Egerton Leigh	)
John Stuart	)
Charles Pinckney	)
Henry Laurens	) Provincial Grand Stewards
Robert Wells	)
John Cooper	)
George Sheed	Provincial Grand Tyler

Most had been members of South Carolina freemasonry for some time and all were prominent local figures. John Stuart (1718-1799), a Scot, had migrated to Charleston in 1748 and formed a partnership, *Stuart & Reid*, with Patrick Reid. The firm was active in slave trading and importing general merchandise and traded until Reid's death in 1754. Stuart's fortunes declined thereafter but despite being bankrupted in 1756 he rebuilt his wealth and eventually acquired more than 10,000 acres across Granville, Colleton and Berkeley counties.

Stuart represented St Helena in the Commons from 1754-57 and served as a captain in the Georgia militia, but he is known best as the Superintendent of Indian Affairs for the Southern District with a direct reporting line to London. The Southern District included every province south of Maryland and the office entitled Stuart to a seat on the royal council of each. Stuart, a loyalist, later fell out with his patriotic contemporaries, including fellow lodge member Peter Timothy, who refused to allow Stuart to publish his news releases in the *Gazette*. Stuart had more amenable friends in the St Andrews Society, which he joined on arrival in the colony and of which he was president from 1772. Regardless, allegations that Stuart was attempting to influence the first nations against the patriotic cause and in support of Britain forced him to flee South Carolina for Florida. Stuart's assets in South Carolina were subsequently seized and declared forfeit.

Samuel Carne (1727-1786),[23] settled in Charleston in 1740 and practiced as a doctor and apothecary.[24] He later diversified into trade, opening a successful merchant house at Cordia Waters and in 1747 moving to larger premises on the Bay. The business gave him the resources to acquire a part-share in two vessels, *Charming Peggy* and *Koulikan*, 20-ton schooners. Carne was appointed Port Physician in 1759 and the following year a commissioner to stamp paper currency. His political career began at the same time with his election to represent St Peter's Parish. He was returned for Christ Church in 1761 where he had a 1,000-acre plantation. Coincidentally, it was put up for sale the following year:[25]

> To be SOLD, at public vendue, on Wednesday the 10th day of November, at the subscriber's plantation in Christ-Church Parish, the said plantation, containing near 1000 acres of land, good for indigo, corn, etc. with some rice land, together with the house, stills, vats, ----houses, barn, and other out-houses.
>
> The agreeable healthy situation of this place is too well known to need any pompous description, and the present possessor of it is so well satisfied of the many profitable advantages that may be made of the distillery; and also of the land, by sawing, lime burning, or raising stock, etc. for the Charles-Town market that was he not about to leave the province, no money should tempt him to part with it.
>
> At the same time and place will be sold, three sets of indigo vats, with a lime vat large enough to supply ten lots. A parcel of healthy valuable young Negroes, amongst which is one pair of sawyers and some sensible boys and young wenches. A small stock of young cattle, about 40 head

---

[23] Carne's date of birth is given variously as 1725 or 1727.
[24] Carne was a partner of Dr Robert Wilson, 1759-70, and Dr Elisha Poinsett, 1770-75. Cf., Laurens, *Papers of Henry Laurens, 1 November 1755 – 31 December 1758*, p. 212, fn. 2.
[25] *South Carolina Gazette*, 9 October 1762.

of sheep, a large parcel of goats, household furniture, a riding chair and draught horses, one soared canow and a smaller one, sundry plantation tools, and utensils for the distillery, with many other articles too tedious to enumerate.

Carne was appointed provincial grand sword bearer and senior warden of Solomon's Lodge in 1754, and in 1760 was elected master of an unnamed lodge, possibly the Masters' Lodge. In addition to freemasonry, he was a member of the Charleston Library Society (1750-67) and South Carolina Society (1746-77). Carne left Charleston for London in 1764 to establish a trading business. Although not as successful as Crokatt, his profits were nonetheless substantial and reinvested in two plantations. *Haggart Hall*, a 1,300-acre estate, and *Crowfield*, 1,440 acres. The cost was an estimated £10,000 sterling. *Crowfield* was sold in 1776, probably as a hedge against the coming hostilities.

Like Stuart, Carne was a loyalist. He declined to take an oath against George III and fled the colony in August 1777, leaving his wife and son in Charleston.[26] He returned with the British in 1779[27] and remained until 1782, hoping to realise his assets and avoid 'the same fate [as the] loyalists of Savannah'.[28] Carne's assets were confiscated when the British withdrew and allotted to his son who had fought in the patriotic cause.[29] Carne was also forced to write-off his outstanding receivables and although he filed a claim with the Loyalist Claims Commission for £4,481, he received nothing and

---

[26] Carne's house was at 4 Orange Street. He acquired it shortly before his departure for England in 1777.
[27] Carne to Christopher Rolleton, 12 October 1780: Samuel Carne Papers, South Caroliniana Library, USC.
[28] Carne to James Blair, *12 July 1782*: Samuel Carne Papers, South Caroliniana Library, USC.
[29] Listed in the *Royal Gazette* 'Confiscations List', 20 March 1782.

was later bankrupted. Alienated from his family politically and geographically, he died in London in 1787.

Peter Leigh's death from fever in 1759 was reported on both sides of the Atlantic.[30] James Michie, his deputy, took over as acting provincial grand master. Michie's position in the colony made him a candidate to succeed Leigh however he died soon afterwards. Benjamin Smith, the senior provincial grand warden, was installed as Leigh's successor in December 1761.

Smith's grand officers were predominantly those who had been appointed a decade earlier and with the exception of Henderson, the master of Charleston's Free School who died in 1763, the line remained in situ until Smith retired.

Hon. Benjamin Smith	Provincial Grand Master
Hon. Egerton Leigh	Deputy Provincial Grand Master
Mr William Henderson	Provincial Senior Grand Warden
Mr William Burrows	Provincial Junior Grand Warden
Robert Wells	Provincial Grand Secretary

SOUTH CAROLINA'S MODERNS LODGES

The 1750s and 1760s were a period of masonic expansion in South Carolina with 'many ... gentlemen of distinction' initiated into freemasonry and on 31 December 1764, a year before the Stamp Act crisis, the *South Carolina Gazette* reported that 120 members were present at the St John's Day

---

[30] *London Evening Post* and *Whitehall Evening Post or London Intelligencer*, 14-16 February 1760, et al. The prior week the press had announced the death of Peter Leigh's brother, Egerton, archdeacon of Hereford Cathedral. The name 'Egerton' was taken in honour of the earls of Bridgwater, into whose family the Leigh's had married.

festival, including William Bull, lieutenant-governor, and the Hon. Lord Adam Gordon, MP for Aberdeenshire, colonel of the 66th Foot.[31]

At least three lodges were working in Charleston: Solomon's Lodge, with George Sheed as master; Union Kilwinning[32] under John Deas; and the Masters' Lodge, with William Gibbs in the chair. Other lodges operated at Beaufort, Dorchester, Georgetown, Ponpon and Saxe Gotha, now Columbia. With 40-50 members per lodge, and disregarding those who were members of more than one, the implication is that South Carolina was home to more than 300 freemasons. A letter from Charleston dated 1784 despatched to the Grand Lodge of England set out a definitive list of Moderns' lodges.[33]

A List of the several Lodges Constituted in the State of South Carolina by the Provincial Grand Masters thereof by Deputation from the Grand Lodge of England from the Year 5736 until the year 5784

Provincial Number	Lodge Name	Date of Constitution [34]
1	Solomon's Lodge, Charleston	1736
2	St George Lodge, Dorchester	1738
3	Prince George Lodge, Winyaw	1743

---

[31] Lord Adam Gordon (*c*.1726-1801) was MP for Aberdeenshire from 1754-68 and for Kincardineshire (1774-88). In 1767 he married the widow of James, 2nd Duke of Atholl. Gordon was a professional soldier, commissioned into the 2nd dragoons in 1741 and eventually promoted to commander in chief of Scotland (1789-98) and governor of Edinburgh Castle. He was colonel of the 66th Foot (1763-1775).

[32] The lodge appears under different guises in the registers of the Grand Lodge of England and the Grand Lodge of Scotland.

[33] UGLE Library & Museum, London: GBR 1991 HC 28/E/6.

[34] In the letter the date of constitution of each lodge is written in the Masonic form and not as shown, i.e., '1737' is written as '5737' and so on; the dates of constitution given for lodges 4 to 7, and 10 and 11, also specify the day and month.

4	Union [Kilwinning] Lodge, Charleston	1755 / 1759[35]
5	Masters' Lodge, Charleston	1756
6	Port Royal Lodge, Beaufort	1756
7	Jacksonborough Lodge, Ponpon	1765
8	Marine Lodge, Charleston	1766
9	Tyrian Lodge, Saxegotha Township	no date given[36]
10	Military Lodge, no location given	1778
11	St John's Lodge, Charleston	1784

Mackey's *History* and Lane's *Masonic Records* differ from the above. Lane confuses Solomon's Lodge in Charleston with the lodge in Savannah later given the same name: 'this lodge is erroneously called Solomon's Lodge, Charles Town, South Carolina … but is correctly indexed under Georgia'. He nonetheless cites 1735 as the date the warrant was issued in England and this is probably correct. Lane also omits St George Lodge in Dorchester but records Union Lodge in Charleston, giving a warrant date of 3 May 1755. Union Kilwinning Lodge, a Scottish-warranted lodge, was chartered the same month.[37] John Deas, apparently the master of both lodges, was later the Moderns' provincial grand master.

Lane notes that the Masters' Lodge at Charleston received its warrant on 22 March 1756 and that at Port Royal Lodge, Beaufort, on 15 September 1756. Jacksonborough Lodge at Ponpon, midway between Beaufort and Charleston, is ignored by Lane and Mackey, with Lane also

---

[35] Union Lodge had an English warrant; Union Kilwinning a Scottish warrant. Mackey argues that the former lodge became the latter. Other sources show two lodges in existence. It is possible that the lodge held two warrants.

[36] The letter notes that the provincial grand lodge minutes for 1766 recording the formation of Tyrian Lodge were lost: 'the reason why the date of its constitution was not nor could be ascertained'.

[37] A few editions of *The Free Masons Pocket Companion* include both Union and Union Kilwinning as English and Scottish respectively. Cf., for example, John Entick, *The Freemasons Pocket Companion* (Edinburgh: William Auld, 1772), pp. 142 & 287.

excluding Marine Lodge. Tyrian Lodge is listed as 'St Mark's lodge', Saxe Gotha, with a warrant dated 8 February 1763. The same date is recorded by Mackey: 'the date of this warrant in one of the registries in my possession is 8 February 1763'.

Lane's *Masonic Records* provides details of two lodges not included in the 1784 list. The first received its warrant on 30 September 1774 and later became an Antients' lodge; the second, No. 498, obtained its warrant in 1761 but ceased to submit returns after 1765. It may also have joined the Antients. Lane does not record either the Military Lodge, No. 10 or St John's Lodge, No. 11.

In summary, Lane's *Masonic Records* lists the following lodges:

Lodge Number[38]	Lodge Name	Date of Constitution	Location
46	not named	1735[39]	Charleston
75	Prince George	1743	George Town
116	Union	1755	Charleston
125	Masters' Lodge	1756	Charleston
126	Port Royal	1756	Beaufort
92	unnamed	1761 (later Antients)	Charleston
163	St Mark's	1763	Saxe Gotha
190	not named	1774 (later Antients)	Charleston
236	not named	1786 (later Antients)	Charleston

One other lodge can be added to those recognising the Grand Lodge of South Carolina: No. 12, La Candeur, established in Charleston on 24 July 1796. It was the last lodge to affiliate with the Moderns and did so on 27 December 1798.

---

[38] The number is given per the 1792 numeration.
[39] Solomon's Lodge, Charleston.

Chapter Four

'Calling Off'

Egerton Leigh

Egerton Leigh (1733-1781), was 20 when he joined his father in South Carolina. An only child, he was educated at Westminster School.[1] A subsequent description as 'late of Lincoln's Inn'[2] is disingenuous and refers to residence within the Inn. There is no evidence that Leigh was admitted a member of Lincoln's Inn, let alone called to the Bar.[3] Non-member residents sub-let rooms from benchers, members of the Inn,[4] and any legal training would have been informal at best.[5]

Despite the absence of a legal qualification, Leigh was admitted to the South Carolina Bar by his father within six months of his arrival in Charleston

---

[1] H. Hale Bellot, 'The Leighs in South Carolina', esp. 175.

[2] Warwickshire County Record Office: CR 1711/67, *1753*, re the Admission of Egerton Leigh, late of Lincoln's Inn, as one of the attorneys of the Court of Commons Pleas of South Carolina by Peter Leigh, Chief Justice of South Carolina. [Dated Charlestown, 1 November 1753.]

[3] Egerton Leigh is not mentioned in the 'Black Books': *The Records of the Honourable Society of Lincoln's Inn* (London, 1899), volume III (1660-1775); nor in the Serle's Court Books (Lincoln's Inn Archives E2 a1) or the Red Books (L .I. Archives E1 a2 & 3). However cf. Warwickshire County Record Office: CR 1711/67, *1753*, 'the Admission of Egerton Leigh, *late of Lincolns Inn*, as one of the attorneys of the Court of Commons Pleas of South Carolina by Peter Leigh, Chief Justice of South Carolina'. Author's italics.

[4] Lincoln's Inn was not itself the freeholder of many of the chambers in New Court and had no control over third party letting.

[5] I am indebted to Guy Holborn, Librarian, Lincoln's Inn Library, for this information. Cf., David Lemmings, *Professors of the Law: Barristers and English Legal Culture in the Eighteenth Century* (Oxford: OUP, 2000), esp. pp. 230-9, for a discussion of the American connections to the Inns of Court.

and the following year was granted the position of clerk of the Court of Common Pleas. But despite the nepotism, it was Leigh's own abilities and connections that established him as a 'go-to' lawyer in the colony. A key element was his relationship with Henry Laurens, his wife's uncle. Leigh had married Martha Bremar, Henry Laurens' niece, the daughter of a successful planter, in January 1756, and Laurens subsequently gave Leigh part of his litigation business. His endorsement allowed Leigh to obtain legal work from other traders including Peter Manigault and Miles Brewton, the latter Benjamin Smith's former business partner. Leigh's law practice generated an income stream of more than £1,000 sterling annually,[6] and his connection to Laurens became so robust that when Leigh visited England in 1764 Laurens wrote to his London agents assuring them of Leigh's reliability and offering surety against his own credit for any loans that Leigh might take.[7]

Leigh was elected to the Commons in 1755 and the same year appointed surveyor general, a role which gave him responsibility for surveying and allocating land grants. He was re-elected in 1757 despite leaving for London to study at the Inner Temple. He remained in England for two years but although his fees are recorded as paid in the Inner Temple account books there is no mention of an admission to the Bar.[8]

In 1759, shortly before Leigh returned to Charleston, two vacancies arose on South Carolina's royal council. William Wragg (1714-1777), had been suspended from the council and then dismissed;[9] and Charles Pinckney

---

[6] Bellot, 'The Leighs in South Carolina', esp. 175.

[7] Robert M. Calhoon and Robert M. Weir, 'The Scandalous History of Sir Egerton Leigh', *William & Mary Quarterly*, 3rd series, 26.1 (1969), 47-74, esp. 51.

[8] Roberts, *A Calendar of Inner Temple Records*, volume 5, p. 88.

[9] William Wragg was a loyalist and supporter of the crown's authority in South Carolina. His dismissal from the royal council made many within the elites question the value of such a position and added to the incremental transfer of political power to the assembly. Cf., W. Stitt Robinson, *James Glen: From Scottish Provost to Royal Governor of South Carolina* (Westport, CT: Greenwood Press, 1996), p. 113.

(1699-1758), a leading attorney and former speaker, had died. Governor Lyttelton nominated Egerton Leigh and George Austin to be their successors and his recommendations were accepted by the Privy Council.[10]

London considered Leigh reliable and subsequently granted him a string of senior legal offices. In 1761, he was appointed sole judge of the Court of Vice-Admiralty and after another visit to London in 1764[11] was made attorney general, taking office in June 1765. As a member of the royal council, Leigh was also a justice of the Quorum (1765, 1767 and 1769) and a judge in Chancery.

Leigh's income from his law practice and fees as surveyor general and from his judicial offices allowed him to acquire *The Retreat*, a 500-acre plantation on the Santee River, a second estate on the Cooper River, and several property lots in Charleston.[12] But despite his investment in the colony, Leigh remained as an outsider. His adherence to parliamentary law and loyalty to Britain was shared by others in South Carolina but it was not the view of the majority and in 1765 it brought him into conflict with the Sons of Liberty who proclaimed Townshend's Stamp Act unconstitutional and a constraint on colonists' rights.

THE STAMP ACT

The Stamp Act made it obligatory for legal documents, including court papers, to be stamped – taxed, with those missing the required embossment

---

[10] K.H. Ledward (ed.), *Journals of the Board of Trade and Plantations, January 1759 - December 1763*, (London: IHR, 1935), volume 11, 1 June 1759.

[11] Calhoon and Weir, 'The Scandalous History of Sir Egerton Leigh', esp. 51.

[12] Egerton Leigh was also awarded a land grant of 1,000 acres in Georgia south of the Altamaha River and 900 acres in the South Carolina backcountry. Despite his seat on the royal council and position as surveyor general, a combination which gave him access to the best land in the province, there is no evidence that he acted exploitatively and his landholdings were a fraction of the size of many of his peers.

deemed void.[13] The legislation was designed to raise revenue to subsidise the cost of keeping Britain's regiments on station in America but many colonists failed to understand why a standing army was needed given that the threat from the French and their allies had diminished following the Treaty of Paris in 1763. The colonies' militias were to hand and, correctly or otherwise, considered adequate. But for the Sons of Liberty the bigger issue was one of principle. The legislation was portrayed as a unilateral extension of parliamentary sovereignty and a threat to the colonists' constitutional control over domestic taxation and expenditure.

London's influence over trade and navigation was accepted as a corollary of being part of the British Empire and had the benefits of naval protection. But the Stamp Act was seen differently. The Sons of Liberty raised what would be a defining issue: whether it was legitimate to raise tax without due representation. But although the dispute was portrayed as a rebuttal of a key tenet of democracy, this is not correct. The British government had invited the colonies' parliamentary agents, their London lobbyists and representatives, to propose alternative means of raising revenues both before the bill reached parliament and during the parliamentary process. But the suggestions put forward were limited and unviable. Indeed, America's assemblies had always failed to produce adequate funds to cover home defence.

George Grenville, the prime minister, saw no alternative to the Stamp Act, a view shared on all sides. The act was passed in the Commons by 205 votes to 49, and unanimously by the House of Lords. The debate demonstrated how the colonies were perceived in Britain. According to Townshend, the act should have been regarded as reasonable and fair; the colonists were 'children planted by our care, nourished up by our indulgence until they are grown to a degree of strength and opulence, and protected by our arms

---

[13] 5 George III, c. 12: *Duties in American Colonies Act 1765*.

[who] grudge to contribute their mite to relieve us from heavy weight of the burden which we lie under'.[14]

It was left to Colonel Isaac Barré[15] who led the minority opposition in parliament to set out an opposing view, one shared by the Sons of Liberty:

> ... planted by your care? No! Your oppression planted them in America. They fled from your tyranny to a then uncultivated and unhospitable [sic] country where they exposed themselves to almost all the hardships to which human nature is liable, and among others to the cruelties of a savage foe, the most subtle, and I take upon me to say, the most formidable of any people upon the face of God's earth
>
> ... nourished by your indulgence? They grew by your neglect of them. As soon as you began to care about them, that care was exercised in sending persons to rule over them, in one department and another, who were perhaps the deputies of deputies to some member of this house, sent to spy out their liberty, to misrepresent their actions and to prey upon them; men whose behaviour on many occasions has caused the blood of those sons of liberty to recoil within them
>
> ... protected by your arms? They have nobly taken up arms in your defence, have exerted a valour amidst their constant and laborious industry for the defence of a country whose frontier while drenched in blood, its interior parts have yielded all its little savings to your emolument ...
>
> The people, I believe, are as truly loyal as any subjects the king has, but a people jealous of their liberties and who will vindicate them if ever they should be violated; but the subject is too delicate and I will say no more.[16]

---

[14] Jared Ingersoll to Governor Thomas Fitch, 11 February 1765, in Edmund S. Morgan (ed.), *Prologue To Revolution: Sources And Documents On The Stamp Act Crisis, 1764-1766* (Chapel Hill, NC: UNC Press, 1959), pp. 24-43, esp. 29-35.

[15] Isaac Barré, an Irish Huguenot, had served in North America and sat in the 2nd Earl of Shelburne's interest.

[16] *Prologue To Revolution: Sources And Documents On The Stamp Act Crisis, 1764-1766.*

Jared Ingersoll,[17] Connecticut's parliamentary agent, had updated Hartford regarding the discussions that had preceded the act. Although a loyalist,[18] he could see both sides of the argument and was clear that the crisis resulted from a lack of understanding on both sides:

> The agents of the colonies have had several meetings at one of which they were pleased to desire Mr Franklin & myself as having lately come from America & knowing more intimately the sentiments of the people, to wait on Mr Grenville together with Mr Jackson & Mr Garth who being agents are also members of parliament to remonstrate against the Stamp Bill & to propose in case any tax must be laid upon America that the several colonies might be permitted to lay the tax themselves. This we did Saturday before last. Mr Grenville gave us a full hearing, told us he took no pleasure in giving the Americans so much uneasiness as he found he did, that it was the duty of his office to manage the revenue, that he really was made to believe that considering the whole of the circumstances of the mother country & the colonies, the latter could and ought to pay something, & that he knew of no better way than that now pursuing to lay such tax, but that if we could tell of a better he would adopt it... he said he had pledged his word for offering the Stamp Bill to the house, that the house would hear all our objections and would do as they thought best; he said, he wished we would preserve a coolness and moderation in America; that he had no need to tell us, that resentments indecently and unbecomingly expressed on one side the water would naturally produce

---

[17] Jared Ingersoll (1722-1781).

[18] Ingersoll was subsequently appointed stamp officer for Connecticut. Public pressure forced him to resign - 'the cause is not worth dying for' – and he was compensated by being appointed judge of the Court of Vice Admiralty for the middle colonies. Cf., William M. Meigs, *The Life of Jared Ingersoll* (Philadelphia, PA: J.B. Lippincott, 1897), p. 17. Ingersoll's son, also Jared (1749-1822), was a prominent supporter of American Independence and later the attorney general for Pennsylvania.

resentments on the other side, and that we could not hope to get any good by a controversy with the mother country; that their ears will always be open to any remonstrances from the Americans with respect to this bill both before it takes effect and after, if it shall take effect, which shall be expressed in a becoming manner, that is, as becomes subjects of the same common prince.[19]

Anti-Stamp Act protests took place in all thirteen colonies but in South Carolina the violence and vilification of stamp officers was particularly widespread. Leigh stood out prominently as the only member of the Bar who opposed opening the colony's courts without stamped papers, and as attorney general and an officer of the crown, attracted additional criticism for refusing to prosecute cases or enter judgments without stamped authority.

OPPROBRIUM AND WORSE

Leigh's inflexibility attracted the contempt of his colleagues at the Bar and of his clients, who removed their business. Criticism of his conflicts of interest was voiced at the same time and the assembly voted in favour of demanding that Leigh either resign as attorney general or from the bench. They also instructed their London agent, Charles Garth, to raise the matter with William Petty, Lord Shelburne,[20] the secretary of state, to stress 'the incompatibility of some of the offices held by Mr Leigh'.[21] Shelburne may have sympathised with Charleston's concerns but his formal response made clear that he could not intervene. Leigh held his offices under patents from the crown and there had been 'no representation of misbehaviour or

---

[19] Jared Ingersoll to Governor Thomas Fitch, 11 February 1765.

[20] William Petty, 1st Marquess of Lansdowne (1737-1805), known as the Earl of Shelburne 1761-84. Prime Minister 1782-3 during the final months of the War of Independence.

[21] *South Carolina Historical and Genealogical Magazine*, 28 (1927), 228

omission of duty'.[22] The government's inability to act was perceived as unwillingness, and Shelburne's confirmation of Leigh's entitlements reinforced Charleston's view that Leigh was no more than a 'downright placeman'.[23]

In the event, Leigh's support for the Stamp Act was for nothing. The act was repealed in March 1766 barely six months after it was implemented. Tax revenues had been non-existent and opposition from British merchants unable to import from or export to the colonies was irresistible. The act's repeal was celebrated in Charleston with a ball and gala dinner - 'a very elegant entertainment' - sponsored by William Bull, the acting governor.[24] But the goodwill London gained from reversing its position was dissipated within weeks with the passage of the American Declaratory Act.[25] The act was viewed as another attempt to subjugate the colonies,[26] with a preamble that set out Britain's legal stall:

> Whereas several of the houses of representatives in his Majesty's colonies and plantations in America, have of late against law, claimed to themselves, or to the general assemblies of the same, the sole and exclusive right of imposing duties and taxes upon his Majesty's subjects in the said colonies and plantations; and have in pursuance of such claim, passed certain votes, resolutions, and orders derogatory to the legislative authority of parliament, and inconsistent with the dependency of the said colonies and plantations upon the Crown of Great Britain: may it therefore please your most excellent Majesty, that it may be declared; and be it declared by the King's most excellent majesty, by and with the advice and consent of the lords spiritual

---

[22] *South Carolina Historical and Genealogical Magazine*, 29 (1928), 45.

[23] Ibid., 216.

[24] Daniel J. McDonough, *Christopher Gadsden and Henry Laurens: The Parallel Lives of Two American Patriots* (Selinsgrove, PA: Susquehanna University Press, 2000), pp. 69, 76-77.

[25] 6 Geo III c. 12: The American Colonies Act 1766, 18 March 1766.

[26] Cf. *Schism*, chapter eight.

and temporal, and commons, in this present parliament assembled, and by the authority of the same, that the said colonies and plantations in America have been, are, and of right ought to be, subordinate unto, and dependent upon the imperial Crown and parliament of Great Britain; and that the King's majesty, by and with the advice and consent of the lords spiritual and temporal, and commons of Great Britain, in parliament assembled, hath, and of right ought to have, full power and authority to make laws and statutes of sufficient force and validity to bind the colonies and people of America, subjects of the Crown of Great Britain, in all cases whatsoever.

And be it further declared and enacted by the authority aforesaid, that all resolutions, votes, orders, and proceedings, in any of the said colonies or plantations, whereby the power and authority of the parliament of Great Britain, to make laws and statutes as aforesaid, is denied, or drawn into question, arc, and are hereby declared to be, utterly null and void to all in purposes whatsoever.

Leigh's stance over the Stamp Act could be viewed as principled, after all he suffered social opprobrium and substantial financial losses. But as a senior crown servant, Leigh had limited options. Chief Justice Skinner informed the Board of Trade how the crown's officials had behaved during the crisis and regarded Leigh's behaviour as exemplary. But while Leigh's standing was enhanced in London, when leaked in Charleston the report trashed Leigh's prospects of rebuilding his law practise. And although he was advised by Laurens that his legal offices continued to raise too many conflicts, Leigh considered that the collapse of his law firm left him with no alternative but to exploit his crown offices to generate income.[27] He ignored Laurens's counsel, a decision that would prove to be disastrous.

---

[27] Calhoon & Weir, 'The Scandalous History of Sir Egerton Leigh', esp. 52.

Chapter Five

A Merchant Prince

Henry Laurens

Writing to his wife from the continental congress in Philadelphia, John Adams, later the second president, described Henry Laurens as 'a great acquisition – of the first rank in his state, Lt. Governor, of ample fortune, of great experience, having been twenty years in their assembly, of a clear head and a firm temper, of extensive knowledge and much travel'.[1] Laurens represented the finest America had to offer; indeed, Adams wished that 'all the States would imitate this example and send their best men'.[2] His view of Laurens was undimmed two years later, a diary entry noting that Laurens's approach was marked by his 'long experience in public life', 'amiable character for honour and probity' and a 'great landed fortune free from debt'.[3]

Henry Laurens (1724-1792), a second generation American, was born in Charleston. The family were French Huguenot émigrés who arrived in South Carolina by way of London, Dublin and New York. Originally from the Protestant enclave of La Rochelle, they had fled Louis XIV's *Dragonnades* in the 1680s. The family's marriages, births and deaths are detailed in the registers of Huguenot churches in London and New York, and begin with the wedding of Henry's grandfather, André Laurens (1667-1715), to Marie Lucas in the French Church in London's Threadneedle Street on 22 February 1688. They moved to Dublin and then New York, where their first

---

[1] John Adams to Abigail Adams, 17 August 1777. *Adams Family Papers: An Electronic Archive*. Massachusetts Historical Society, www.masshist.org/digitaladams, accessed 23 July 2013.

[2] Ibid.

[3] John Adams, *Diary*, 12 March - 31 July 1779. *Adams Family Papers: An Electronic Archive*.

son, Jean Samuel (1696-1747), was born. In 1715 Jean Samuel married Esther Grassett (1700-1742), the daughter of another La Rochelle émigré.[4] The wedding took place a fewt weeks before the family left for Charleston, the largest Huguenot community in North America.

Henry Laurens (1724-1792)
John Singleton Copley, 1782
Detail from a photograph by the author of the original portrait
in the National Portrait Gallery in Washington, DC

The Laurens family was middling. A letter from Henry Laurens to a correspondent in Poitiers recalled that his grandfather had 'saved so much money as enabled him to set up four sons and one daughter ... [and to] put them

---

[4] Copies of the church records are contained in the relevant publications of The Huguenot Society of London (now The Huguenot Society of Great Britain and Ireland) and the Huguenot Society of America; cf. specially Alfred V. Wittmeyer (ed.), *Registers of the Births, Marriages and Deaths of the Eglise Francoise a la Nouvelle York* (Baltimore, MD: Genealogical Publishing Co., 2010), reprint.

above low dependence'.⁵ André died shortly after moving to Charleston and Jean Samuel, the eldest son, became head of the family. A saddler and leather worker, he later established his own business, growing it to a level where it was reputedly the largest in the colony.

The family assimilated into Charleston society and became members of the Episcopal St Philip's church, rather than the Huguenot French Church, with Jean anglicising his name to 'John'. His rising status is reflected in his election as a churchwarden in 1733 and appointment as one of Charleston's Firemasters. When Esther died in April 1742 John remarried.⁶ His second wife, Elizabeth Wicking, was English, which suggests a move into mainstream colonial society. John retired shortly afterwards and the management of his saddlery business was passed to his younger brother, Peter, and Benjamin Addison, an employee, with John retaining ownership.⁷

Henry was the third of John and Esther's six children but their first son. In 1744, aged 20, following 'the best education which that country afforded', he was sent to England to begin an apprenticeship at *Crokatt & Co*. He returned to Charleston in 1747 to find that his father had died barely three weeks earlier. Appointed executor and residual legatee under the will, Henry handled probate of the 'valuable lands, a large number of notes and accounts, and a stock so large that it had to be sold in lots to dealers up and down the coast as far as New York'.⁸ The value of the estate is hard to determine. The inventory was large, appraised at over £5,000 in local currency, but could not be sold quickly nor were all the outstanding receivables of

---

⁵ Quoted in David Wallace, *The Life of Henry Laurens* (New York, NY: G.P. Putnam & Sons, 1915), pp. 12-4. 25 February 1774.

⁶ A.S. Salley (ed.), *Register of St Philip's Parish, Charles Town, South Carolina, 1720-58* (Charleston, S.C.: published privately, 1904).

⁷ *South Carolina Gazette*, 12-19 July 1742.

⁸ Wallace, *The Life of Henry Laurens*, p. 12.

£19,000 recoverable. Asset rich but cash poor, Laurens was unable to pay the £1,000 legacy owed to his stepmother for more than a year.[9]

Laurens delayed his return to London and a breakdown in correspondence with Crokatt had the consequence that Crokatt withdrew his offer of a partnership. Crokatt had insisted that Laurens accept the offer before April 1748 and having not received a reply withdrew it in favour of another candidate. Historians have accepted at face value Laurens's account that his 'holding' letter failed to reach Crokatt, but this explanation raises questions. Important letters were commonly sent in duplicate or triplicate by different vessels in order to ensure delivery against the risks of capture, sinking or delay due to bad weather. More realistic explanations might be that Laurens had failed to send a duplicate or that had simply deferred writing. Regardless, in October 1748 after a 'disagreeable and fatiguing passage of nine weeks', Laurens and Crokatt met in London. Laurens's account of his father's death and explanation for the missing letter mollified Crokatt but as Laurens wrote to his stepmother, it was no longer possible for Crokatt to reverse his decision regarding the partnership.[10]

Laurens had known before leaving Charleston that the chance of Crokatt reversing his decision to withdraw his offer was negligible and had provisionally accepted another offer of partnership from George Austin. Laurens now wrote to Austin to accept his offer formally and confirm that he would 'follow his direction in business'.[11] Born in Shropshire, Austin (*c.*1700-1774) had settled in South Carolina in the 1730s and over the following decade built a thriving trading business. Laurens describes him as 'a worthy honest gentleman' and Crokatt as a merchant he 'could not hold in higher regard'.[12]

---

[9] Joseph P. Kelly, 'Henry Laurens: The Southern Man of Conscience in History', *South Carolina Historical Magazine*, 107.2 (2006), 82-123.

[10] Henry Laurens to Elizabeth Laurens, 16 December 1748, in Henry Laurens, *Papers of Henry Laurens, 11 September 1746 - 31 October 1755*, pp. 179-81.

[11] Ibid.

[12] Ibid.

Austin's commercial success was based on slave trading and in the late 1740s he led demands in the assembly for the repeal of the import duties imposed following the Stono Rebellion.[13] Success appeared probable and Austin positioned himself to benefit once the slave trade recommenced.

As a sole trader, Austin's interest in Laurens as a prospective partner lay not just in his potential as a colleague but also in the utility of his imminent departure for England. Austin would have found it impossible to run his business in South Carolina and at the same time resurrect trading contacts in England that had lain dormant for six years.[14] With Laurens's departure, Austin had a prospective solution.

Although Crokatt cautioned Laurens to consider alternatives, including 'offers to settle in London … which he thought much more agreeable than going back to Carolina', Laurens was adamant that he would join with Austin: it was 'out of my power to accept new proposals from any person whatsoever, let the prospect of advantage be ever so great'.[15] His resolve is explained by the profit he anticipated would flow once the slave trade had been reinstated.[16] With the partnership confirmed, Austin wrote to Laurens with instructions and a list of contacts, and over the following six months Laurens journeyed from London to Bath, Bristol and Liverpool to market *Austin & Laurens*'s trading and factoring services. Old contacts were revived and meetings arranged with prospective counterparties and clients, each of whom received a letter written in nearly identical terms:

> Sir, by a letter from Mr George Austin to his friends in England which you have had for perusal you are informed that gentleman and myself are entered into a co-partnership at Charles Town in South Carolina where I beg leave to make a tender of our services to your good self and friends

---

[13] He represented St Bartholomew's Parish and thereafter St Philip's.
[14] Kelly, 'Henry Laurens: The Southern Man of Conscience in History', esp. 106.
[15] Ibid.
[16] Ibid.

assuring you we shall be careful to conduct with integrity any of your concerns that may be put under our directions. As you have been pleased to hint to me some thoughts of sending a ship from Africa to Carolina with negroes and desire to know our terms for consignment in that branch the following are what we have to offer: to load the ship which imports the slaves with such produce as to be had at the season, pay coast commission there, make good all debts and remit accordingly to the times of payment if freight to be obtained and as much as can be procured in Bills of Exchange as can be procured with cash arising from the sales, to give security in England for remitting the proceeds, our commission 10 per cent as customary.

I can venture to assure you that there is a pretty good prospect for sale of negroes in that colony as rice promises to be a good commodity, the quantity heretofore exported being lessened by the planters' attention to indigo and from the success of the first attempt in that article we expect it will for the future make a very considerable addition in our remittances to Great Britain. Our House will be under the name of George Austin & Henry Laurens. We shall be glad to open a correspondence with yourself or friends and endeavour that nothing be wanting in us to increase the same to mutual interest.[17]

Laurens even wrote to Crokatt to solicit his trade:

Our House at Charles Town will be under the name of George Austin & Henry Laurens. We shall be very glad of the opportunity to open a correspondence with your good self and your friends and shall endeavour to act so as may increase the same to mutual interest.[18]

---

[17] Ibid., Laurens to Richard Farr, Bristol, 18 February 1748, pp. 210-1.
[18] Ibid., Laurens to James Crokatt, 7 January 1749, pp. 201-2.

Laurens drummed up business by advising his prospective counterparts that Southern planters were willing to buy slaves in quantity and ready to pay in rice and indigo: 'I think that there's a prospect of most advantage to be made by the Guinea Trade as we have reason to expect good sales for Negroes in that colony, rice promising fair to be a good commodity the quantity heretofore exported being greatly reduced by our attention to Indigo'.[19] And following correspondence from Austin in February 1749, Laurens advertised that 'I have one letter which says that Negroes would sell at a monstrous price and I can't learn of any ship from this port [Bristol] gone with slaves'.[20]

Laurens returned to Charleston in the second half of 1749. He married the following year. Eleanor, the only surviving child from Elias Ball's second marriage, had inherited a fifth share of a large estate that included the 10,000-acre *Comingtee* plantation in Berkeley County; land and land grants in Berkeley and Craven counties; property lots in Charleston; and more than forty slaves. She was also Austin's sister-in-law and Laurens thus became Austin's brother-in-law as well as his business partner.[21]

Austin & Laurens grew rapidly and profitably. By the early 1750s it was the largest of the many merchant traders importing slaves into South Carolina, with 61 cargoes between 1751-61.[22] By way of comparison, *Middleton & Brailsford*, their nearest competitor, handled 37 cargoes over the same period.[23] Austin retired in 1762 to settle in England and from that point Laurens traded on his own account. Over the following seven years his firm ran

---

[19] Ibid., Laurens to Foster Cunliffe, 20 January 1749, p. 204; also, Laurens to Richard Farr, 18 February 1749, et al.

[20] Ibid., Laurens to James Pardoe, Bristol, 21 February 1749, p. 213.

[21] Henry and Eleanor had twelve children, four of whom survived into adulthood. Henry's letters to his eldest son, John, named for Laurens's father, form a substantial part of Laurens's later correspondence.

[22] It traded as *Austin, Laurens & Appleby* from 1759 when Austin's nephew joined the partnership.

[23] Higgins, 'Charles Town Merchants and Factors Dealing in the External Negro Trade 1735-1775', 205-17.

another 7 slave consignments, a figure that excludes dozens of cargoes facilitated for third parties.

Austin & Laurens was equally successful in the other legs of the Atlantic trade, exporting agricultural commodities, principally to England, and importing manufactured goods from Britain, wine from Europe, and rum and sugar from the Caribbean. The firm acted both as a commission agent and as a principal, trading on its own account. From 1749-59, it was ranked one of South Carolina's top three importers of general merchandise with over 120 cargoes. Between 1760-62, *Austin, Laurens & Appleby* handled another 46 cargoes and Laurens was responsible for 30 more from 1762-70.[24]

Each part of the business was vastly remunerative. Wholesale factors earned a 5% commission on the import and export of general merchandise, and a 10% commission on slaves, albeit that they paid-away local freight and handling charges. And being central to the flow of market information also allowed Laurens to trade profitably as a principal.[25] His activities were buccaneering and, in line with the time, free from the concept that one should avoid or manage conflicts of interest.

Laurens's letters to his correspondents and clients during the 1750s and 1760s open a window on his agency business and on trading conditions, and include details of slave and agricultural prices and business intelligence. In the mid-1750s, he wrote of 'the expectation of a sudden war with France' and how this might affect the demand and price of slaves: 'the rice planter will have but little encouragement to purchase slaves but those who run upon indigo, which are no inconsiderable number, won't be at all discouraged'.[26] Laurens's comments on the vagaries of indigo planting are also well-observed and he marketed his connections and encouraged his correspondents by noting that 'a large share of these chaps always apply to us when we are possessed

---

[24] Stumpf, 'South Carolina Importers of General Merchandise, 1735-1765', 1-10.
[25] Wallace, *The Life of Henry Laurens*, p. 47.
[26] For example, Laurens to William Whalley, 12 May 1755 in *Papers of Henry Laurens, 11 September 1746 - 31 October 1755*, pp. 245-6.

of slaves so that we should not fear of making as speedy and good sales as anybody can here if a war should alter the present system of things'. Indeed, just over two weeks later, Laurens wrote to advise that 'a number of small indigo planters finding a ready sale for their crops at 32/6 to 35/ per lb ... brought them in such large sums they were all mad for more negroes and gave for very ordinary Calabar men £250 cash'; he nonetheless cautioned that although some 'fine men' had recently sold for as much as £40 sterling, the price should not be taken as a likely outcome and that 'our people will not currently give that price'.[27] Towards the end of June, Laurens once again suggested that his buyers might wish to take advantage of an upturn in the indigo market: 'the cultivation of indigo creates such a demand ... that at a sale we had on the 24th ... we sold a great many men at £40 sterling [and] the cargo which was from Angola averaged £33.17 sterling. Such a price has not be heard of for many a day for Angola slaves'.[28]

Laurens provides insights into harvest conditions, the prevalence of disease, the need for quarantining vessels, and the vagaries of the weather, especially hurricanes, which could delay or re-route cargoes. Extreme weather was a common cause of shipboard fatalities and traders budgeted to lose a tenth of each slave cargo, although losses were often higher.[29]

He also gives advice, in 1755, for example, noting that 'if you should hereafter ship rum ... send it in the largest hogsheads you can obtain; the saving in freight and the cost of the casks must be obvious to you but a more essential point is this, several of our buyers won't if they can help it take a hogshead that gauges less than 15 or 16 gallons. Such will bring them when empty 30/ for packing skins when those that are smaller won't bring anything'.[30]

---

[27] Ibid., Laurens to Wells, Wharton and Doran, 27 May 1755, pp. 257-8.
[28] Ibid., Laurens to Rawlinson and Davison, 28 June 1755, pp. 277-8.
[29] Ibid., Laurens to Richard Prankerd & Co., 5 July 1755, p. 287.
[30] Ibid., Laurens to Wells, Wharton & Doran, 12 August 1755, p. 314.

Laurens was elected to represent St Philip's in 1757. He was 33. He was re-elected in each of the following two elections but his support for James Grant, the commander of British forces in the Cherokee Expedition, over Thomas Middleton, the provincial commander, caused dissent locally and in 1761 he failed to be returned. Grant had been tasked by Jeffrey Amherst, the commander-in-chief of Britain's forces in America, to move against the Cherokee who had taken Fort Loudon, posing a threat to the frontier posts and settlements that protected the Low Country, and accused Middleton of misconduct and incompetence. Despite his pro-Grant stance, Laurens was returned to the assembly in 1762 and re-elected thereafter, serving almost continuously through to the creation of the provincial congress in 1775 and the general assembly of 1776.

Politics was a core activity for the colony's elites and the machinations of the assembly and council were designed to advance personal and family interests. The role of women in politics was negligible. Laurens's wife was not unusual in having twelve pregnancies in twenty years. It destroyed her health and she died in 1770, a month after giving birth to Mary Eleanor, the second of her daughters to survive to adulthood. Many wives died far younger.

The key to influence in South Carolina, as elsewhere, was money. The constitutional war which Charleston fought with London and its officials was on a fiscal battlefield and both sides understood that power resided in the right to control taxes and distribute the proceeds. The formulation and passage of the annual money bills was the front line. The argument over who controlled the colony's purse strings dated back to the 1720s. Indeed, in December 1725 the assembly objected to the council's entitlement to amend a money bill, arguing that it should have the same constitutional rights as the House of Commons, its counterpart in Britain. The dispute culminated in a formal declaration by the assembly in the mid-1730s:

Resolved, That it is the Opinion of this House that it is the inherent right of every Englishman not to be charged with any Taxes or Aids of Money, but what are given and granted by his Representative in Parliament.

Resolved, That the House of Commons have the Sole Right and Power over the Moneys of the People, and of giving and granting or denying Aids or Moneys for the Public Service.

Resolved, That the House of Commons have the first commencement and consideration and the sole modelling in their House of all Laws for imposing Taxes, and levying and raising aids of Money upon the People for the defence and support of the State and Government.

Resolved, That the foregoing Privileges are some of the Fundamental Laws, Rights, Liberties and Customs of the People of England, confirmed by many Statutes and Acts of Parliament.

Resolved, That His Majesty's Subjects of this Province are entitled to all the Liberties and Privileges of Englishmen.

Resolved, That the Commons House of Assembly in this Province, by Laws and Statutes of Great Britain made of force in this Province, and by Acts of Assembly of this Province, and by ancient Usage and Custom, have the same Rights, Powers, and Privileges in regard to introducing and passing Laws for imposing Taxes on the People of this Province as the House of Commons of Great Britain have in introducing and passing Laws on the People of England.[31]

Although it objected to such resolutions formally, in practice the governor, royal council and London were obliged to acquiesce. Governor Glen complained that almost all official positions were at the disposition of the assembly, with the Treasurer, Commissary, Comptroller and Indian Commissioner given as examples. And although Glen exaggerated the argument, his basic

---

[31] Quoted in William Roy Smith, *South Carolina as a Royal Province, 1719-1776* (New York: Macmillan, 1903), pp. 296-7.

analysis was accurate: 'little by little, the people have got the whole administration in their hands and the Crown is by various laws despoiled'.[32]

Laurens's approach to politics was pragmatic but his unwillingness to accept a position on the royal council in 1764 in recognition of the support he had offered to Grant, and his unenthusiastic response to the Stamp Act in 1765, indicates that a more radical stance was emerging: 'conclude not hence that I am an advocate for the stamp tax ... I would do a great deal to procure a repeal of the law'.[33] His opposition was moderate however and he was reluctant to condone the Sons of Liberty and the Charleston mob's invasion of private houses, including his own, in a search for stamps. The destruction of property and burning of effigies was anathema to Laurens as it was to 'every man of property'.[34]

Charleston's nine days of anti-Stamp Act protests ended with the resignation of the colony's stamp officers. The act was repealed and Laurens was delighted to take advantage of the improved terms of trade: 'our rice planters have gained a vast ascendant over the British and fairly turned the edge of the stamp tax upon them'.[35]

EGERTON LEIGH AND THE WAMBAW, BROUGHTON ISLAND AND ANN

Laurens's reputation for patriotism may not have been enhanced by his objections to the Sons of Liberty's tactics but it was in the ascendance the following year when three of his ships, the *Wambaw*, *Broughton Island* and *Ann*, were

---

[32] Glen to Board of Trade & Plantations, 1748. Cf. James L. Underwood, *The Constitution of South Carolina: the Relationship of the Legislative, Executive and Judicial Branches* (Columbia, SC: USC Press, 1989), p. 11.

[33] Laurens to Joseph Brown, 11 October 1765: HSP, Henry Laurens Papers, MSS.

[34] Laurens to Joseph Brown, 22 October 1765: HSP, Henry Laurens Papers, MSS.

[35] Laurens to William Fisher, 27 February 1766: [Frank] Etting Papers, HSP, MSS.

arrested by the Charleston Customs Collector, Daniel Moore (1701-c.1772). Originally a Barbados planter, Moore had returned to England and in 1747 purchased Widmere Manor in Buckinghamshire. He bought election to the House of Commons, becoming MP for Great Marlow, the local constituency, and sat as a government supporter for seven years from 1754. However, following electoral defeat and short of money, Moore lobbied Newcastle for a place overseas: 'I flatter myself that my past behaviour will entitle me to your Grace's countenance and protection'.[36] An application for Customs Collector in Jamaica was rejected but Moore's persistency resulted in the award of the same position in South Carolina, where he was granted a seat on the royal council.

Moore expected to use his offices for personal gain and his first attempt of extortion occurred within days of his arrival in Charleston when on 4 April 1767 he demanded £20 for a certificate to authorise payment of a bounty on exported hemp, and additional fees to authorise payments on indigo.[37] Charleston's merchants were furious. They contested the legality of the charges, filed suit against Moore in the Courts of General Sessions, Common Pleas and Vice Admiralty, and publicised their complaint in a pamphlet: *A Representation of Facts, Relative to the Conduct of Daniel Moore, Esquire; Collector of His Majesty's Customs at Charles-Town, in South Carolina.*

Gabriel Manigault and John Neufville, two of Charleston's leading merchants, sued Moore personally for illegally demanding 'fees, gratuities or rewards for signing several indigo certificates' and demanded that he be dismissed and fined.[38] The case was tried by Egerton Leigh in the Court of Vice Admiralty. He acquitted Moore on a technicality but in the hope of walking a middle line, judged Manigault and Neufville's suit to have been reasonable and ordered Moore to pay their costs.

---

[36] Cf., www.historyofparliamentonline.org/volume/1754-1790/member/moore-daniel-1701, accessed 5 December 2014.

[37] *Papers of Henry Laurens, 1 September 1765 - 31 July 1768*, volume 5, pp. 238-9.

[38] Maurice A. Crouse, 'Gabriel Manigault: Charleston Merchant', *South Carolina Historical Magazine*, 68.4 (1967), 220-31, esp. 230.

Moore sought income elsewhere and on his instructions George Roupell, the Customs Searcher, detained one of Laurens's smaller vessels, the *Wambaw*, a 15-ton schooner. The ship was co-owned with Benjamin Perdrieau, a fellow Huguenot, and John Comming Ball, Laurens's brother-in-law and manager of two of his plantations. The vessel had left Charleston in May 1767 carrying tools and provisions for Laurens's plantation at on the Altamaha River in Georgia, nine miles from Frederica. The Charleston Customs Office had allowed the ship to leave without a certificate or bond that any 'non-enumerated goods' would be landed at a colonial port. Unlike 'enumerated goods' subject to export and import duties and shipped exclusively to British or colonial ports, non-enumerated goods were untaxed and shipped freely. But smuggling and fraud, the passing-off enumerated goods as non-enumerated, had led Britain to pass additional Navigation Acts that required ships carrying such goods, even ballast, to register with the Customs Office before departure and post a bond. Having off-loaded in Georgia, the *Wambaw* returned to Charleston, empty except for ballast, where it was seized.

On Moore's orders, Roupell followed up by arresting the *Broughton Island*, a new 30-ton schooner also owned by Laurens, which had also returned from Altamaha with ballast. Roupell, with Moore's approval, announced that he aimed to break the spirit of the Charleston merchants and to 'sweat some of those merchants before the summer was over'.[39] The *Wambaw* and *Broughton Island*'s arrest translated that undertaking into action. The seizures also provided the means by which Moore hoped to pay Leigh's judgment against him for costs in favour of Manigault and Neufville.

Following the seizures, Manigault and James Laurens, Henry's brother, offered security for the *Wambaw* and *Broughton Island*, a strategy which in the past had been accepted. Roupell and Moore declined, but recognising the weakness of their position offered to release the ships if 'it were asked as a

---

[39] Henry Laurens to James Grant, 12 August 1767 in Laurens, *Papers of Henry Laurens, 1 September 1765 - 31 July 1768*, pp. 277-9.

favour'. Unwilling to enter into a compromise given their ongoing dispute over fee irregularities, Manigault and Laurens refused.[40] Moore then suggested that Roupell might allow the *Wambaw* and *Broughton Island* to 'slip away in the dark'. This would have been a tacit admission of guilt and the offer was refused.

With no prospect of resolution, the cases were scheduled before Leigh in the Court of Admiralty. Laurens's lawyers argued that the *Wambaw* had been seized improperly not merely because the deputy collector had allowed the vessel to sail from Charleston without a certificate and implied that she might return in the same way, but because Laurens had complied with the law by giving a bond in Georgia before two Frederica merchants and magistrates. Given the circumstances Leigh would have been obliged to find for Laurens had he not mentioned that the *Wambaw's* ballast was to be sold. Leigh used the admission to find Laurens guilty. He ordered that the vessel be auctioned with one third of the proceeds going to the crown, a third to the governor and a third to Roupell. Worse, Laurens was ordered to pay legal costs, including Leigh's court fees of £277. The total came to some £700, more than the value of the vessel itself. Laurens was outraged at what he considered an invidious judgment and unfair order for costs. Indeed, a case tried by Leigh only days before led to the confiscation of a French vessel for smuggling without any order for costs and with the sailors' outstanding pay settled from the proceeds of sale.

The *Broughton Island* trial took place a week after Leigh had condemned the *Wambaw*. Despite having asserted that the two cases were identical, Leigh acquitted Laurens, judging that there was no case to answer. Moreover, he declared that the seizure had been frivolous and opened the way for Laurens to counter-sue. But notwithstanding his judgment, Leigh ordered Laurens to pay two-thirds of the legal costs, including Leigh's court fees of £216 15s. Roupell was ordered to pay the balance.

---

[40] Wallace, *Life of Henry Laurens*, pp. 138-9.

Leigh's judgments satisfied neither side. Laurens faced the loss of one of his vessels and had received an order for costs in both cases. Roupell and Moore had failed to win the *Broughton Island* case despite having succeeded over the *Wambaw*. And they were liable for one third costs. Following the verdicts, Moore disclosed that he had paid Leigh for a legal opinion as to whether to seize the *Broughton Island* and that Leigh, as a private attorney rather than attorney general, had advised that they should.

Leigh's advice was at odds with his own judgment and Moore threatened to complain to London to 'overset the judge'. Although Moore may have misrepresented Leigh's £50 retainer, which Leigh argued was for general advice, he had nonetheless given advice despite the conflict of interest. Operating as the colony's attorney general, running a private legal practice, and sitting on the bench of three of South Carolina's courts, including the Court of Vice Admiralty, was an extreme example of judicial dysfunction, even for the eighteenth century. Laurens asserted that the advice Leigh had offered Moore had been swayed by the fees that he expected to receive as the judge in both cases.[41] And although the accusation could not be proven, the conflict was irrefutable.

Leigh regarded his position as defensible. A year before he had released a coastal sloop, *Active*, for failing to clear Customs in accordance with the new Navigation Acts. Leigh had ruled that the acts were not intended to unnecessarily restrain legitimate American commerce and should not be applied *strictly* to intra-colonial coastal trade. Although Leigh believed his judgment to be fair and did not argue that the law should be ignored, his ruling was swayed by a wish to preserve his position with his clients in Charleston's merchant community. For obvious reasons the judgment was not received positively by Charleston's Customs Office nor by London, to whom they complained. Leigh's ruling was referred to the British attorney general and Leigh was censured and instructed that his future judgments would need to

---

[41] Ibid., pp. 140-1.

demonstrate support for the Excise and its officers. It provides the context for Leigh's judgments in favour of Moore and Roupell.

Assailed by Charleston's merchants, Moore's position in the colony was untenable and he used the excuse of his dispute with Laurens to return to England. He had served six months in the colony and having expressed a reluctance to return, was dismissed as Customs Collector the following year.

Leigh believed that his judgments in the *Wambaw* and *Broughton Island* cases, taken together, achieved a compromise that would be seen as fair. He was naïve. His findings alienated both sides and by failing to declare a probable cause of seizure - that Roupell had reasonable grounds for believing that the *Broughton Island* had been operating illegally - he allowed Laurens's lawyers to sue for damages. Calhoon and Weir have suggested that this was a deliberate ploy by Leigh.[42] If so it worked, and proceedings were issued against Roupell by Laurens to recover his losses.

Unlike Moore, Roupell was not a placeman. He had migrated to South Carolina in the 1740s and been elected to the assembly in 1755 to represent St Helena Parish. Equally importantly, he was married to Elizabeth Prioleau, the daughter of Samuel Prioleau (*d*.1752), an influential merchant, planter, assemblyman and a prominent freemason.[43] But with Laurens as the plaintiff, Roupell was unable to obtain a lawyer willing to defend him. Consequently, Leigh, as attorney general, had no choice but to represent Roupell since he was being sued as an officer of the crown.

The position was now absurd. Leigh was to argue a case against a judgment that he had delivered. Worse, as Roupell protested to the Customs Commissioners, Leigh 'had left such an opening when judge, that [as] attorney general [he] could not close it'.[44] With feeling against the Excise running high, Laurens was awarded a settlement so large that

---

[42] Calhoon and Weir, 'The Scandalous History of Sir Egerton Leigh', esp. 55.
[43] Mackey, *History*, p. 18.
[44] Ibid.

Roupell was unable to pay. Compounding Roupell's problems, Moore's successor, Roger Hatley, was unwilling to pay the damages from Customs Office funds, an obvious course of action, without London's unequivocal authorisation.

Not knowing when or whether this might be granted, Hatley suggested an alternative means of raising monies and on 17 June 1768 he delayed receipt of a bond for goods that had been loaded onto the *Ann*, another of Laurens's vessels, and encouraged Roupell to seize the ship. Roupell did so but via intermediaries offered to release it if Laurens withdrew his demand for damages. Laurens refused, and the case went to court with Leigh adjudicating once again.

Laurens was his wife's uncle, a one-time friend, a masonic brother, and a figure Leigh could not afford to antagonise further. He was also a client. On the other hand, given the protests that Charleston's Customs Officers had raised in London against Leigh's rulings, Leigh could not risk alienating Hatley or Roupell. The wrong decision would lead London to intervene.

The circumstances surrounding Hatley's connivance with Roupell raised the possibility that Laurens could argue that the *Ann* had been taken without probable cause and counter-sue for damages. In order to eliminate that prospect, Leigh asked Roupell to confirm formally that he had acted in good faith. On this basis, given that a bond had not been posted and that the *Ann* was technically in violation of the law, Roupell could argue probable cause. Unfortunately, that did not prove the charge against Laurens since the Navigation Acts allowed bonds to be given after loading but before sailing. Moreover, it was standard practice that when a bond was given for enumerated goods (the *Ann* was carrying rice), no additional bond was required for non-enumerated goods. When this was pointed out by Laurens's lawyers, Leigh was obliged to find in Laurens's favour and to discharge the *Ann*. And although Leigh had protected Roupell from being counter-sued personally by Laurens, he criticised Roupell from the bench: 'there was more of design ... on the part of some officers than ... any intention to commit fraud on the part of the claimant'.[45]

But despite winning the case, Laurens was again ordered to pay costs, including Leigh's fees as judge. Neither side was happy. Roupell had avoided counter-suit but had been publicly humiliated and remained liable to Laurens for the *Broughton Island* damages that he could not afford. And Laurens had been penalised again via an order for costs and had wasted additional time in litigation.

Roupell filed a complaint with the Treasury, charging Leigh with failure to support the Charleston Customs Office and acting to prejudice revenue collection in the colony. It was an accusation London took seriously and a response from the Admiralty followed:

> It having been represented to my Lords Commissioners of His Majesty's Treasury that difficulties have been found to attend the condemning vessels seized in the Province of South Carolina, owing to the same person acting in the double capacity of judge of the Vice Admiralty Court, and attorney general; and their Lordships having suggested to my Lords Commissioners of the Admiralty the necessity of appointing some other person judge, that the interest of the crown may not suffer from the want of the attorney general to support the officers of the Revenue in the discharge of their duty: my Lords do therefore command me to desire your Lordship will please to acquaint Mr. Leigh, who holds both those offices, that on account of the said objection it is necessary he should decline one of them.[46]

Leigh was obliged to resign from the bench but allowed to remain attorney general.

---

[45] Ibid., 56.
[46] Quoted in Bellot, 'The Leighs in South Carolina', quote 178-9.

Notwithstanding that Leigh's third judgment had praised Laurens's personal integrity, Laurens criticised Leigh's performance in a pamphlet - *Extracts from the Proceedings of the Court of Vice-Admiralty in Charlestown, S.C.* - published in Philadelphia and Charleston six months later. The delay allowed Laurens to claim that he was not driven by pique so much as belief that justice should be objective and seen to be objective. It also prevented Leigh from prosecuting Laurens for contempt of court.

The pamphlet offered a biting indictment of Leigh's judicial conduct:

> This last act of the judge's proceedings, added to his Honour's total neglect of the Deputy Collector's untrue and evasive deposition, must increase the abhorrence of American subjects against the establishment and jurisdiction of courts of Vice-Admiralty in their present extent ... What claimant and owner, conscious of their own integrity, acquitted from all suspicion of fraud, 'trepaned' and 'surprised' by the custom house officers, thus cunningly dismissed with compliments upon their conduct and characters, with partial restitution, exorbitant fees and with effectual bar against recovering satisfaction for damages, could refrain from expressing the highest dissatisfaction at the proceedings and final sentence of a double minded judge thus greedily running after the error of Balaam; or could forbear complaining as we complain against judge and officers all, who, jugglers like, trick us and trick one another![47]

Despite the criticism, Leigh sought to offset the loss of court fees by increasing his salary as attorney general. Leigh proposed that it be raised to £500 sterling, a level twice that originally set by the assembly, via an amendment to the Circuit Court Bill. Effectively blackmailing the assembly, Leigh

---

[47] Henry Laurens, *Extracts from the Proceedings of the Court of Vice-Admiralty in Charlestown, S.C. ... and some general observations on American Customs House officers and courts of Vice Admiralty* (Philadelphia, PA: published privately, 1769).

threatened to ensure that London would reject the bill if his terms went unmet.[48]

Laurens's relationship with Leigh deteriorated further in March 1769 when a rejoinder to *Extracts* was published.[49] Leigh's *The Man Unmasked* accused Laurens of a 'specious show of an exalted kind of virtue' and of using 'sly dollars', charging that Laurens had no regard for the law, friendship, or alliances or ties of blood. Laurens was accused of seeking 'to gain a popular name' and characterised as 'a man in the meridian of his days'.[50]

Leigh's justification of his actions and insults inflamed the quarrel. Leigh had charged Laurens with hypocrisy, arguing that while Laurens had ceased to be active in the slave trade his decision had been made only after he had accumulated vast wealth and that he was prepared to retain that wealth regardless of its origins. Laurens, forced to defend himself, did so in a second extended edition of *Extracts* in which he posed the rhetorical question: 'what benefit is it to the public to know the motives and principles from which I quitted the African branch of commerce'. Laurens's answer was that his reasons for leaving the trade were economic and not moral.

Leigh was in a fight with one of the most powerful merchants in the colony. He could not win. He was forced to close his private chancery practice and without Laurens's protection and friendship, and on bad terms with the colony's merchants, planters and most lawyers, he was virtually isolated.

SCANDAL, DECLINE AND LEIGH'S EXIT FROM SOUTH CAROLINA

Leigh returned to England with his family in June 1771 to lobby for a peerage, arguing that only this would retrieve his and the crown's standing in the

---

[48] Wallace, *Life of Henry Laurens*, pp. 144-5.
[49] Egerton Leigh, *The Man Unmasked: Or, The World Undeceived in the Author of a Late Pamphlet* (Charleston, SC: published privately, 1769).
[50] Ibid.

colony.[51] His request was not received warmly but a few weeks before his departure Leigh made a final plea to Sir Stanier Porten, the under-secretary at the Southern Department,[52] arguing that the grant of a suitable honour 'would not only re-introduce him into the province with more weight as to himself, but in an especial manner in his public stations'.[53] The government relented and leaked the prospect to the press: 'we hear that the Hon. Egerton Leigh Esq., his Majesty's Attorney General etc. of South Carolina will shortly be created a baronet in this kingdom'.[54] The award was granted in September and was known in Charleston by the time Leigh returned at the end of October. However any boost to his status would be undermined by a sex scandal. While in London Leigh slept with his ward, his wife's younger sister, another of Laurens's nieces.

Whether Leigh had seduced her or *vice versa* is irrelevant; their liaison in 1771 resulted in a pregnancy and in an attempt to disguise the affair Leigh arranged that Mary would return separately to Charleston. Some months later shortly before her due date, Leigh placed Mary on a ship for England, hoping that she would give birth at sea. But her labour began shortly into the voyage and the vessel turned back. When an attempt was made to disembark, Leigh initially prevented it. Whether as a consequence or not, the child died within a week of birth.

Laurens discovered that Leigh was the father and deemed the death murder. He also suspected that Leigh had hoped or intended that both mother and child would succumb on the voyage. Although Leigh denied complicity for a year, he finally confessed and attempted to apologise, offering financial

---

[51] *General Evening Post*, 30 May - 1 June 1771.
[52] W.P. Courtney, 'Porten, Sir Stanier (*bap.* 1716, *d.*1789)', rev. Ian K. R. Archer, *ODNB*.
[53] National Archives, State Papers Domestic 37/9, Leigh to Lord Rochford, *29 July 1772*; to Sir Stanier Porten, 7 August 1772.
[54] *Middlesex Journal or Chronicle of Liberty*, 9-11 June 1772.

recompense.⁵⁵ Outraged, Laurens rejected Leigh's offer of a settlement as a gratuitous insult. Leigh's attempts to reach a rapprochement were also rejected.

> I have now received advices from my brother informing me that notwithstanding Mr Leigh had owned himself guilty of the horrible fact charged upon him by Miss Bremar in several letters to his mother and sister and desired them to make up the affair with me upon the best terms they could, of which I received a full account from Miss Leigh in presence of a third person. Notwithstanding the conviction of himself which appears in a letter which he wrote to me dated in May last, in short, notwithstanding all the proofs that can be possibly given in a case of this nature and the belief and persuasion of everybody in Carolina of his guilt in consequence of which he is abandoned and detested by everybody, yet he is wicked and hardened enough to deny the truth on that side of the water under the most solemn assertions. My brother writes that Mr Leigh cannot remain in the country where he is universally detested, that he believes he would leave it instantly but dread meeting me on this side, that as soon as he hears I am embarked for Carolina he will come from thence.
>
> I must confess that he has disappointed me. I thought it barely possible under so many proofs as stand against him that he might make a bold and impudent denial but I had no idea of the possibility of such wickedness and folly in any man as that of perpetrating so horrible a deed then to deny it to one man in terms which clearly convict him, own it to other persons, at the very same time and both under his hand.⁵⁶

That Leigh's 'wickedness' occurred after he had been granted a baronetcy gave the scandal political consequence. And once it became known in the

---

⁵⁵ Calhoon & Weir, 'The Scandalous History of Sir Egerton Leigh'.
⁵⁶ Henry Laurens to Edwards Pierce, *6 December 1773* in *The Papers of Henry Laurens* (Columbia, SC: USC Press, 1992), volume 9, pp. 193-4.

colony, his behaviour was deemed indefensible. James Laurens expressed the feeling of many in his comment that 'Sir E.L. has been hard pushed by the remaining few who hold any conversation with him for a vindication of himself and, impossible as that is, he would make people believe that he is going to set about it ... a confession of his crime would leave him without the countenance of a single man here ... therefore he denies the fact more resolutely than ever with oaths etc'.[57] Henry Laurens also reflected a widespread view when he wrote to Edwards Pierce, Mary's prospective fiancé, that Leigh was 'the most wicked man and the greatest fool that ever I heard or read of, in a man of tolerable education and sense'.[58] And when writing to his son the following year, he noted that public condemnation had not been lifted: 'not a word more yet of Leigh but that he is exceedingly despised'.[59]

Leigh manufactured a dispute with the assembly over who had the ultimate authority to raise tax in an attempt to shore-up his reputation in England but in Charleston it had the opposite effect. He was ostracised and in June 1774 Leigh applied again for a leave of absence.

A letter from John Laurens to his father details a chance meeting with Leigh in London in November 1774. It offers an insight into Leigh's state of mind and makes clear that any hope that Leigh may have entertained of recovering his standing was false.

> I must tell you, what has happened between Sir Egerton Leigh and me. As I was standing in one of the Committee Rooms with a Counsellor of my Acquaintance, I discovered the baronet with his face turned towards

---

[57] James Laurens to Henry Laurens, 2 November 1773 in *The Papers of Henry Laurens*, volume 9, p. 138.

[58] Ibid., Laurens to Edwards Pierce, 31 March 1773, quote, 63-4.

[59] Henry Laurens to John Laurens, *8 October 1773*, 'Letters from Hon. Henry Laurens to His Son John, 1773-1776', '*South Carolina Historical and Genealogical Magazine*, 3.2 (1902), 86-96, quote from 90.

me. A little rapid reasoning in my own mind, made me think proper to give him the usual compliment of the hat, which he did not return; pride hindered me from changing my countenance to any other than a look of contempt and indifference, though I felt that spice of mortification which I believe most people would be sensible of upon a similar occasion. After a minute or two had passed and we had advanced nearer to the scene of business, he came up to me, took off his hat and made a very decent apology for not knowing me. He thought it had been a gentleman unknown to him bowing to some other person in the crowd. In effect, the sun had shone so directly into his eyes through a neighbouring window that I suppose he could not know, then pass'd complimentary inquiries from each party about friends. I had not then received your Letter. The next day he paid me a visit and was admitted before I knew who it was. He introduced himself by saying that if I had not yet heard from you, he could tell me that you were arrived. I was much obliged to him but had received a letter soon after I parted from him yesterday. After some conversation, he said he hoped I would come and see him, that Lady Leigh particularly entreated it. I bowed and told him he was very kind, made him no promise and turned the conversation to something else. I was booted and prepared for a ride with Mr Manning, so that his stay with me was not long. At taking leave, he again pressed me to come and take a dinner with him in a friendly way and to appoint a day for that purpose begged that I would promise him; feared that I had some reason for not coming that I did not choose to express; asked me whether you would have any objection to it. Upon the whole he was so very solicitous, that I was obliged to tell him that you did not think it proper. He said he was sensible that there could not be on a sudden that cordiality on our parts but that he hoped you would permit it to come by degrees; begged me to write on the subject to you; asked me if you would take it amiss of him if he were to write you a Letter. I answered you would be glad to hear from him. He took his leave in an affectionate manner. I must confess that from my knowledge of the people I would rather do them service at a distance, than be within the reach of their civilities.[60]

Leigh had known for some time that his future in the colony was in the balance. He had limited prospects for raising capital to develop his land and had sold his principal estate, *The Retreat*, before leaving for London. When his son enrolled at Westminster School in June 1771, Leigh gave his address as Rugby Hall in Warwickshire not South Carolina,[61] and by December 1771 he had sold other assets, including his townhouse and furniture. On his return to England in 1774, Leigh desperately sought an appointment in another colony. He blamed but did not name Laurens: 'a powerful faction to whose insults [he had become] subject on the score of his public stations'.[62] But Leigh's infidelity had not only set Laurens against him but much of Charleston. And with Leigh still provincial grand master, it had a devastating impact on freemasonry's reputation in the colony.

In 1771 and 1772, Leigh's installation and the St John's Day feast had been well-attended and marked 'with unusual splendour'.[63] Two hundred masons, 'the largest number that had ever appeared before the public', processed through Charleston from Leigh's house where the provincial grand

---

[60] John Laurens to Henry Laurens, 15 November 1774, in 'Letters from John Laurens to His Father, Hon. Henry Laurens, 1774-1776', *South Carolina Historical and Genealogical Magazine*, 5.4 (1904), 197-208. Laurens's view of Leigh remained negative; he regarded Leigh as 'that wretch in Charles Town' and looked to him 'to own his guilt and ... do justice to the injured party'. Cf. Henry Laurens to Mary Bremar, 29 October 1773, in *The Papers of Henry Laurens* (Columbia, SC: USC Press, 1992), volume 9, p. 137-8.

[61] Bellot, 'The Leighs in South Carolina', 184.

[62] Quoted in Bellot, 'The Leighs in South Carolina', 183-4.

[63] Mackey, *History of Freemasonry*, pp. 43-4.

lodge had been held and a breakfast taken, before moving to Holliday's Tavern, Leigh in a coach and the freemasons following in sedan chairs. Solomon's Lodge was opened and the meeting followed by a service at St Philip's and an entertainment at Pike's New Rooms in Church Street. The day was capped by a grand feast hosted at Holliday's Tavern with some 150 attendees.[64]

In 1773, with knowledge of Leigh's adultery and hypocrisy now widespread, there was no meeting of provincial grand lodge nor any other masonic celebration: 'we had neither a pompous ode[65] [nor] procession of masons ... the brethren are ashamed of their Grand Master and we have not heard a word of masonry for many months'.[66] Although Mackey wrote that 'the annual ... and quarterly communications ... continued', there are no records of any such meetings from 1773 until 1776.[67] Indeed, Laurens writing to his son, John, in 1774 confirmed that there had been 'no procession [and] no talk of Masonry' in Charleston: 'in short, the fraternity are quite ashamed of their Grand Master'.[68]

A few lodges remained active, including the loyalist Union Kilwinning, which held a benefit evening on 11 May 1774, an event that took place with the permission of the lieutenant-governor.[69] In 1777 a rival Grand Lodge of the State of South Carolina was constituted, the first occasion on which the word 'state' was used in connection with South Carolina freemasonry. A

---

[64] Ibid.

[65] The 'ode' refers to a loyalist poem composed by Leigh in 1770 and set to music, and performed before the provincial grand lodge.

[66] James Laurens to Henry Laurens, 29 December 1773, in *The Papers of Henry Laurens*, volume 9, pp. 211-3.

[67] Mackey, *History of Freemasonry*, p. 46.

[68] Henry to John Laurens, *21 February 1774* in *The Papers of Henry Laurens* (Columbia, SC: USC Press, 1992), volume 9, pp. 298-305.

[69] *South Carolina & American General Gazette*, April 1774.

new grand master, Barnard Elliott,[70] a patriot, was elected and around one hundred masons attended a grand banquet.

South Carolina freemasonry was not alone in rejecting Leigh. The South Carolina Society took a similar stance, principally as a result of Laurens's influence. Laurens had been a member since 1753 and served as steward, junior and senior warden. He had also involved the society in his court disputes with Leigh, gifting it more than £480: the fees which Leigh 'might or could have justly and legally demanded' in connection with his litigation in the Vice Admiralty Court.[71]

Only one South Carolina society was willing to permit Leigh to remain a member: the St Andrew's Society. Its hundred plus members were dominated by loyalists, including John Stuart, its president, James Simpson, vice-president, Alexander Hewatt, William Holliday, George Roupell and Robert Wells. Only a minority, perhaps fifteen members, were patriots. The society suspended its meetings during the initial phase of the revolution but when Charleston was recaptured by the British in 1780 it reconvened and opened its doors to the British officers in the city. Sixty-four new members were admitted, all loyalists, of whom more than twenty were British, including Colonel Nisbett Balfour, the commander in Charleston.[72] The

---

[70] Barnard Elliott (1740-1778), a successful South Carolina planter, was an assemblyman (1769-72), before being appointed a member of the royal council, from which he resigned in 1775. Elliott was elected to the first and second provincial congress and fought against the British as a captain in the 2nd South Carolina Regiment, lieutenant-colonel of the 4th Regiment, and commander of Fort Johnson.

[71] Henry Laurens to the Stewards, Wardens and Members of the South Carolina Society, 19 September 1769, in *The Papers of Henry Laurens*, volume 7, pp. 138-9.

[72] J.H. Eastbury, *History of the St Andrew's Society in Charleston, South Carolina* (Charleston, SC: privately published, 1929). Although difficult to gauge with precision, loyalists probably comprised less than a fifth of South Carolina's white population. See Robert Stansbury Lambert, *South Carolina Loyalists in the American Revolution* (Clemson, SC: Clemson University Digital Press, 2010), 2nd edn., pp. 222-6.

former provincial grand lodge was also resurrected when Leigh returned to Charleston during the occupation as a member of the military advisory council but his appeal for the return of civilian rule with himself installed as governor was ignored.

Leigh died in British-occupied Charleston in September 1781. His reputation had been tainted by what was seen as blind loyalism and his position in society destroyed by his adultery and its denial. The hostility directed against Leigh personally was extended to the institutions he fronted. This included South Carolina's provincial grand lodge, whose diminished status from 1773 can be attributed directly to Leigh's decline and fall. Leigh has been traduced by American historians, characterised as an egregious example of a British placeman, an assessment that can be regarded as essentially correct.

Laurens Once More

Unlike Leigh, Laurens's status had soared to the point of celebrity. Within freemasonry he had been treasurer of Solomon's Lodge and in 1754 had accepted a position as provincial grand steward under Peter Leigh. The offices suggest a personal and financial commitment to the Craft. But it did not last. Lauren's relationship with freemasonry, his principal activity outside business other than the South Carolina Society and the church,[73] was compromised fatally by Leigh's conduct.

---

[73] Apart from freemasonry and the South Carolina Society, Laurens', social activities were highly limited. Laura Frech notes that he 'did not enjoy balls, concerts, or horse races, tried to avoid playing cards for money and refused to indulge in idle conversation', nor did he participate in 'the more frivolous social activities of the colonial capital'. Frech confirms the views of others that Laurens took life seriously, was a devout Christian and moralist, and focused principally on his businesses, his family and a close circle of friends. His relationship with Leigh and with freemasonry can be understood best in this context. Cf. Laura P. Frech, 'The Republicanism of Henry Laurens', *South Carolina Historical Magazine*, 76.2 (1975), 68-79.

Laurens returned to South Carolina from Europe in late 1774. He was elected president of the first provincial congress, appointed to the first council of safety and became president of the second. He later served in the first, second, third, fourth and sixth general assemblies from 1776-85, notwithstanding his imprisonment in London for most of 1781. Although the consequence of separation from Britain was a major concern for Laurens and he was acutely aware of the threat war posed to commerce, he committed to the revolutionary cause and fought in defence of Charleston in June 1776 while simultaneously seeking to prevent civil war between the majority patriots and minority loyalists.

In 1777, with Leigh and the British having left Charleston, the Grand Lodge of the State of South Carolina was constituted, the first occasion on which the word 'state' was used in connection with South Carolina freemasonry. A new grand master, Barnard Elliott,[74] a patriot, was elected and around 100 freemasons attended a celebratory banquet.

Laurens represented South Carolina at the second continental congress from January 1777-79, and was president from November 1777 to December 1778, when the articles of confederation were approved and an alliance with France ratified. Asked to sail to the Netherlands to negotiate a trade treaty, Laurens was captured by the Royal Navy on route, charged with treason, and imprisoned in the Tower of London from October 1780 to December 1781. Although initially refused release, bail was negotiated by Benjamin Franklin and Laurens was exchanged for Lord Cornwallis, the captured commander of Britain's forces in America. He joined Franklin and Adams at the peace conference in Paris, arriving two days before the treaty was signed which confirmed Independence.

---

[74] Elliott was an assemblyman (1769-72) before being appointed a member of the royal council from which he resigned in 1775. He was elected to the first and second provincial congresses and fought against the British as a captain in the 2nd South Carolina Regiment, lieutenant-colonel of the 4th Regiment, and commander of Fort Johnson.

Laurens returned to America in 1784 and to Charleston in 1785. The death of his son, John, a lieutenant colonel in the Continental Army, killed at the age of 27 at Combahee River in 1782, had broken him. Laurens declined to serve in South Carolina's assembly and refused to attend the constitutional convention in Philadelphia. He died at *Mepkin*, his country estate, on 8 December 1792

Chapter Six

The Georgia Project

A Buffer Colony

The origin of the Georgia colony - 'the uncultivated parts of Carolina which is to be called *Georgia*' – can be dated back more than three decades before 1733 when James Oglethorpe disembarked from the *Ann* with the first clutch of 114 settlers.[1]

Proposals to establish a buffer settlement had been circulated since the 1700s. Robert Montgomery in a *Discourse Concerning the Design'd Establishment of a New Colony to the South of Carolina* wrote of the 'natural sweetness and beauty' of a land he depicted glowingly as 'our future Eden',[2] and in his *Description of the Golden Islands* three years later he praised what he described as the 'finest English plantation in America' with 'rich lands' and 'commodiousness of living'.[3] He was not alone. Another proposal had been advanced by Jean Pierre Purry, a Swiss merchant trader, who in a memorial to the Duke of Newcastle set out his scheme for a colony stretching from the Atlantic coast to the Mississippi. Purry argued that his proposal would counter French military and political influence in Louisiana and provide Britain with profitable exports and the benefit of self-sufficiency in silk within thirty years.[4] Unlike many others, Purry recognised that the most sellable aspect of the proposed colony was strategic: defending South Carolina's exports of naval stores, deerskins and rice, and safeguarding the profitable import trade in British goods from French and Spanish attack.

---

[1] Cf. *Grub Street Journal*, 10 February 1732; *Daily Journal*, 2 November 1732.

[2] Robert Montgomery, *A discourse concerning the design'd establishment of a new colony to the south of Carolina, in the most delightful country of the universe* (London, 1717).

[3] Robert Montgomery, *A description of the Golden Islands, with an account of the undertaking now on foot for making a settlement there* (London: J. Morphew, 1720).

[4] Jean Pierre Purry, *A Memorial* (1724).

The Carolinas and Georgia
Detail from Emanuel Bowen, Geographer to His Majesty, and John Gibson, Engraver,
An Accurate Map of North America following the Paris Treaty of 1763
London, 1763

But despite the logic of a buffer colony, there were numerous obstacles, including the need to secure government and parliamentary support, and obtain the agreement of South Carolina's legislature and its planters and merchants. The exercise required extensive lobbying but progress was made, with arguments in favour of colonisation driven by the prospect of profit and a concern for the resettlement of the worthy poor. Public interest was encouraged and enhanced by what was portrayed as the altruism of those involved in the prospective colony, especially the Georgia Trustees.[5] Their willingness to forego remuneration or a financial interest in the colony guided others to copy their stance. The 'great humanity of the design' was

---

[5] *London Evening Post*, 3-5 February 1732 et al.

such that Newcastle 'most generously refused to accept the fees due to him [for processing the scheme], which are very considerable ... since they were to come out of money appropriated to the assistance of the unfortunate'.[6] Unlike the misdeeds of the Charitable Corporation which had suffered fraud and collapsed, the Georgia project was to be a *'truly* charitable corporation',[7] 'for the Poor are thereby to be relieved and provided for without paying 10 per cent or one farthing for what they get, and it is said that his Majesty and the Royal family are to contribute largely towards the settling of this new colony'.[8]

THE GEORGIA TRUSTEES AND THE GEORGIA CHARTER

The Georgia project was positioned publicly as a benevolent endeavour: 'the trustees are appointed in order to relieve such British subjects as are by misfortune rendered incapable of supporting themselves and their families here, and to give a safe and comfortable retreat to foreigners persecuted for conscience' sake, and to augment the numbers of the subjects of Great Britain by preserving of the first and drawing over the latter. Every person preserved by perishing by want is a Subject gained as well as every foreigner who is allured to settle in the British dominions. The trustees are to facilitate the settling [of] these people in Georgia under a regular form of government, to grant lands to them and their heirs forever, to have them instructed and encouraged in the raising of raw silk, wine, flax, hemp and such other gross materials as may be useful to the trade of England, and to prevent them from making any manufactures that may interfere with it. One and twenty noblemen and gentlemen are named by the charter as trustees and their number is to be augmented ... by the addition of several others of very great rank and distinction, and none of the trustees are to

---

[6] *Grub Street Journal*, 15 June 1732 et al.
[7] Ibid.
[8] *Fog's Weekly Journal*, 1 July 1732.

have any advantage whatsoever by this design, except that of relieving the miserable'.[9]

But the colony's benefits were also viewed through a more cynical lens: '[it] will in a few years considerably lessen the poor tax by relieving great numbers of unfortunate people and by giving employment to manufacturers in England for furnishing [the colonists] with all kind of necessities'.[10]

In January 1732 George II signed the Georgia Charter and the act passed through Newcastle's office in May.[11] A wave of publicity encouraged the public to support the venture with private donations and from 1732 into 1733, substantial contributions were highlighted in the press, including the anonymous gift of £100 that was delivered to the first meeting of the trustees at their Old Palace Yard offices.[12]

Encouraged by the support, the trustees granted commissions to the great and good to solicit funds on their behalf.[13] Sir Gilbert Heathcote (1652-1733), MP for St Germans, a merchant and former governor of the Bank of England, at a meeting of the Bank's Court of Governors, proclaimed the benefits of providing relief to 'necessitous people' and the 'future advantages arising to England by strengthening the American colonies and increasing the trade and navigation of England'.[14] Heathcote led by example, 'giving

---

[9] *Daily Journal*, 4 July 1732.

[10] *Grub Street Journal*, 20 July 1732.

[11] An account of the Georgia colony written for the Trustees makes it clear that the rationale for going ahead was twofold: to increase trade with British North America; and to improve South Carolina's security - a colony 'frequently ravaged by Indian enemies'. The relief of worthy poor suffering from 'misfortune or want of employment' and the resettlement of those seeking a new start in the New World were second tier objectives. Cf. *An account, showing the progress of the colony of Georgia in America from its first establishment* (London, 1741).

[12] *London Evening Post*, 22-24 June 1732.

[13] *Daily Journal* and *Daily Post*, 26 August 1732 et al.

[14] *Daily Courant*, 2 September 1732.

a very handsome benefaction to the design [which] was followed by all the directors then present'.[15] In the light of his trading interests, especially his estates in Jamaica, his donation may not have been entirely disinterested, but his support was influential. Heathcote had been a staunch Whig for decades and was one of Britain's wealthiest men with a fortune estimated at over £700,000.[16]

A Masonic Connection

Given the reportedly philanthropic nature of the colony and the publicity its backers attracted, it is unsurprising that Georgia's supporters attracted London's elites, including prominent freemasons. James Vernon (1677-1756), one of the first Georgia Trustees, was one of the most active supporters. He attended some two hundred meetings of the Common Council, the colony's executive committee, and over five hundred meetings of the Georgia Corporation.

Vernon's father had been an MP, secretary of state and Teller of the Exchequer,[17] and his own connections were similarly comprehensive, extending from parliament and the court, where he was Clerk to the Privy Council, to the Royal Society[18] and the City of London.[19] As a member of Martin Folkes's lodge at the Bedford Head in Covent Garden, Vernon was also linked to freemasonry's inner circles.[20] Although his political influence

---

[15] Ibid.

[16] www.historyofparliamentonline.org/volume/1715-1754/member/heathcote-sir-gilbert-1652-1733.

[17] He was secretary of state for the Northern Department, then the Southern Department. Cf. www.historyofparliamentonline.org/volume/1690-1715/member/vernon-james-i-1646-1727.

[18] Elected FRS 1702: *Sackler Archives*.

[19] Cf. Berman, *Foundations*, pp. 98-103.

[20] Ibid.

waned in the mid-1720s when he was suspected of colluding with the patriotic Whig opposition, his sinecure as a Commissioner of the Excise was restored in 1728 after the intercession of the Duke of Devonshire and a reconciliation with Walpole.

Vernon's activities in the 1730s focused mainly on his charitable undertakings. He was a trustee of Dr Thomas Bray's charity – the Society for Promoting Christian Knowledge - and the Georgia project. He persuaded John Perceval, later Lord Egmont, to chair the Georgia Council, and secured the backing of the Grand Lodge of England who ordered that collections be made on behalf of the colony. Thomas Batson, the deputy grand master, George Payne's brother-in-law and a member of the Horn Tavern, steered the matter through grand lodge on 13 December 1733:

> Then the Deputy Grand Master opened to the Lodge the Affairs of Planting the new Colony of Georgia in America and having sent an Account in Print of the Nature of such Plantation to all the Lodges, and informed the grand lodge that the Trustees had to Nathaniel Blackerby Esq. and to himself Commissions under their Common Seal to collect the Charity of this Society towards establishing the Trustees to send distressed Brethren to Georgia where they may be comfortably provided for.
>
> Proposed: that it be strenuously recommended by Masters and Wardens of regular lodges to make a generous collection among all their members for that purpose.
>
> Which being seconded by Br Rogers Holland Esq. (one of the said Trustees) who opened the Nature of the Settlement, and by Sir William Keith, Bt., who was many years Governor of Pennsylvania, by Dr Desaguliers, Lord Southwell, Br. Blackerby and many other worthy brethren, it was recommended accordingly.
>
> The Deputy Grand Master and Br. Blackerby, Treasurer, informed the Grand Lodge that they would wait upon the Noblemen and other Persons

of Distinction who are members of this Society for their Contribution to the charity of Georgia.[21]

The initial call for funds was followed up at the next quarterly communication of grand lodge on 18 March 1734:

> Resolved: That the Masters of all regular Lodges who shall not bring in their contribution of charity do at the next Quarterly Communication give the reasons why their respective Lodges do not contribute to the Settlement of Georgia.[22]

Of those named, Rogers Holland (c.1701-1761), a past grand warden, a lawyer, was MP for Chippenham (1727-37); and Sir William Keith (1669-1749), a member of the French Arms lodge in Madrid and the Hoop and Griffin in Leadenhall Street, a former lieutenant-governor of Pennsylvania. Nathaniel Blackerby (16..?-1742), a past deputy grand master and currently grand treasurer, another member of the Horn, was also treasurer of the Commission for Building Fifty Churches. And Lord Southwell was Thomas Southwell, 2nd Baron Southwell (1698-1766), a member of the Irish Privy Council and governor of County Limerick. He had been in England since June 1731[23] following his appointment as Master of Horse to the Princess Royal on her marriage to the Prince of Orange.[24]

---

[21] *Grand Lodge Minutes I*, pp. 235-6.
[22] *Grand Lodge Minutes I*, p. 238.
[23] *London Journal*, 12 June 1731.
[24] *London Journal*, 29 September 1733; *London Evening Post*, 4 October 1733. Although newspaper reports described him as 'late Grand Master of Ireland' and 'late Provincial Grand Master of Ireland', neither tag was accurate. He was a senior member of Irish Grand Lodge and became GM of Ireland just under a decade later in 1743.

Other masonic supporters included J.T. Desaguliers, a past grand master and deputy grand master; John Laroche (c.1700-1752), a merchant and MP for Bodmin (1727-52), a member of the Prince Eugene's Head Coffee House in St Alban's Street; and George Heathcote (1700-1768), a member of the Rummer. Heathcote was a Jamaica merchant and opposition Whig MP who represented Southwark (1734-41), and the City of London (1741-47), and was elected Lord Mayor in 1742.[25] He resigned from the Georgia Council in 1738 complaining that the trustees were subservient to Walpole.[26] Another member of the Horn and former grand warden, George Carpenter, 2nd Baron Carpenter of Killahy in Co. Kilkenny (c.1695-1749), had been MP for Morpeth (1717-27) before succeeding to the title in 1732. He was elected to the Georgia Council in 1732 and had acted as chair[27] but became disillusioned and resigned in 1738.[28]

More than half of Georgia's first trustees were MPs. Most had served on Oglethorpe's parliamentary committee to 'enquire into the state of the gaols', including Edward Digby (1693-1746), Tory MP for Warwickshire (1726-death), a close friend of John Ward, later Lord Dudley & Ward, grand master of English Grand Lodge. The majority were Whigs, including

---

[25] George Heathcote's election to the Royal Society in 1729 was sponsored by James Douglas and William Sloane, both freemasons, and Hans Sloane, William's uncle and the president of the Royal Society.

[26] www.historyofparliamentonline.org/volume/1715-1754/member/heathcote-george-1700-68.

[27] *Daily Journal*, 2 September 1732.

[28] Carpenter was re-elected against his wishes the following year and resigned again in 1740. Other trustees also resigned, including Robert Hucks (1699-1745), MP for Abingdon (1722-41), who left the Council in 1738 in protest at the expropriation of land in Georgia for the benefit of the Church of England. Robert More (1703-1780), MP for Bishop's Castle (1727-41), who resigned in 1736 for the same reason, as did John White (1699-1769), MP for East Retford (1733-68), although both continued to act as trustees.

a number personally loyal to Walpole.[29] Twenty-two trustees were appointed in 1732 under the Georgia Charter, a further fifteen in 1733 and another nine in 1734. Twenty-six more were appointed between 1737-49. The Charter allowed the trustees twenty-one years before control reverted to the crown and until that time their authority was virtually absolute.

JAMES OGLETHORPE

The principal champion of the project and the man acknowledged as Georgia's founding father was James Oglethorpe (1696-1785). Born into a pro-Jacobite family, Oglethorpe adopted a loyal Tory stance and was from 1722-54 MP for Haslemere where the family had a large estate. Although his name is absent from the lists of members submitted by constituent English lodges to grand lodge in the 1720s and 1730s, and from other masonic records, legend holds that Oglethorpe was a freemason. This is improbable but as the senior administrative figure in the colony he permitted the founding of the first masonic lodge at Savannah. Given the financial and political support for Georgia from the masonic community in England, and that James Vernon, one of the key trustees, was an influential freemason, Oglethorpe would have been sympathetic to freemasonry regardless of whether or not he was a freemason himself.

THE LODGE AT SAVANNAH

Georgia freemasonry also holds to a tradition that Oglethorpe delivered the warrant for the lodge at Savannah[30] on his return from England in February

---

[29] They included Francis Eyles (1704-1750), MP for Devizes (1727-42), described by Egmont as one of Walpole's 'creatures'; William Sloper (1709-1789), MP for Great Bedwyn (1729-41); and Thomas Tower (1698-1778), MP for Wareham (1729-34) and Wallingford (1734-41).

[30] Now known as Solomon's Lodge, No. 1, Savannah. Cf. W.B. Clarke, *Early and Historic Freemasonry of Georgia, 1733/4-1800* (Georgia, GA, privately published, 1924).

1736. It is more likely that it was entrusted to Roger Lacy.[31] Lacy was a member of the King's Arm's lodge at St Paul's and of the Swan Tavern in Long Acre. He was one of twelve grand stewards in 1731 and appointed provincial grand master for Georgia in 1735.[32] His selection was analogous to that of John Hammerton who became provincial grand master of South Carolina the following year,[33] and both were well-known at grand lodge.[34]

Although Egmont's diary entry that Lacy was the first colonist to migrate to Georgia at his own expense is almost certainly incorrect,[35] it indicates his financial and social status. Lacy constructed an estate, *Thunderbolt*, on a bluff above the Wilmington River near Savannah and built a small fort for its protection. He impressed Oglethorpe who in June 1736 instructed him to identify a suitable site for a trading post further up the Savannah River and tasked him with supervising its construction and fortification. He appointed him Indian Agent for the area, with command of a constable and small force to maintain peace with the Cherokee and police the Indian trade. The trading post, Augusta, was operational by 1738. Lacy contracted fever in July that year and died at *Thunderbolt* a month later.[36]

---

[31] Also written as 'Lacey'.

[32] *Grand Lodge Minutes I*, p. 142.

[33] They were among eight who were appointed PGMs in North America between 1730-50, the first of whom was Daniel Cox, PGM for New York, New Jersey and Pennsylvania. He was followed by Henry Price (New England, 1733); Roger Lacy (Georgia, 1735); Robert Tomlinson (New England, 1736); John Hammerton (SC, 1736); Richard Riggs (New York, 1737); Thomas Oxnard (North America, 1743); and William Allen (Pennsylvania, 1749).

[34] 15 December 1730: *Grand Lodge Minutes I*, p. 137.

[35] Egmont, *Diary of the Earl of Egmont*, volume II, p. 193. However, E. Merton Coulter & Albert B. Sayle (eds.), *A List of the Early Settlers of Georgia* (Athens, GA: University of Georgia Press, 1983), p. 81 records that James Lacy [Roger Lacy's brother/father?] 'arrived 1 February 1733/4. Settled at Thunderbolt on a grant of 500 acres made him 21 December 1732. Dead.'

[36] Cf. Edward J. Cashin, *Colonial Augusta: "Key of the Indian Country"* (Macon, GA: Mercer University Press, 1986) pp. 31-2, 60-2, 78, 100, 109.

Freemasonry in Savannah initially took a different path to that in Charleston. Although intended originally as a gentlemanly activity, Savannah had a more raw frontier flavour that reflected the colony's youth and its tenuous position close to the front line with Spanish Florida. Indeed, Georgia freemasonry was almost a parody of that in South Carolina. It was accused of being a drinking club and became a source of jealousy and dispute in the colony, and letters from the settlers to the trustees in London suggest that the lodge had as many detractors as supporters.

Some colonists viewed lodge membership as a means of achieving personal aspirations and social validation. Elisha Dobree, for example, wrote in 1735 that 'the body of Freemasons has accepted me as a brother', believing acceptance into the lodge offered evidence of his moral character and standing, a perception reinforced by a subsequent statement that he had 'been chosen arbitrator in several affairs ... of the greatest consequence'.[37]

Many took a different view. An anonymous letter the same year recorded a long list of grievances, including allegations of collusion between the magistracy and the lodge: 'in difficult cases a special jury is called, the majority of which are Freemasons, which have often been challenged, but as no other reasons could be alleged against them but their being Freemasons the court has over-ruled the objection'.[38] The same month, Paul Amatis, a silk maker, one of the first settlers, complained that the trustees' ban on liquor was widely flouted: 'the following persons are known publicly to sell rum ... Edward Jenkins; John Ambrose; John Fallowfield; Patrick Houston; James Gould, chief clerk of your public store; [Thomas] Christie ... and several others ... The reason some of the above gentlemen do not pay a fine is because they are intimate to Mr Causton. I don't say because they are

---

[37] Elisha Dobree to Egmont, 15 January 1735: *Egmont Papers*, volume 14201, p. 165: University of Georgia Libraries: djvued.libs.uga.edu/egmont/.

[38] Anonymous to Egmot, 5 June 1735, *Egmont Papers*, volume 14201, pp. 354-5.

Freemasons'.[39] Whether or not as a consequence, Amatis 'took a disgust' to life in Georgia and relocated to Charleston'; he died there in December 1736.[40]

And there were other complaints. Thomas Jones who arrived in Georgia in 1738 and succeeded Causton as the trustees' store keeper,[41] grumbled that the freemasons were Jacobites who had 'found fault with all the measures that have been taken by the government ever since the [Glorious] Revolution (excepting during the few years of Bolingbroke's Ministry) [and had] set up a freemason's club, a St Andrew's club and other tippling societies'. Jones's grouses were exaggerated, reflecting his background as a parish constable in the rookeries of Holborn, an area awash with gin shops and beer houses. His view was also marked by envy: 'from what fund they are supported in this expensive way of living is yet a secret'.[42]

Robert Parker, writing to the trustees in December 1734, noted that there were 'about thirty or forty Freemasons. They have a fine supper every Saturday night and often two or three in the week besides. Where such an expense can be born I am at a loss to know. One night among other disorders they went to the Guard, cut the Captain down the Head and disarmed the rest carrying the arms away. When they came to reflect on it on the morrow, to make things up, they called a lodge at night and admitted Gough, the Captain, a freemason, so I suppose the thing dropped. I might go on with

---

[39] *Egmont Papers*, volume 14201, pp. 358-9. Thomas Causton was the colony's store keeper, bailiff and chief magistrate, appointed by Oglethorpe.

[40] E. Merton Coulter & Albert B. Sayle, *A List of Early Settlers of Georgia* (Baltimore, MD: Genealogical Pub. Co., 1983), reprint, pp. 1-2.

[41] Jones had previously served as the unpaid and part-time High Constable of Holborn, the law official for the parish appointed by the local magistracy: LMA: MJ/SPP/005 *1721/2*.

[42] Thomas Jones (Savannah) to Jo. Lydes (London), 18 September 1740, *Egmont Papers*, volume 14205, p. 66.

other particulars but I have already said enough to fill you with indignation at what passes at Savannah'.[43]

Parker was also motivated by resentment. He had been wealthy, an elected alderman at Lynn in Norfolk, but having paid his passage to Georgia to make his fortune he failed and quit in July 1736.[44] His note of the number of men involved - 'thirty or forty' – is important. The figure was a substantial percentage of the number of adult men in Savannah and those excluded would have felt aggrieved. Georgia's population in the mid-1730s was less than 2,000. Half lived in Savannah, of whom three-quarters or more were servants, women or children, all of whom were excluded from lodge membership.

Causton's journal provides a contrasting perspective. In his entry for 24 June 1737 he describes the St John's Day lodge meeting earlier in the day, noting that after morning church service and a sermon preached by John Wesley, then in the colony with his brother, Charles, the freemasons 'lunched, breaking up about 3 o'clock ... [and] Mr Wesley dined with us and received the thanks of the society for his suitable sermon'.[45]

Causton, a calico printer, had been part of the first wave of settlers who had sailed on the *Ann*. Oglethorpe promoted him to first bailiff and store keeper in September 1733 following the death of Joseph Hughes, the previous incumbent. The appointment was contentious and dismayed several settlers, and residual ill-feeling lay behind subsequent accusations of profiteering and embezzlement. True or not, Causton was 'turned out of both offices ... for abusing his trust'.[46]

---

[43] Robert Parker to the Trustees, undated December 1734, *Egmont Papers*, volume 14201, pp. 154-8.

[44] Coulter & Sayle, *A List of Early Settlers of Georgia*, p. 39.

[45] Thomas Causton, *Journal*, 24 June 1737: *Egmont Papers*, volume 14203, p. 24.

[46] Coulter & Sayle, *A List of Early Settlers of Georgia*, p. 9.

Persuaded by the stream of anti-masonic correspondence from Georgia and reinforced by an undercurrent of antipathy towards the Grand Lodge of England in London, Egmont developed a jaded view of Georgia freemasonry, writing in 1739 that 'the Freemason's company having spent all their money is now broke up, but while it subsisted they met every Saturday morning at the tavern and revelled there until 2 o'clock on Sunday morning, when they would go reeling home'.[47] And in 1741, comment again on masonic profligacy, Egmont noted that spending £15 or £16 a night at the tavern 'in balls and Freemasons' feasts [was] enough to ruin richer men than they'.[48]

Georgia's Malcontents and the Battle to Legalize Slavery

Freemasonry decayed in Georgia in the 1740s as a function of the colony's economic decline. The colony's parlous condition resulted from the trustees' ban on slavery. Oglethorpe was fully opposed to it being lifted and his intransigence led to a division among the settlers, with Oglethorpe supported nominally by the Scots at the Darien settlement and Salzburgers at Ebenezer, but facing hostility from the 'malcontents' in Savannah. This was not the only resentment that Oglethorpe encountered:

> We hear from Georgia that an attempt was lately made there to murder the Hon. James Oglethorpe, Esq., Governor and General Commander of that place. This conspiracy was carried out by six or seven of the last raised recruits that went from England; they complained that they had not had the allowance that was promised them and grumbled very much and seemed inclined to mutiny, on which the Governor went and demanded of the regiment the reason of their behaviour, when one of the fellows

---

[47] John Percival, *Diary of the 1ˢᵗ Earl of Egmont, 1739-47* (London: HMSO, 1923), p. 67.
[48] Ibid., p. 174.

presented his piece and fired, but it misfired the governor, and an officer happening to be by, drew his sword and ran the fellow through the body and killed him on the spot, upon which the rest ran away, but five of them were soon taken and laid in irons.[49]

The prohibition of chattel slavery had been one of the tenets on which Georgia had been founded. But almost from the date of first settlement the issue had led to conflict, with rival factions in Savannah and London circulating pamphlets and lobbying against and in favour of the ban. Georgia's malcontents argued that the colony's problems were due almost entirely to slavery's prohibition. They were broadly correct. The economic turnaround from the 1750s was linked directly to the ban being lifted.[50]

The trustees' argument in favour of banning slavery was based on three principles. First, they envisioned Georgia would be a virtuous 'middling' colony where the extremes of slave-based plantation wealth and its corollaries of 'lethargy and luxury' would be absent. In this analysis, prohibition had a moral purpose, notwithstanding that the well-being of the slaves themselves was not considered. Second, it was argued that allowing slavery would encourage the Spanish to foment revolution and facilitate an attack on the colony. This would pose a danger to both Georgia and South Carolina. And third, linked to both arguments, the trustees had a concept of Georgia as a densely settled farming *qua* military community, believing that this improved the colonists' ability to resist encroachment from Spanish Florida. The three principles fed through to the limits the trustees placed on land ownership, with land grants restricted to the acreage that a man and his family could be expected to farm successfully, limits that could not assuage settler aspirations.

---

[49] *London Evening Post*, 23-25 January 1739.
[50] Betty Wood, *Slavery in Colonial Georgia, 1730-1755* (Athens, GA: University of Georgia Press, 1984).

There is no evidence that the trustees were opposed to slavery *per se* nor that they were abolitionists. Oglethorpe had accepted a directorship of the slave-trading Royal African Company in 1731 and became its deputy governor in 1732, notwithstanding that he sold his shares later the same year.[51] Oglethorpe also owned a plantation in South Carolina on which slaves were worked,[52] and both his and his fellow trustees' concerns over slavery were limited to and ended at Georgia's borders.

The trustees' approach to Georgia's governance was also influenced by their belief that the colony's innate fertility and natural advantages were sufficient to allow settlers to produce cash crops at low cost with relative ease. But this sylvan ideal was not rooted in reality nor did it stand up to economic logic. South Carolina's climate and soil were virtually identical to that in Georgia, but where Georgia struggled with subsistence farming and an expensive white labour force, South Carolina benefited from the economies of scale of large plantations and a low-cost slave labour. Until slavery was permitted or abolished in both colonies, Georgia could not compete with South Carolina and could only fail economically.

Among the trustees' other constraints was the need to safeguard the colony's annual grant from parliament. In order to ensure that the subsidy would be paid, the trustees had an obligation to demonstrate publicly that the colony was in the national interest: that it protected South Carolina; provided a refuge to the deserving poor; and would in due course become self-sufficient rather than demanding a continuing subsidy. In the light of the malcontents' protests, it became clear that a number of these points were contradictory. If the malcontents' arguments was accepted and the ban on slavery reversed, it raised the issue of whether the colony could retain its

---

[51] Cf., among many references, Phinizy Spalding (ed.), *Oglethorpe in Perspective. Georgia's Founder after Two Hundred Years* (Tuscaloose, AL: University of Alabama Press, 1989), p. 69.

[52] Donnie D. Bellamy, 'The Legal Status of Black Georgians During the Colonial and Revolutionary Eras', *Journal of Negro History*, 74.1/4 (1989), 1-10, esp. 2.

status as a strategic buffer against Spanish encroachment. But if it were rejected, the ban meant that parliamentary funding could be presented as an indefinite ongoing commitment since the colony would continue to remain uncompetitive with South Carolina.

The trustees' distance from the colony and the lack of reliable information translated to condescending and incompetent rule. Opposition from within and without Georgia swelled and in the early 1740s the trustees' fears were crystallised as the malcontents' arguments began to gain traction. Together with a loose coalition of South Carolina's planters and merchants, the trustees' opponents lobbied hard against the ban on slavery. Oglethorpe himself unintentionally helped open the door to the opposition. His military success against the Spanish at Bloody Marsh in 1742 was seen as having reduced the threat from Florida and weakened the military argument against slavery's introduction.

The malcontents' principal advocates were Thomas Stephens, son of the secretary of the colony, who had migrated to join his father in Savannah in 1737,[53] and Patrick Talifer, who left Georgia for South Carolina in frustration at the trustees' restrictions. It was Talifer who drafted *A True and Historical Narrative of the Colony of Georgia*[54] to rebut William Stephens's optimistic *A State of the Province of Georgia*.[55] Despite its faux content, Stephens had attested to the truth of *A State of the Province* 'upon Oath in the Court of Savannah' and the document was deployed as an advertorial and acclaimed the 'great numbers' of mulberry trees being planted for silkworms, 'greatly

---

[53] William Stephens (1671-1753), Tory MP for Newport, Isle of White, 1702-1727. Despite his seemingly high social status, Stephens had substantial debts and after losing his commission for victualing the Navy in 1714 he was obliged to accept a series of relatively mediocre employments.

[54] Patrick Talifer, Hugh Anderson et al, *A True and Historical Narrative of the Colony of Georgia...* (Charles Town, SC: privately published, 1741).

[55] *A State of the Province of Georgia* (London: W. Meadows, 1740)

increased' vines, and an 'advantageous' deerskin trade. Stephens also reminded his readers of the colony's strategic advantages:

> The French are striving to get [the Cherokee] from us, which if they do, Carolina must be supported by vast numbers of troops or lost. But as long as we keep the town of Augusta, our party in the Cherokees can be so easily furnished with arms, ammunition and necessaries that the French will not be able to gain any ground there.
>
> The Creek Indian live to the Westward ... one hundred and twenty miles from the nearest French fort ... they are esteemed to be fiercely attached to his Majesty's Interest.
>
> Beyond the Creeks lie the brave Chickasaw who inhabit near the Mississippi River and possess the banks of it. These have resisted both the bribes and the arms of the French and traders sent by us live among them.
>
> At Augusta there is a handsome fort where there is a small garrison ... one reason that drew the traders to settle the town ... was the safety they received from this fort.

Talifer's *True and Historical Narrative* set out an alternative analysis. He spelled out the colonists' difficulties, detailed their complaints against the ineptitude of the trustees' governance and railed against their failure to respond to the colonists' concerns: 'the grand sin of withstanding, or any way opposing authority, (as it was called, when any person insisted upon his just rights and privileges) was punished without mercy'.[56]

Talifer argued that the colony's economic survival required change. He was deeply critical of the status quo, offering evidence that 'no proper measures were ever taken for advancing the silk and vine manufactures',[57] that 'Mr. John Wesley who had come over and was received by us as a Clergyman

---

[56] Talifer, *A True and Historical Narrative of the Colony of Georgia*, p. 26.
[57] Ibid.

of the Church of England ... frequently declar'd, that he never desir'd to see Georgia a Rich, but a religious colony;[58] and, most damagingly, that 'we have ... settled in this colony in pursuance of the description and recommendation given of it by you in Britain; and from the experience of residing here several years, do find that it is impossible that the measures hitherto laid down and pursued for making it a colony can succeed. None of all those who have planted their land have been able to raise sufficient produce to maintain their families in bread kind only, even tho' as much application and industry have been exerted to bring it about, as could be done by men engaged in an affair on which they believed the welfare of themselves and posterity so much depended... It is very well known, that Carolina can raise everything that this colony can; and they having their labour so much cheaper will always ruin our market, unless we are in some measure on a footing with them'.

Talifer's arguments had support in the City of London and of a minority in parliament, but the trustees' greater influence prevented the malcontents from securing changes to Britain's position on Georgia. The trustees' position was nonetheless damaged by Talifer and their political injuries were compounded by another pamphlet published the following year: Thomas Stephen's *The Hard Case of the Distressed People of Georgia*.[59]

Stephens emerges in the late 1730s and early 1740s as the malcontents' most effective advocate. Wood argues that 'if any one person can be credited with responsibility for the introduction of black slavery into Georgia then Thomas Stephens, the son of the Secretary of the Colony, was the man'.[60] Various factors underpinned his opposition to the trustees, including a personal gripe - his unhappiness at Oglethorpe's reaction to his complaint of an alleged fraud, but there is little doubt that Stephens shared the malcontents'

---

[58] Ibid., pp. 29-30.

[59] Thomas Stephens, *The Hard Case of the Distressed People of Georgia* (London, 1742).

[60] Betty Wood, 'Thomas Stephens and the Introduction of Black Slavery in Georgia' *Georgia Historical Quarterly*, 58.1 (1974), 24-40.

analysis of Georgia's problems and was willing to put his reputation on the line as their advocate.

Stephens returned to London in October 1739 to recuperate from ill health. He updated the trustees on conditions in the colony and briefed Egmont in private. He emphasised that Georgia's problems were rooted in the limits the trustees had placed on land tenure and compounded by the behaviour of colonial officials and the trustees' failure to address the colonists' 1738 petition in favour of lifting the ban on slavery. Stephens advised that the petition set out an accurate assessment of Georgia's problems and that only the introduction of slavery would provide a sustainable solution.[61] He confirmed that the colonists' desire to introduce slavery was simply an attempt to allow Georgia to compete with South Carolina and not to undermine the trustees' will on the matter *per se*. Stephens also suggested that a compromise - 'proper limitations' - on the number of slaves imported into Georgia would be acceptable to the colonists but was plain that a continuation of prohibition would not.

Egmont and the trustees disregarded Stephens. His analysis conflicted with what was being reported by his father and by James Oglethorpe, whose views on the issue were fixed. Stephens was also at odds with what the trustees believed intuitively and his comments were dismissed accordingly: 'the trustees, observing his conduct, had no more to say to him ... upon which he said in a huff, he would justify himself to the public. So we expect he will appear in print against us'.[62]

Stephens returned to Savannah in April 1741. He reported on what had occurred and promised the settlers that were they to appoint him their agent in London he would act as their advocate without pay and petition parliament directly. Funds to support his prospective campaign were raised

---

[61] Cf. *Manuscripts of the Earl of Egmont, Diary of the Earl of Egmont*, (London: HMSO, 1923), volume 3, pp. 86-9, 174-6.

[62] Ibid., p. 121; also 174.

in Georgia and South Carolina, and Stephens left the colony for London the following October.

In 1742 following the publication of *A True and Historical Narrative of the Colony of Georgia* and in the wake of Walpole leaving office, the Commons voted down the Georgia Trustees' annual petition for funding, a decision that prompted Egmont's resignation as chair. Stephens took advantage and in April 1742 published *The Hard Case of the Distressed People of Georgia*.

The pamphlet condemned the trustees' policies as 'utterly impracticable' and reiterated Talifer's critique. Stephens argued that Georgia could not survive - let alone prosper - without access to black labour, and dismissed out of hand the contention that slavery would increase the military threat to the colony. He asserted instead that the trustees had been derelict and had 'haughtily and contemptuously' rejected the colonists' accurate appraisal of Georgia's economic condition.

The trustees responded by going on to the offensive. Despite having resigned as chairman, Egmont demanded that Stephens's petition be heard before the House of Commons. This was agreed. Stephens presented his case in May 1742 and the trustees responded the following month. At the end of June, having heard both arguments, the Commons vindicated the trustees. Egmont, in his *Diary*, noted on 24 June 1742 that despite significant opposition 'the House of Commons came to a resolution in their Committee that the petition of Thomas Stephens contains false, scandalous and malicious charges tending to asperse the characters of the Trustees for establishing the colony of Georgia in America'.[63]

A second resolution proposing the introduction of black slavery into Georgia was rejected.

Stephens was ordered to attend the House to be admonished and on 30 June was brought to the Bar where 'the Speaker severely reprimanded

---

[63] Ibid., p. 265.

him'. But the episode was not as clear cut as some commentators have assumed. Notwithstanding the trustees' nominal victory, the Speaker refused permission for Stephens' reprimand to be published. And as Samuel Tufnell (1682-1758), MP for Great Marlow,[64] a Walpole ally, later reported to Egmont, Stephens had been 'impudently standing in the Lobby ... with a gay countenance' the day after the rebuke. The trustees and Egmont had been fatally wounded and despite the ostensible triumph, Egmont noted the reality: '7 July, 1742 — I resigned my office of Common Councillor of Georgia, partly by reason of my ill health and partly from observing the ill behaviour of the Ministry and Parliament with respect to the colony'.[65]

Egmont advised the trustees to surrender the Georgia charter. Despite the Commons having resolved in their favour, Egmont was aware that the government was unwilling to support the trustees in the long term but preferred 'to have the power of disposing of the Colony as they please'.

Stephens continued to campaign on behalf of Georgia's settlers for another year but made limited headway. A follow-up pamphlet, *A Brief Account of the Causes that have retarded the Progress of the Colony of Georgia in America*, repeated the points made in *Hard Case* and included thirty-six appendices to substantiate his claims that the colony had failed to prosper as a result of the trustees' constraints. He lambasted the trustees' absolutism, their unworkable restrictions on landholdings, the ban on slavery, the absence of true justice in the colony's courts, and the inadequacy of Georgia's defences. And although acknowledging that the trustees had enacted a number of minor reforms, Stephens argued that these had been inadequate and that the

---

[64] Samuel Tuffnall was senior warden of the lodge at the Bell Tavern in Westminster. Cf. Grand Lodge *Minutes I*, pp. 18, 34.

[65] *Diary of the Earl of Egmont*, pp. 265-7.

colony continued to suffer accordingly. He also condemned his father's role in perpetuating the myth of Georgia's economic success.[66]

Stephens left London at the end of 1743. He could not bear the prospect of returning to Georgia and instead settled in South Carolina.

---

[66] Cf. Julie Anne Sweet, 'William Stephens versus Thomas Stephens: A Family Feud in Colonial Georgia', *Georgia Historical Quarterly*, 92.1 (2008), 1-36.

The Lodge at Savannah, No. 139
Details from, John Pine's *Engraved List of Lodges*,
London 1736

Chapter Seven

A Schism in Georgia

The Introduction of Crown Rule and the Legalization of Slavery

At the end of the 1740s, in the face of a stagnant economy and continuing and growing opposition within parliament, the Georgia Trustees conceded that it was no longer feasible to maintain their ban on slavery. In 1749 they petitioned the crown to request that Georgia's anti-slavery legislation be repealed.[1] The following year parliament voted to suspend Georgia's annual subsidy and in response, twelve months before the charter ended formally, the trustees handed back the colony to the crown.

Direct rule ushered in a conventional legislative structure with a governor, an appointed royal council and an elected Commons House of Assembly. Within months a slave code was introduced modelled on that in South Carolina,[2] and land grants liberalised. Until this point Georgia had attracted almost no interest from planters and merchants looking for new commercial opportunities. The prospects had been less than appealing: a virtually uninhabited colony marked with small, inefficient farms and operating within an economic straight-jacket.

Economic Take-Off

Slavery had existed illicitly in Georgia, albeit on a small scale, but its legalisation was transformative for the colony. In the wake of what was perceived as a generational opportunity, inward migration took-off. Entrepreneurial planters from South Carolina hurried to acquire land in the colony, many

---

[1] Slavery was legalised on 1 January 1751 by royal decree.

[2] *An Act for the better ordering and governing Negroes and other slaves in this province.*

establishing estates just south of the Savannah River. Henry Laurens acquired 6,000 acres on the Altamaha and Turtle Rivers,[3] and brought with him other investors from South Carolina including Henry Middleton, John Grayson, John Harvey and Miles Brewton. Between 1750 and 1760, the number of white settlers in Georgia almost doubled from under 4,000 to over 7,000. And the level continued to rise over the following decades, increasing to 12,000 in 1770 and to over 56,000 by 1780, including 21,000 slaves.[4]

The number of merchants and traders expanded in tandem. In the 1740s there had been barely a handful in the colony - perhaps five. But by the mid-1750s more than a dozen had businesses in Savannah and competed to export the surplus that the colony was beginning to produce. Credit was made available to planters and retailers, and a rising tide of prosperity encouraged the importation of manufactured and other goods.[5]

In the 1760s, the *Georgia Gazette* carried advertisements from 24 merchants. Many were based in Savannah: *John Graham & Co.*; *Cowper, Telfairs*; *Gordon, Netherclift*, the Georgia branch of a Charleston house dealing mainly in deerskins: *Read & Mossman*; *George Baillie & Co.*; *Samuel Douglass & Co.*; and *Inglis & Hall*. Others had offices in nearby Sunbury: *John Graham*; *Darling & Munro*; and *Spalding & Mackay*, later *Spalding & Kelsall*.[6]

Georgia's leading merchant was James Habersham (c.1712-1775), a former Wesleyan missionary from Yorkshire who had been jointly responsible

---

[3] Cf. David R. Chesnutt, 'South Carolina's Penetration of Georgia in the 1760s: Henry Laurens as a Case Study', *South Carolina Historical Magazine*, 73.4 (1972), 194-208.

[4] Cf. www2.census.gov/prod2/statcomp/documents/CT1970p2-13.pdf: *Estimated Population of American Colonies: 1610-1780*, Series Z 1-19, Colonial and Pre-Federal Statistics.

[5] Paul M. Pressly, 'Scottish Merchants and the Shaping of Colonial Georgia', *Georgia Historical Quarterly*, 91.2 (2007), 135-68.

[6] Pressly, 'Scottish Merchants and the Shaping of Colonial Georgia'.

for running the colony's Bethseda orphanage.[7] Habersham founded *Harris & Habersham* in partnership with Francis Harris (*d*.1771), a former assistant to the trustees' storekeeper. The firm was the first to establish direct shipping links to England and benefited hugely after the repeal of the anti-slavery law.

Habersham's personal wealth soared and he acquired landholdings exceeding 15,000 acres, much of which was developed into rice plantations, and purchased some 200 slaves. Habersham's wealth also brought political influence and in 1754 he was appointed secretary of the colony and a member of the royal council, becoming its president in 1767.

Georgia's success attracted capital from London, Bristol and elsewhere, setting off a cycle of investment and further economic growth. Land clearance brought tens of thousands of acres under cultivation, expanded output and led directly to a rise in the number of slaves. Most were sourced via Charleston's slave markets where Georgia became a key re-export destination.[8] And with more slaves and greater output came further profits. As in South Carolina, Georgia's planters and merchants reinvested their wealth, creating larger and more profitable plantations and funding private and public infrastructure.

British military victories in Europe and the Americas, and the peace treaties that followed, nudged Georgia towards border security. The most important was the 1763 Treaty of Paris which opened America's interior to agriculture and trade, and ceded East Florida to Britain. The colony pivoted away from defence towards expanding cultivation and settlement, and the combination of a more responsive government and access to capital and slaves allowed Georgia's output to climb.

---

[7] Bethseda was founded in 1740 by George Whitefield (1714-1770), a Calvinist Methodist. He was pro-slavery and added his voice to those demanding the legalisation of slavery in Georgia. Cf. Boyd Stanley Schlenther, 'Whitefield, George (1714-1770)', *ODNB* (online edn., May 2010).

[8] Higgins, 'Charles Town Merchant and Factors Dealing in the External Negro Trade'.

Rice exports increased ten-fold from less than 2,300 barrels annually in the mid-1750s to more than 25,000 barrels per annum in the 1770s, while deerskin exports grew thirty-fold, expanding from around 10,000 lbs to over 300,000 lbs per annum.[9] In value terms, exports rose from £27,000 sterling in the early 1760s to more than £121,000 a decade later.[10] And with vessels arriving almost daily, the ports of Savannah and Sunbury developed in tandem with improved harbour facilities and multiple wharves and warehouses. Savannah established produce markets and slave markets, allowing a larger proportion of trading profits to be internalised within the colony.[11] And prosperity brought increased confidence and further capital investment and loans, with an estimated £260,000 owed to British merchants alone by 1776.

As the economy pressed forward, Georgia's society became more stratified. In common with South Carolina, the key to social position and financial success was land ownership. Crown policy now permitted larger land grants, with the head of a family receiving 100 acres plus a further 50 acres for each additional family member, including slaves, up to a maximum of 1,000 acres. Easier access to credit facilitated an expansion in the area of land under cultivation and resulted in a concentration of landholdings, with the colony's larger planters buying up smaller estates and using their political connections to acquire additional land.

Within two decades the colony's wealth had become narrowly held and by the mid-1770s less than 60 colonists, around 5% of landowners, owned some 350,000 acres. Within this group a small number had estates of 25,000 acres or more across multiple plantations. John Graham, the lieutenant-governor, owned over 26,500 acres worked by 270 slaves. Jonathan

---

[9] Cf. Paul M. Pressly, *On the Rim of the Caribbean: Colonial Georgia and the British Atlantic World* (Athens, GA: University of Georgia Press, 2013).

[10] Wood, *Slavery in Colonial Georgia, 1730-1775*, pp. 74-130.

[11] The minimum number of slaves carried by slave-trading vessels from West Africa was around 150-200; until Georgia could absorb such numbers as a single unit, the trade was indirect via Charleston.

Bryan, a South Carolinian, owned an even larger plantation empire extending to around 32,000 acres worked by 250 slaves.[12] Bryan also acquired political influence and was appointed to the royal council where, unlike South Carolina, political power was concentrated in the 1750s and early 1760s.

Bryan's fellow council members were James Habersham, Francis Harris, Noble Jones, James Mackay, James Edward Powell, William Clifton and Sir Patrick Houstoun, all appointed in the 1750s; and William Knox, Gray Elliott[13] and John Graham, appointed the following decade.[14] Most were planters and more than half were members of the 'Lodge in Savannah', Georgia's first and that time only masonic lodge.[15] There was no conspiracy. Freemasonry had simply risen to the apex of Savannah Society and lodge membership had become a status symbol.

THE LODGE AT SAVANNAH REOPENS

The newly elevated financial standing of Georgia's merchants, planters, officials and professionals led directly to freemasonry's re-launch in Savannah as an elite fraternal association.

Clarke's *Early and Historic Freemasonry of Georgia* contains a reproduction of the 1757 lodge membership list. The evolution of the lodge reflected Georgia's financial hardship in in the 1730s and 1740s and its later economic revival. The first group of members is recorded as having been initiated, passed and raised between 1734-38, and the second, the majority, in 1756 and 1757. The implication is that freemasonry was dormant in the 1740s

---

[12] Alan Gallay, 'Jonathan Bryan's Plantation Empire: Land, Politics, and the Formation of a Ruling Class in Colonial Georgia', *William and Mary Quarterly*, Third Series, 45.2 (1988), 253-79.

[13] Also written as 'Grey' and 'Elliot', respectively.

[14] Gallay, 'Jonathan Bryan's Plantation Empire'.

[15] Elliott, Graham, Habersham, Houstoun, Jones, Powell.

and revitalised only in the mid-1750s with the introduction of a new cohort of wealthy members.

Other than the correspondence referred to in chapter six and the issuance of a lodge charter, little is known about the early years of Georgia freemasonry. Clarke suggests that Lacy's death in 1738 led to the role of provincial grand master becoming 'vacant' until Gray Elliot was appointed in the late 1750s. But this is conjecture. No minutes survive from the 1730s or 1740s, nor from the late 1750s until the 1780s, albeit that those from the mid-1750s do confirm that Elliot visited the lodge in 1756 and that he was admitted as a member in 1757.[16]

Clarke records that Elliot was appointed provincial grand master in 1757 by Lord Aberdour, grand master of English Grand Lodge, although grand lodge's own records show the appointment having occurred in 1760.[17] The actual date is less important than the fact that in the course of 1756 and 1757 almost thirty new members joined the lodge, bringing the total membership to thirty-six. The incomers transformed Georgia freemasonry and in addition to the colony's principal law officers, including Charles Pryce, later the attorney general, and Charles Watson and William Spencer, the lodge contained at least six members of the royal council: Gray Elliot; John Graham; James Habersham; Sir Patrick Houstoun, the colony's register and receiver of the quit-rents; James Edward Powell; and Noble Jones.

NOBLE JONES

Noble Jones (1702-1775) was the first freemason to be initiated in Georgia and his membership of the lodge dates back to 1734 and the beginning of the colony.[18]

---

[16] Ibid, p. 56

[17] *Masonic Year Book, Historical Supplement* (London: UGLE, 1969), 2nd edn., p. 47.

[18] Noble Jones was initiated a freemason alongside John Farmer, Charles Pryce, and Daniel and Moses Nunes, the latter two being the first Jews to be made freemasons in Georgia.

He was a stalwart of Savannah freemasonry and following Elliot's death in 1771 was appointed provincial grand master.[19] He retained the title until his own death in 1775.

Jones was a master carpenter and with his family and servants had sailed with Oglethorpe on the *Ann*. He acquired influence as an Indian Agent and self-taught physician, and as the colony's surveyor-general, albeit that Oglethorpe later removed him from the post, deeming him 'deficient in setting out the people's lands'.[20] Jones nonetheless regained favour and served as a captain in the militia with responsibility for the Narrows, the southern coastal approach to Savannah, where *Wormsloe*, his 500-acre plantation, was used as a garrison for defence.[21] Following the introduction of crown rule, Governor Reynolds[22] appointed him the colony's treasurer and a judge, and invited him to join the royal council.

In common with his fellow members of the council, Jones was an ardent loyalist. He and much of his generation benefited from crown rule and gained wealth and status under British protection. There was an appreciation of how the colony had moved forward economically and, despite the Treaty of Paris, many believed British naval and military protection to be a necessity.

Opposition to Britain's mercantilism was commonplace but older Georgia settlers were reluctant to support the revolutionary sentiments expressed in other colonies and by the younger generation in their own. The lack of a consensus on the issue led to the absence of representatives from Georgia at the first continental congress in 1774. And although delegates

---

[19] Letter of William Young, Master of Solomon's Lodge, No. 63, Georgia, *11 June 1771*. UGLE Library: GBR 1991 HC 28/G/14. Also UGLE Library: GBR 1991 HC 28/G/15, copy of letter sent to Georgia authorising Noble Jones's installation as PGM and discussing the fees involved.

[20] Egmont, *Diary of the First Earl of Egmont*, volume II, p. 287.

[21] Noble Jones was granted the freehold of Wormsloe ('the Wormslow') by George II. Jones's descendants extended the plantation to 1,200 acres.

[22] John Reynolds (1713-1788), a naval officer, served as governor of Georgia 1754-57.

were elected to the second congress, the lack of any unanimity on what stance to take resulted in a majority of those nominated declining to attend. One exception was Lyman Hall (1724-1790), a rabidly anti-English Scot representing St John's Parish, home to Sunbury, Georgia's second port.[23]

Georgia was also the last province to sign the Continental Association, leading delegates from other colonies to vote to cease trade with the province in the belief that it was acting in bad faith.

But where Jones and his fellow council members remained largely loyalist, their sons were patriots. A generational political schism had opened up in the 1760s with the introduction of the Stamp Act, and it grew worse in the 1770s under Governor James Wright.

Governor James Wright

Wright was the third and arguably most effective governor of Georgia.[24] Born in London, he had grown up in South Carolina where his father was chief justice, had studied law and been appointed the colony's attorney general. He returned to London in 1757 as South Carolina's agent and impressed, being offered the position of lieutenant-governor of Georgia in 1760 and succeeding as governor a year later.

Despite strong ties to South Carolina, including a Carolinian wife, Wright became committed to Georgia's interests, a stance thrown into relief by his protests to London when Thomas Boone, South Carolina's governor, proposed to issue land grants south of the Altamaha River in 1763. Wright's opposition was instrumental in securing the land for Georgia.[25] Wright was also dedicated to the colony financially having sold his estates in South Carolina to invest in Georgia. He acquired eleven plantations, around

---

[23] Lyman Hall was admitted to a seat in Congress in 1775.

[24] He succeeded Henry Ellis who served from 1758-60.

[25] 'Protest and Caveat of Sir James Wright against Governor Thomas Boone of South Carolina', *Georgia Historical Quarterly*, 2.1 (1918), 43-46.

24,500 acres, and owned 520 slaves,[26] a significant percentage of the total in the colony.[27] Wright's main crop was rice and his annual production of up to 3,000 barrels made him one of the colony's wealthiest planters.

James Wright (1716-1785)
Print after portrait attributed to Andrea Soldi c.1775

Wright's term as governor began during the Anglo-French war and at its conclusion he presided over a congress at Augusta attended by the governors

---

[26] Julia Floyd Smith, *Slavery and Rice Culture in Low Country Georgia, 1750-1860* (Knoxville, TN: University of Tennessee Press, 1985), esp. 20-5.

[27] Cf. Wood, *Slavery in Colonial Georgia, 1730-1775*.

of Virginia, North and South Carolina, and some 900 members of the first nations. The peace treaty that followed made land between the Savannah and Ogeechee rivers available for settlement and complemented the Treaty of Paris which extended Georgia's boundaries west to the Mississippi and south to the St Marys River, channelling settlers into the backcountry.[28]

Wright gained kudos for the settlement but Townshend's Stamp Act raised more contentious issues that were less easily resolved. Notwithstanding that Georgia was the only colony in which the Stamp Act was implemented, the Stamp Act split Georgia and boosted the opposition faction in the assembly. Despite its repeal, a patriotic momentum built up, leading the assembly to complain that four new parishes from territory ceded to Georgia had no representatives in the assembly and were thus being taxed improperly. Although Wright agreed to issue writs for elections, he deferred doing so in order to obtain London's approval. Manufactured or genuine, the assembly expressed outrage at the delay and refused to pass a tax bill. Wright dissolved the assembly in retaliation. London's permission was forthcoming and the argument resolved, but the antipathy that had been unleashed created other problems, one of which was Wright's handling of Creek raiding parties on the frontier.

Wright responded to attacks on outlying settlements by securing the agreement of the Southern colonies to impose a total ban on the Indian trade. It was a shrewd tactic. The Creeks had become dependent on trade and Wright's move brought them to the negotiating table in search of a compromise. But Wright's agreement to reopen trade in return for an undertaking that the raiders would be punished by the tribe and the 1763 treaty upheld was criticised heavily by those who believed that he should have used his tactical advantage to obtain settler access to land west of the Ogeechee.

---

[28] Despite the prohibition on incursion onto Indian lands, Georgia's settlers encroached beyond the permitted borders within a decade and Wright was forced to procure a new treaty in 1773 that made available additional land in north-west Georgia.

It has been argued that the decision turned sentiment in Georgia against Wright and substantiated the view that Britain and its placemen were an impediment to the colonists' economic and territorial ambitions.[29]

Wright had been among the most prominent South Carolina freemasons, master of Solomon's Lodge and provincial grand master, as well as provincial grand secretary and provincial grand treasurer. But there is no evidence that he was a member of or attended the lodge at Savannah. And although the royal council was dominated by freemasons, this was a function of their standing in the colony and not masonic collusion. There are two possible reasons for Wright stepping back from freemasonry. First, as the crown's representative in Georgia, he may have considered it appropriate to maintain a distance; and second, from the early and mid-1760s the lodge at Savannah altered from a largely loyalist organisation to one dominated by patriots, many of whom were prominent within the Sons of Liberty.

NOBLE WIMBERLY JONES

One of the principal patriotic freemasons in Savannah was Noble Wimberly Jones (*c.*1723-1805),[30] a leading assemblyman and Noble Jones's son. He had been elected in 1755 and in the mid-1760s emerged at the head of the Sons of Liberty and of others opposed to the Stamp Act. Jones was also involved in the appointment of Benjamin Franklin as Georgia's London agent, which was viewed by the administration as a hostile act. As Hinds notes, 'Jones ... was not a neutral presiding officer but a very strong Liberty Boy'.[31] Wright response was to refuse to accept Jones as speaker of the assembly, an act that was constitutionally improper. When the Commons

---

[29] Edward J. Cashin, 'Wright, Sir James, first baronet (1716-1785)', *ODNB* (on-line edn., Jan 2008).

[30] Also written as 'Wymberley'.

[31] Asher C. Hinds, 'The Speaker of the House of Representatives', *American Political Science Review*, 3.2 (1909), 155-66.

retaliated by passing a resolution condemning the governor's actions Wright dissolved the assembly, and he did so again on each occasion that Jones was re-elected between 1771 and 1773.

Wright's obduracy was counter-productive and led to a political stalemate. Jones and other opposition members of the Sons of Liberty responded by calling provincial congresses.[32] The first was short-lived and poorly attended, but pro-patriotic sentiment grew with news of Lexington and Concord and over 100 delegates attended a second congress with representatives from almost every parish and district within Georgia. They convened at Tondee's Long Room in Savannah,[33] a tavern owned by Peter Tondee (c.1723-1775) a fellow patriot and an active freemason.[34]

PETER TONDEE

Tondee provides another bridge between political radicalism and freemasonry, especially Antients freemasonry. Tondee had co-founded the Union Society with Richard Milledge and Benjamin Sheftall, another freemason, in 1750.[35] The organisation was established to protect Georgia's white arti-

---

[32] The first provincial congress met on 18 January 1775 and the second on 5 July some weeks after news of the opening battles of Lexington and Concord had reached Georgia.

[33] The tavern was situated at the corner of Broughton and Whitaker Streets.

[34] Born in London to Huguenot parents, Peter Tondee (c.1723-1775), migrated to Georgia with his father and brother, Peter, on the *James*, the second vessel commissioned by the trustees. The family had paid their own fare. Orphaned within two months, Tondee was brought up at the Bethesda orphanage and apprenticed as a carpenter. He became a master carpenter and was appointed inspector of lumber at Savannah.

[35] Of insufficient status and wealth to be elected to the assembly, Tondee held the position of Messenger to the Commons, responsible for formal communications between the Commons and the council and for maintaining the fabric of the assembly building.

sans from competition from slave craftsmen, and when that was no longer considered a threat, it became a benevolent society. A number of its members gravitated towards freemasonry and in 1774 they established Unity Lodge, with Tondee elected as its first master. The lodge was the second to be established in Georgia and met at Tondee's Long Room, as did the Sons of Liberty and the lodge at Savannah which, in 1770, was renamed as 'Solomon's Lodge'.

Tondee's association with the revolutionary cause in Georgia was significant, with his tavern described 'a minor hotbed of revolutionary politics'.[36] The overlap between freemasonry and patriotism was pronounced in Georgia, nowhere more than in the provincial congresses and the committees of safety.

REVOLUTION AND WAR

Georgia's second provincial congress elected Archibald Bulloch (1730-1777), a lawyer and the master of Solomon's Lodge, as its president,[37] and George Walton (c.1749-1804), another lawyer and the lodge secretary, as its secretary.[38] Bulloch became Georgia's first president and commander-in-chief; Walton, a signatory to the Declaration of Independence, was appointed Georgia's chief justice and from 1789-90 served as governor.

---

[36] Cf. georgiahistory.com/education-outreach/online-exhibits/featured-historical-figures/additional-featured-historical-figures/peter-tondee, accessed 14 September 2014.

[37] Arthur Bulloch had moved to Georgia from South Carolina in 1758; he was elected as assemblyman a decade later.

[38] George Walton, one of Georgia's most successful lawyers, originally from Virginia.

The provincial congress agreed that when it was not in session authority would be delegated to a council of safety – an executive cabinet. The provincial congress also chose five delegates to represent Georgia at the second continental congress. Three were members of Solomon's Lodge: Noble Wimberly Jones; Archibald Bulloch; and John Houstoun, Sir Patrick Houstoun's third son. The *Proceedings of the Georgia Provincial Congress* records the names of the delegates to each provincial congress, among whom were numerous freemasons. In addition to Bulloch, Jones and Houstoun, Savannah's representatives include Joseph Habersham, William Young, Samuel Elbert, Oliver Bowen, George Houstoun, John Martin and William O'Bryan. Matthew Roche was one of two representatives from Vernonborough; John Morrell, represented Sea Island; Francis Henry Harris, Little Ogeechee; John Morel, George Walton and John Treutlen, St Mathew's Parish; Stephen Drayton, William Maxwell and William Le Conte, St Philip's Parish; and Peter Tondee, Christ Church Parish.

Members of Solomon's Lodge, Unity Lodge and Grenadier's Lodge also dominated the council of safety. Of its sixteen members in 1775, fifteen were freemasons,[39] all chosen as the leading members of their communities.

Reports of the skirmishes in Massachusetts cemented the upsurge in patriotism and the divisions between first and second generation Georgians grew wider. The political schism between Noble Jones and Noble Wimberly Jones was repeated in many other households with the Habersham, Harris and Houstoun families divided along the same line. Indeed, the most prominent member of the Sons of Liberty in Georgia other than Wimberley Jones

---

[39] George Walton, Edward Telfair, John Martin, William Ewen, John Bohun Girardeau, Oliver Bowen, Stephen Drayton, John Smith, Ambrose Wright, Noble W. Jones, Jonathan Bryan, Samuel Elbert, William Gibbons, Joseph Habersham and Francis Henry Harris were or are understood to be freemasons.

was Joseph Habersham, a member of the council of safety and later commander of the 1st Georgia regiment.[40]

In May 1775, Habersham and Jones with George Walton and James Jackson, also members of Solomon's Lodge, and four other Sons of Liberty, broke into Savannah's powder magazine to steal 600 lbs of gun powder. And Habersham participated in the arrest and detention under house arrest of James Wright in January 1776. Wright's escape to the *Scarborough* and return to England marked the end of British executive authority in Georgia and at the end of February 1776, Georgia's patriots had political and military control of the province. A convention was held to agree the state's first constitution and the provincial congress was reconstituted as a House of Assembly. With a nod to political symmetry, Noble Wimberly Jones was again elected as speaker.

The British landed below Savannah in December 1778 and overcame the city's defences. From the coast they marched to Augusta in the expectation of backing from loyalists on the frontier and pro-British first nations tribes. Support was not forthcoming and with patriotic reinforcements arriving from the north, the British retreated. Their occupation of Augusta had lasted just two weeks. A victory at Briar Creek in March 1779 secured a station on the coast and allowed royal government to resume. Wright returned as royal governor and in June 1779 convened a royal assembly. The British withstood a siege by French and American forces in September 1779 and turned it back in October. They advanced the following spring. Charlestown was captured in May 1780 and although Wright warned against leaving Georgia and South Carolina exposed, Cornwallis marched his army north to North Carolina and Virginia. Augusta was recaptured by patriotic troops in June 1780, who

---

[40] The single loyalist among the Habersham brothers was George Habersham. Although a member of the council of safety and Savannah's delegate to Georgia's Secession Convention, he switched allegiance in 1779 after the British occupation of Savannah. Post-war he was subject to punitive taxation.

then filed east to besiege Savannah. The British withdrawal from Georgia and South Carolina began the following year and was completed in July 1782 with Savannah's surrender. The treaty ending the war was signed in September 1783 in Paris.

A copy of the by-laws of Solomon's Lodge sent to the Grand Lodge of England in the early 1770s before Independence concludes with a list of subscribing members.[41] Up to a fifth appear to have been loyalists, part of the older generation, although their identification is not always clear. One example is that of William Young, the master of the lodge. A William Young was expelled from Georgia after the war and his estate forfeit, but another with the same name, his son, was a member of the council of safety and elected to the first provincial congress.[42]

INDEPENDENCE

The Act of Attainder, Banishments and Confiscation passed by the Georgia Assembly on 19 August 1783 names 225 loyalists, at least seven of whom were freemasons and members of Solomon's Lodge.[43] Aside

---

[41] Cf. UGLE: GBR 1991 HC/28/G/13: William Jones, Robert Kirkwood, William Young, Adrian Leyer, Henry L. Bourquin, James Farley, John Adam Treutlen, William Watt, Thomas Lee, Charles Pryce Jr., James Alexander, David Brydie, Thomas Ried, Matthew Roche, Thomas Lee Jr., Samuel Savory, Matthew Roche Jr., John Martin, John Leightenstone, William Stephens, Philip Delegall, David Delegall, Oliver Bowen, Henry Yonge Jr., Henry Preston, John Holmes, John Simpson, Thomas Moodie, Timothy Lowten, George Fraser, Nathaniel Hall, James Houstoun, Thomas Netherclift, George Houstoun, Archibald Bulloch, John Inglis, John Litton Jones, William Le Conte and John Langford Cf., also, Linda Mills Hawes & Albert S. Britt Jr. (eds.), *The Search for Georgia's Colonial Records* (Savannah, GA: Georgia Historical Society, 1976), volume XVIII.

[42] Mrs Howard H. McCall, *Roster of Revolutionary Soldiers in Georgia* (Baltimore, MD: Genealogical Publishing, 2004), volume III, p. 252, (reprint).

[43] Cf. archives.gnb.ca/Exhibits/FortHavoc/html/GeorgiaAttainder1782.aspx?culture=en-CA, accessed 12 September 2014.

from Young, they include Sir Patrick Houstoun, Thomas Ried,[44] John Martin, Henry Yonge Jr., John Simpson and Nathaniel Hall. Each was expelled and their assets confiscated. Other loyalists including as Philip and David Delegall were subject to confiscation orders,[45] albeit some were treated less harshly.[46] But the dominant influence in Solomon's Lodge from the early 1770s was patriotic and the majority of its members fought for Independence.

MILITARY SUCCESS AND POLITICAL INFLUENCE

The political influence of Georgia's freemasons from the mid-1770s is extraordinary. One example is that of John Adam Treutlen (1734-1782). Treutlen had come to Georgia as an indentured servant in the Salzburg community and had prospered, becoming a successful merchant. He was a member of the provincial congress, nominated to the council of safety and rode a wave of popularity in 1777 to election as governor.

Another was Oliver Bowen (1742-1800),[47] a merchant, a member of the council of safety and a representative for Savannah at the provincial congress. Commissioned a captain in the militia in February 1776, Bowen was given 'letters of recommendation' to the governor of Cape Francois and empowered to negotiate a trading relationship.[48] He was at the same time 'authorized to contract with any merchants … for armed vessels to the amount £3,000 … and directed to purchase arms, ammunition and other

---

[44] This is the given spelling.

[45] Robert & George Watkins, *A Digest of the Laws of the State of Georgia* (Philadelphia, PA: R. Aitken, 1880), pp. 242-6.

[46] For example, Henry Preston, the prothonotary, the principal clerk to the courts, and Thomas Moodie, the deputy secretary.

[47] Bowen was born in Rhode Island.

[48] *Proceedings of the Georgia Council of Safety, 1775-1777* (Savannah, GA: Georgia Historical Society, 1901), volume V, part 1, p. 101.

warlike stores to the amount £6,000 ... and to charter vessels sufficient to carry rice ... or other produce of this Province'.[49]

Bowen was promoted to commodore in January 1777 following an assembly vote and tasked with commanding a fleet to protect Georgia's coast. After the war he received a 1,000-acre bounty to add to his 'vast property' in the state.[50] Bowen's wartime exploits include his requisitioning of a schooner to capture *Phillippa*, a British supply vessel, in July 1775,[51] and the fire ship deployed in an attempt to set ablaze nine rice-carrying vessels captured by the British. Bowen maintained his masonic commitments and in 1785 was appointed a grand steward of the Grand Lodge of Georgia.

Samuel Elbert (1740-1788), was similarly commissioned a captain in the militia. He had been apprenticed to John Rae (1708-1772), an Irish-born merchant, one of the 'malcontents' who had signed Talifer's *True and Historical Narrative*. After the introduction of crown rule, Elbert was granted land near Augusta, which he subsequently represented in the Commons.[52] Rae's support gave Elbert traction in the Indian trade and he went on to become a successful merchant, planter and slave owner. His marriage to Rae's daughter, Elizabeth, consolidated his position; the wedding took place at *Rae's Hall*, his father-in-law's estate outside of Savannah.

In 1772 having received military training in England, Elbert established a grenadier company in the Georgia militia. Despite having taken an oath of loyalty to the British crown, Elbert was elected to represent Savannah at Georgia's provincial congress and chosen to serve on the council of safety,

---

[49] Ibid.

[50] Ibid., 14.

[51] Dan Ailes, 'Oliver Bowen: Revolutionary Patriot and Hero' in *The Savannah Biographies*, Armstrong State University, Savannah, GA: library.armstrong.edu/Bowen_Oliver_0.pdf.

[52] George Fenwick Jones, 'Portrait of an Irish Entrepreneur in Colonial Augusta: John Rae, 1708-1771', *Georgia Historical Quarterly*, 83.3, (1999), 427-47.

heading the committee responsible for supplying arms and ammunition.[53] He was appointed commander-in-chief of Georgia's militia in January 1776,[54] and subsequently given command of the Continental Army in Georgia, leading the defence of Savannah in December 1778.

Elbert was wounded, captured, and remained a prisoner of the British until June 1781, when he was exchanged following the British withdrawal from Charleston. He was elected to the continental congress in 1784 but declined to serve citing poor health; he was nonetheless elected governor in 1785.

Elbert was a co-founder of Unity Lodge with Peter Tondee and from 1776 until his death served as Georgia's grand master.

William Stephens (1752-1819), the grandson of the former secretary to the Georgia Trustees and sometime president of the Georgia colony, succeeded Elbert as grand master in 1788. Another captain in the state militia, Stephens was a prominent lawyer and in 1775 became clerk of the Commons House of Assembly. He was appointed Georgia's attorney general in 1776, its chief justice in 1780,[55] and made a Federal District Court judge for Georgia the following year. Stephens was elected Georgia's president in 1787 and later held office as mayor of Savannah from 1793-95. He was a past master of both Solomon's and Union lodges. He was re-elected grand master in 1793 and re-elected annually thereafter until his retirement in 1813.

Samuel Stirk (1756-1793), one of three brothers, another lawyer and later the state's attorney general (1782), had served in the militia, becoming a lieutenant colonel, and in 1777 was appointed to Georgia's executive council. Although elected a delegate to the continental congress in 1781, he did not attend. Stirk was subsequently elected grand secretary.

---

[53] *Proceedings of the Georgia Council of Safety*, pp. 24, 26.

[54] His second in command was Stephen Drayton, commissioned lieutenant colonel; Joseph Habersham, commissioned a major, was third in line. Ibid., p. 28.

[55] *Biographical Directory of Federal Judges*: www.fjc.gov/history/home.nsf/page/judges.html, accessed 23 September 2014.

Other politically influential freemasons include John Houstoun (c.1747-1796), twice elected governor (1778-9 and 1784-5) and in 1790 Savannah's first elected mayor.[56] One of four brothers who fought in the Georgia militia, he represented Savannah in the provincial congress, was a member of the council of safety, and represented Georgia at the continental congress.

Joseph Habersham (1751-1815), later US Postmaster General, a fellow member of the provincial congress and council of safety, worked alongside Elbert, Bowen and Edward Telfair to procure arms for Georgia,[57] and was promoted to a colonelcy in the Continental Army. Following the war, three Habersham brothers were elected members of the House of Assembly, and Joseph and John represented Georgia at the Confederation Congresses.

George Handley (1752-1793), an English migrant who joined the Continental Army shortly after arriving in Savannah in 1775, was commissioned a lieutenant in the militia and ended the war as lieutenant colonel. He married Sarah Howe, Samuel Elbert's niece, in 1780.

Handley was captured shortly after his marriage and spent much of the next two years as a prisoner of the British. He left the army after his release and was appointed a justice of the peace in Augusta, where he had his main estate. Handley was subsequently elected an assemblyman and invited to serve on the executive council (1785-6). He was a delegate to the convention at Augusta on 2 January 1788 at which Georgia ratified the US Constitution. The same month Handley became president of the executive council and served as state governor for a one-year term. His advancement followed General James Jackson's decision to decline the post.[58] Jackson agreed to serve a decade later and was governor from 1798-1801 and sub-

---

[56] Joseph Gaston Bailie Bulloch, *A History and Genealogy of the families of Bayard, Houstoun of Georgia...* (Washington, DC: privately published, 1949).

[57] *Proceedings of the Georgia Council of Safety*, esp. p. 26.

[58] General James Jackson (1757-1806), received the British surrender at Savannah.

sequently a US Senator. He was succeeded as governor by General Josiah Tattnall (1762-1803), another Georgia freemason.[59]

THE GRAND LODGE OF FREE AND ACCEPTED MASONS FOR THE STATE OF GEORGIA

Robert Gould wrote that freemasonry influenced Georgia more than any other of the thirteen American colonies and that the colony was a 'direct outgrowth of Masonic influence'.[60] Although the last comment is inaccurate, the former is correct and many of those who held a leadership role in Georgia were active freemasons. The overlap had everything to do with the crossover between relatively small elite that dominated Georgia.

In the 1770s, Solomon's Lodge included Arthur Bulloch, Noble Wimberly Jones, John Morel, Joseph Habersham, John Houstoun and George Walton, all members of the Sons of Liberty and of Georgia's provincial congresses and council of safety. Indeed, when the British recaptured Savannah they published a list of leading rebels among whom were thirteen freemasons.[61] The contribution they made to the war ensured that freemasons were

---

[59] Cf. Lucian Lamar Knight, *Georgia's Roster of the Revolution: Containing a List of the States Defenders; Officers and Men; Soldiers and Sailors; Partisans and Regulars; Whether Enlisted from Georgia Or Settled in Georgia After the Close of Hostilities* (Atlanta, GA: Index, 1920), for details of lodge members including Thomas Netherclift (1750-1827), a merchant who served as an officer in the Georgia militia, as did James Alexander, John Litton Jones and John Inglis, the last a naval officer. Cf., also, James M. Johnson, *Militiamen, Rangers and Redcoats: The Military in Georgia 1754-1766* (Macon, GA: Mercer University Press, 2003); and George White, *Historical Collections of Georgia* (Baltimore, MD: Genealogical Publishing Company, 1865).

[60] Robert Freke Gould, *History of Freemasonry Throughout the World* (New York, NY: Charles Scribner's Sons, 1936), volume 5, pp. 135-57, quote from p. 150.

[61] The fourteen comprised Oliver Bowen, Samuel Elbert, John Habersham, Joseph Habersham, John Houstoun, Sir Patrick Houstoun, Noble W. Jones, Benjamin Lloyd, William O'Bryan, Mordecai Sheftall, William Stephens, Samuel Stirk and George Walton.

viewed positively and that Georgia's lodges would continue to be considered premier fraternal societies.

Post-Independence, Georgia's freemasons included William Pierce, William Houstoun, George Walton and Nathaniel Pendleton, all delegates to congress that drafted the US Constitution; and William Stephens, Joseph Habersham, James Powell, George Handley and Henry Osborne, who ratified it.[62]

Nowhere in Georgia was freemasonry more influential than in Savannah. At the end of the war, the city was placed under the authority of a committee of seven, each of whom had been elected to represent of one of the city's wards. Their first chairman in 1787 was William Stephens, and the second, Samuel Stirk, who held office from 1788-89. In March 1790, Savannah's mayor was elected by public vote for the first time with John Houstoun heading the poll. A majority of the mayors that followed over the next two decades were also members of Solomon's Lodge: Thomas Gibbons (who served in 1791-2, 1794-5 and 1799-1801); Joseph Habersham (1792-3); William Stephens (1793-4 and 1795-6); and Matthew McAllister (1798-9).[63]

In 1786 four lodges combined to establish the Grand Lodge of Free and Accepted Masons for the State of Georgia:[64] Solomon's Lodge, Unity Lodge, Grenadiers Lodge and Hiram lodge, No. 42, constituted in 1785 by the Grand Lodge of Pennsylvania.[65]

The first slate of grand officers included several familiar names: Major General Samuel Elbert, grand master; William Stephens, deputy grand

---

[62] Gould, *History of Freemasonry Throughout the World*.

[63] www.savannahga.gov/DocumentCenter/View/1971 from Thomas Gamble Jr., *A History of the Government of Savannah, Georgia, from 1790 to 1901* (Savannah, GA: City Council, 1900).

[64] The Grand Lodge of Georgia was incorporated in 1796 by the Georgia legislature.

[65] Cf., Norris S. Barratt and Julius Sachse, *Freemasonry in Pennsylvania, 1727-1907* (Philadelphia, PA: Grand Lodge of Philadelphia, 1909), volume II, p. 107.

master; Mordecai Sheftall, senior grand warden;[66] Brigadier General James Jackson, junior grand warden; James Habersham, grand secretary; George Handley, grand treasurer; and Samuel Stirk and John Martin, grand stewards.

Handley subsequently co-founded and became master of Columbia Lodge in Augusta. In common with other Georgia freemasons, he received masonic funeral honours at his death in 1793.

> George Handley, Esq. Sheriff of Richmond county. As a benevolent and worthy member of society his death will be generally regretted, by his family and particular friends severely lamented. His remains being removed to this city were followed to the grave by the Grand Lodge of this state, Solomon's, Hiram's, and Union Lodges, of this place, and every masonic respect paid his memory as a brother, formerly Grand Treasurer, and Past Member of Columbia Lodge at Augusta. The Union Society and the Society of the Cincinnati, of which the deceased was a Member, with a number of other respectable inhabitants, attended the funeral.[67]

At its meeting in December 1786, Georgia's grand lodge agreed to abolish permanent appointments in favour of the annual election of grand officers. Following this, Samuel Elbert stood down as grand master and was

---

[66] Sheftall was a prominent member of Georgia's Jewish community. Jews had not been encouraged to settle in Georgia but neither were they prohibited and when forty-two arrived from Europe in 1733 Oglethorpe allowed them to remain. Jewish migrants achieved influence in the colony, including public office. The majority were Spanish and Portuguese Jews, fleeing the Inquisition, and a minority German. One of the more senior figures during the war years was Mordecai Sheftall, a merchant and trader, who fought for the patriots and was promoted Deputy Commissary General to the Continental Army in Georgia and South Carolina. He was captured with his son and imprisoned by the British; they were subsequently exchanged for two British officers.

[67] *Augusta Chronicle and Gazette of the State*, 28 September 1793

succeeded by William Stephens. General James Jackson was elected deputy grand master; Sir George Houstoun, senior grand warden; Thomas Elfe, junior grand warden;[68] James Habersham, grand treasurer; and Samuel Stirk, grand secretary. The decision and the names of the new appointees were reported at length in *The Gazette of the State of Georgia*.

Masonic Symbolism and the State Seal of Georgia

Georgia's state seal was adopted in 1799. It features three columns supporting an arch, three steps, and a militiaman with a drawn sword; the same imagery is present on the seal of the Georgia Supreme Court.

The arch represents the state's constitution and the columns the three branches of government: the legislative, guided by wisdom; the judicial, guided by justice; and the executive, exercising moderation. The presence of a soldier points to the defence of the state constitution.

But the seal also has masonic symbolism; indeed, it was designed by Daniel Sturges, a freemason who in 1797 became Georgia's surveyor general.[69] Among the allusions that freemasons then and now would recognise are the three columns signifying 'wisdom', 'strength' and 'beauty', and representing the sun, the moon and the master of the lodge situated in the south, west and east. They also allude to the 'furniture' of the lodge: the square, the compasses and the volume of the sacred law.

The columns support an arch representing the lodge and the universe. The soldier symbolizes the tyler with his sword drawn 'to keep out all cowans and intruders to freemasonry'.

An extract from *The Explanation of the First Degree Tracing Board* provides a more detailed explanation of the symbolism:

---

[68] Probably the son of Thomas Elfe, a Charleston cabinet maker.
[69] Farris W. Cadle, *Georgia Land Surveying History and Law* (Athens, GA: University of Georgia Press, 1991), p. 180.

Our Lodge is supported by three great pillars. They are called Wisdom, Strength and Beauty: Wisdom to contrive, Strength to support and Beauty to adorn; Wisdom to conduct us in all our undertakings, Strength to support us under all our difficulties and Beauty to adorn the inward man.

The Universe is the Temple of the Deity whom we serve. Wisdom, Strength and Beauty are about His throne as pillars of His works. His Wisdom is infinite, His Strength omnipotent and Beauty shines through the whole of the creation in symmetry and order. The heavens He has stretched forth as a canopy; the earth He hath planted as His footstool; He crowns His Temple with Stars as with a diadem and His hands extend their power and glory. The Sun and Moon are messengers of His will and all His law is concord.

The three great Pillars supporting Mason's Lodges are emblematical of the Divine attributes; they further represent Solomon, King of Israel, Hiram, King of Tyre, and Hiram Abif. Solomon, King of Israel, for his Wisdom in building, completing and dedicating the Temple at Jerusalem to God's service; Hiram, King of Tyre, for his Strength in supporting him with men and material; and Hiram Abif, for his curious and masterly workmanship in beautifying and adorning the same. But as we have no noble orders in architecture known by the names of Wisdom, Strength and Beauty, we refer them to the three most celebrated, the Doric, Ionic and Corinthian.[70]

---

[70] Explanation of the First Degree Tracing Board.

CHAPTER EIGHT

SLAVERY IN THE COLONIAL SOUTH AND PRINCE HALL FREEMASONRY

It is impossible to consider the history freemasonry in South Carolina and Georgia without reflecting on the context in which it flourished. For the whole of the eighteenth century a majority of South Carolina's population comprised slaves. And in Georgia, the slave population rose from almost nil in the 1730s to around half the total population.[1]

It is ironic that the plantation system - the South's major economic advantage – was also its principal problem. The South's social and political structure was a product of slave dependency and a function of the machinery needed to control a hostile labour force. The psychological costs, including a need to rationalise slavery as a morally acceptable condition, led to a utilitarian pro-slavery philosophy that festered at the heart of Southern society and yet was at the same time a mainstay of white social cohesion.

Despite the intense concentration of wealth among the plantocrat elites, populist resentment within the white community was limited. One reason was that in the early decades of the eighteenth century financial and social mobility allowed even indentured servants to transition to the heights of polite society. But the principal factor was that poor whites could look down on an underclass of black slaves and thus validate their sense of superiority.

Early reports of white contact with Africans were designed intentionally to give an impression of a sub-human race. In the seventeenth century, for example, Topsell's *History of Four-Footed Beasts and Serpents*[2] deliberately com-

---

[1] Colonial and Pre-Federal Statistics, Series Z 1-19: Estimated Population of American Colonies: 1610-1780.
[2] Edward Topsell, *The History of Four-Footed Beasts and Serpents* (London: G. Sawbridge, 1658).

pared African men to apes: the 'men have low and flat nostrils, are libidinous as apes that attempt women, and having thick lips the upper hanging over the neather, they are deemed fools'.[3] And in later decades, faux ancient history and even the bible were used to rationalise slavery and discrimination, with blacks portrayed as descendants of Noah's outcast son, Ham, cursed to be 'servants of servants' into perpetuity.[4] It was in this artificial context that slavery could be justified by slave owners and slave traders and considered 'moral'.

Another false but widely broadcast image was of the 'kindly planter' and 'appreciative slave'. This fantasy was peddled knowingly by the South for its own purposes or was otherwise no more than an expression of plantocrat self-delusion. The number and frequency of runaways, the endemic risk of slave insurgency, and the ferocity and violence with which the South's slave laws were enforced all give the lie to the concept of a contented black workforce.

Slavery and the prejudice and racism that was its counterpart became cemented into the Southern psyche. It found expression in the social and economic histories of the South that positioned servitude and suppression as structures suitable for Southern agriculture on the implied basis that the slaves who constituted a majority of South Carolina's population and a significant minority of Georgia's were in some sense not a part of the economic and social fabric. Nonetheless, such histories *were* accurate where they concluded that the white population that imposed slavery and fought to preserve that institution were not following a moral or intellectual norm but pursuing instead an economic agenda to maintain their vested property interests. As Blackburn and others argued, the slave economy was

---

[3] Ibid., p. 2.
[4] Genesis 9:25.

not a morality tale but market-driven;[5] in Valentijn's description it was 'the world's oldest trade'.[6]

In the Americas, the Portuguese and Dutch had led the way, especially in Brazil. The English and Scottish followed suit in Barbados and other Caribbean sugar colonies, as did the French and Spanish.[7] America's Deep South emulated and extended their collective example. The immorality of the practice was understood at the time. The signatures to Georgia's *Darien Petition* of 1739 may have been obtained improperly,[8] but the author, whoever that may have been, could nonetheless voice the sentiment that 'it is shocking to human nature, that any race of mankind and their posterity should be sentenced to perpetual slavery'.[9]

The moral argument that slavery was a product of its time is specious.

This chapter does not purport to be an exhaustive study of slavery but rather examines the hypocrisy of slave ownership and slave owners through the eyes and lives of three men whose reputations belie the reality: David Ramsay, George Washington and Henry Laurens.

---

[5] Robin Blackburn, *The Making of New World Slavery* (New York, NY: Verso, 1997).

[6] Francois Valentijn, *Oud en Nieuw Oost-Indien*, S. Keijzer (ed.) (The Hague, NL: H.SC. Susan, 1856), volume II, p. 46.

[7] Among many sources, cf., Marcus Vink, "The World's Oldest Trade": Dutch Slavery and Slave Trade in the Indian Ocean in the Seventeenth Century, *Journal of World History*, 14.2 (2003), 131-77; Seymour Drescher, 'The Long Goodbye: Dutch Capitalism and Antislavery in Comparative Perspective', *American Historical Review*, 99.1 (1994), 44-69; and for a broad overview, Orlando Patterson, 'Slavery', *Annual Review of Sociology*, 3 (1977), 407-49.

[8] Cf. Harvey H. Jackson, 'The Darien Antislavery Petition of 1739 and the Georgia Plan', *William and Mary Quarterly*, 3rd series, 34.4 (1977), 618-31, esp. 629.

[9] Cf. R. Reese (ed.), *The Clamorous Malcontents. Criticisms and Defences of the Colony of Georgia, 1741-1743* (Savannah, GA: Beehive Press, 1973). Cf. also, Michael D. Chan, 'Alexander Hamilton on Slavery', *Review of Politics*, 66.2 (2004), 207-31.

David Ramsay

White Pride & Avarice are great obstacles in the way of Black Liberty.[10]

David Ramsay (1749-1815), a physician, historian and politician, was speaker of South Carolina's senate and a signatory to the act that incorporated the state's two grand lodges on 20 December 1791. Born in Pennsylvania and educated at Princeton, Ramsay moved to Charleston in 1774 to open what would become a successful medical practice. Described by Shaffer as 'schooled in revolutionary republicanism and reformist ideals' and a man who 'opposed slavery both as a moral evil and as inconsistent with and detrimental to a republican society',[11] Ramsay's attitude towards slavery was far more nuanced. It altered over time and was influenced by and eventually accommodative of the views of his Carolinian peers.

Ramsay assimilated successfully into Charleston society. He was elected to the assembly just two years after his arrival and fought as a surgeon in the Continental Army where he was captured by the British. Released, he subsequently served two terms in the continental congress from 1782-83 and again from 1785-86. Ramsay was also a member of South Carolina's senate, elected speaker for three terms. But perhaps most importantly, Ramsay married into one of South Carolina's most eminent families, that of Henry Laurens.

Ramsay's thinking on slavery held a mirror to the views of the progressive Northern elites rather than that of his Southern neighbours. As a consequence, his abolitionist views were rarely expressed other than privately in correspondence with Northern friends, including Benjamin Rush,[12] a fel-

---

[10] David Ramsay to Benjamin Rush, 21 March 1780, in Robert Brunhouse, 'David Ramsay, 1749-1815: Selections from His Writings' *American Philosophical Society - Transactions*, ns, 55.4 (1965).

[11] Arthur H. Shaffer, 'Between Two Worlds: David Ramsay and the Politics of Slavery', *Journal of Southern History*, 50.2 (1984), 175-96, quote from 175.

[12] Melvin Yazawa, 'Rush, Benjamin (1746-1813)', *ODNB*.

low Philadelphian, physician, and later patriot politician to whom Ramsay wrote that he hoped that 'there will not be a slave in these states fifty years hence'.[13]

More surprisingly, Ramsay also wrote in similar terms to Thomas Jefferson,[14] reflecting that 'all mankind ... [is] originally the same and only diversified by accidental circumstances'.[15] His thinking echoed that of Charles-Louis de Secondat, Baron Montesquieu, tangentially a member of Richmond's Horn Tavern lodge, whose philosophical sentiments in *Spirit of the Laws*[16] resonated with many progressive thinkers:

> Slavery, properly so called, is the establishment of a right which gives to one man such a power over another as renders him absolute master of his life and fortune. The state of slavery is in its own nature bad. It is neither useful to the master nor to the slave; not to the slave, because he can do nothing through a motive of virtue; nor to the master, because by having an unlimited authority over his slaves he insensibly accustoms himself to the want of all moral virtues and thence becomes fierce, hasty, severe, choleric, voluptuous and cruel.
>
> In despotic countries where they are already in a state of political servitude, civil slavery is more tolerable than in other governments. Every one ought to be satisfied in those countries with necessaries and life. Hence the condition of a slave is hardly more burdensome than that of a subject.
>
> But in a monarchical government where it is of the utmost importance that human nature should not be debased or dispirited there ought to be no slavery. In democracies where they are all upon equality; and in aristocracies where the laws ought to use their utmost endeavours to

---

[13] Ramsay to Rush, 20 June 1779.
[14] P.S. Onuf, 'Jefferson, Thomas (1743-1826)', *ODNB*.
[15] Ramsay to Jefferson, 3 May 1786.
[16] Anonymous [Montesquieu], *De L'Espirit des Loix* (Amsterdam: Chatelain, 1748).

procure as great an equality as the nature of the government will permit, slavery is contrary to the spirit of the constitution: it only contributes to give a power and luxury to the citizens which they ought not to have.[17]

But as all men are born equal, slavery must be accounted unnatural, though in some countries it be founded on natural reason and a wide difference ought to be made between such countries and those where every natural reason rejects it, as in Europe, where it has been so happily abolished.[18]

Despite Ramsay's commitment to reformist politics, his life in Charleston necessitated an accommodation with South Carolina's slave-owning planters and merchants. Notwithstanding his objection to the principle, Ramsay was unwilling to oppose the slavery other than obliquely. Indeed, it can be argued that he was ultimately acquiescent: one consequence of his marriage to Martha Laurens was Ramsay becoming a substantial slave owner in his own right.

Like other northern progressives and federalists, Ramsay accepted the *realpolitik* that with the South's entrenched attitudes, outright opposition to slavery would be counter-productive. The overweening influence of the pro-slavery majority was confirmed by the refusal of South Carolina legislature to support the arming of even a small number of slaves to fight against the British in return for a promise of their future emancipation. Despite the idea being promoted by Henry Laurens's son, John, with the support of Philadelphia's continental congress, when the proposition was put before South Carolina's assembly in 1779, 1780 and again in 1782, it was defeated on each occasion.

The results confirmed that despite the prospect of South Carolina's military defeat and the re-imposition of British rule, arming blacks and the potential abolition of slavery was viewed as the greater danger. The legislature's

---

[17] Ibid., chapter I.
[18] Ibid., chapter VII.

perspective is unsurprising. The wealth amassed by South Carolina's plantocracy was founded on and maintained by slaves, and there was a genuine fear that everything would be lost by freeing slaves on even the most modest scale.

Their control of the Commons gave South Carolina's elites the ability to manage public debate and control the political system. From their own perspective they had every reason to stand firm. Had Britain succeeded in re-taking and holding South Carolina and Georgia, or had the thirteen colonies been defeated in their quest for independence, the Southern plantocracy would have remained in place with their economic interests largely intact. Conversely, and regardless of whether America gained independence or otherwise, if slavery had been compromised institutionally there was a powerful risk that the financial and social basis on which the South's prosperity and status rested would have been destroyed.

After Independence and notwithstanding revolutionary declarations in praise of liberty and equality, South Carolina's slave trade resumed 'without anything being said on the subject'.[19] And although Ramsay continued to look for arguments to arrest its progress, this was far from straightforward. Ramsay may have considered the slave trade 'infamous' and been determined to 'have no concern with it', but he understood that it would be futile to make an argument based on ethics. And Ramsay had a personal agenda to consider. His medical practice and political offices gave him a status in Charleston that represented a major investment of financial and social capital, and Ramsay was unwilling to place this at risk. He may have had misgivings about 'the renewal of this trade' but he was not prepared to condemn slavery in public. To do so would have alienated his clients and social peers in Charleston.[20] Ramsay was however willing to express opposition using more circuitous and socially acceptable arguments.

---

[19] Ramsay to Rush, 22 August and 9 September 1783.
[20] Ibid.

Following the war, the expected revival in the rice trade did not materialise and planters who had imported slaves using debt and extended credit suffered as a consequence. With demand depressed and economic growth static, Ramsay argued that a temporary halt to slave imports would repair the economy and restore growth. Ramsay's proposition was lost narrowly in the first instance by 49 votes to 51, but the economy remained weak and two years later the proposal was revived and Ramsay persuaded the legislature to agree to a three-year ban. His analysis proved relatively accurate and the proscription of slave imports was renewed triennially until 1803. But despite the success, the ban on slave imports was never regarded as more than a temporary measure and underlying attitudes were unchanged. When the South's economy recovered in the nineteenth century the slave trade resumed. Slavery itself had never been threatened.

Ramsay married Henry Laurens's eldest surviving daughter, Martha, in 1787. It was his third marriage. His first wife, Sabina Ellis, had died barely a year after their wedding in 1776, and his second wife, Frances Witherspoon,[21] in 1784. Martha brought a dowry of landholdings across South Carolina and Georgia and more than 100 slaves who worked on her plantations. Others served at Ramsay's Charleston townhouse. The engagement and marriage also brought Ramsay closer to South Carolina's ruling cousinage and to state and national politicians including Charles Pinckney (1757-1824), Arthur Middleton 1742-1787), and John Rutledge (1739-1800).

Pinckney was married to Eleanor, Martha's younger sister. He had represented South Carolina at the continental congress and now sat in the state legislature. He served as governor on three occasions, 1789-92, 1796-98 and 1806-08. Middleton, was a past member of the council of safety and succeeded his father at the continental congress. He was also a signatory to the Declaration of Independence. Married to Mary Izzard, he was one

---

[21] Frances Witherspoon was the daughter of John Witherspoon (1723-1794), a signatory to the Declaration of Independence and president of the College of New Jersey, now Princeton.

of the South's largest land and slave owners and despite losing more than 200 slaves during the war, still retained more than 740 working on his plantations and in his houses.[22] Married to Elizabeth Grimké, the daughter of Frederick Grimké, Rutledge had been president of South Carolina in 1776 and would be governor in 1797. A lawyer and judge, he was later chief justice of South Carolina's Court of Common Pleas and nominated chief justice of the Supreme Court.[23] All three men were adamantly pro-slavery and it is improbable that Ramsay would have wished to distance himself.

Ramsay was not alone in wishing to avoid offending Southern sensibilities.[24] Slavery was a key issue in post-Independence America and most Northern politicians were aware of the requirement to reach a political accommodation with their Southern allies. Despite victory over Britain, there was a strong sense of American nationalism and Ramsay and others understood the need for a political and cultural consensus that might generate a sense of unity among the former colonies.[25] In Cohen's words, these sentiments would '[prompt] the nationalists ... to develop a notion of American identity that rested on two major premises: that politics, culture, and society were inextricably intertwined so that a change in any one would subtly alter the others; and that culture was a significant force in shaping human consciousness, an idea which offered a powerful incentive to use literature as a means of exhortation'. Ramsay's *History of the American Revolution* was

---

[22] Edgar & Bailey, *Biographical Directory*, pp. 456-7.

[23] Rutledge's nomination was not approved by the US Senate as a result of his opposition to the Jay Treaty.

[24] But see Arthur H. Shaffer, 'David Ramsay and the Limits of Revolutionary Nationalism' in Michael O'Brien and David Moltke-Hansen (eds.), *Intellectual Life in Antebellum Charleston* (Knoxville, TN: University of Tennessee Press, 1986), pp. 45-84, especially in connection with Ramsay's thwarted political ambitions.

[25] Lester H. Cohen (ed.), Ramsay, *The History of the American Revolution* (Indianapolis, IN: Liberty Fund, 2012).

central to this thesis and written not as a history *per se* but to foster nationhood and as an instrument for promoting unity'.[26]

The History of the American Revolution opens a window onto the arguments deployed by Ramsay and other Northern federalists in connection with slavery. Political schisms between and within the thirteen states had created and sustained numerous competing factions supporting conflicting interests driven by financial self-interest. Many federalists believed that if such divisions persisted there was a risk that a constitutional union would fail at the first hurdle and the states revert to individual autonomy or coalesce into regional blocs. At the same time, social and cultural differences between North and South, sustained misunderstandings which reinforced division. As a federalist, Ramsay wanted the union to be a pivot on which America's future turned and believed it to be essential that 'we should consider the people of this country … as forming one whole, the interest of which should be preferred to that of every part'.[27]

But there were divisive issues that could not be resolved by words alone. Although the federalist imperative was to allow 'the prejudices, peculiarities and local habits of the different states [to] be respected and tenderly dealt with', slavery was the most crucial area of divergence.[28] Ramsay's *History* was written to bolster patriotic republicanism, construct a common federal denominator, and create the concept of a people unified in 'republican habits and sentiments' of liberty, industry, morality, equality and the natural rights of man. But in seeking to advocate this vision, Ramsay had to circumvent internal conflicts over social class and religion, and to tread lightly with 'the slavery of the Africans, to which America has furnished the temptation and the many long and bloody wars which it has occasioned'.[29]

---

[26] David Ramsay, *The History of the American Revolution* (Philadelphia, 1789).
[27] Cohen, Ramsay, *The History of the American Revolution*, foreword, fn. 6.
[28] Ibid.
[29] Ibid., p. 29.

Ramsay acknowledged that slavery 'was not by law forbidden anywhere', but he could allow himself to remark that 'there were comparatively few slaves ... to the Northward of Maryland' and that in the South 'we behold such a crowd of woes, as excites an apprehension, that the evil has outweighed the good'. Ramsay was torn between the moral arguments against slavery and the risk of creating tension between North and South that would cause the collapse of the federal union at its inception.

His answer lay in economic analysis - positioning slavery as an institution that in the longer term lacked utility:

> The peaceable and benevolent religion of the Quakers induced their united opposition to all traffic of the human race. Many individuals of other denominations in like manner discountenanced it but the principal ground of difference on this head between the Northern and Southern Provinces arose less from religious principles than from climate and local circumstances. In the former they found it to be for their interest to cultivate their lands with white men, in the latter with those of an opposite colour. The stagnant waters and low lands which are so frequent on the shores of Maryland and Virginia and on the coasts and near the rivers in the Southern Provinces generate diseases which are more fatal to whites than blacks. There is a physical difference in the constitution of these varieties of the human species.[30]
>
> It is certain, that a great part of the low country in several of the provinces must have remained without cultivation if it had not been cultivated by black men. From imagined necessity founded on the natural state of the country, domestic slavery seemed to be forced on the Southern provinces. It favored cultivation but produced many baneful consequences. It was particularly hostile to the proper education of youth. Industry, temperance and abstinence, virtues essential to the health and vigor of both

---

[30] Ibid., p. 35.

mind and body were with difficulty practised where the labour of slaves procured an abundance not only of the necessaries but of the delicacies of life and where daily opportunities and facilities were offered for early excessive and enervating indulgences. Slavery also led to the engrossing of land in the hands of a few. It impeded the introduction of labouring freemen and of course diminished the capacity of the country for active defence and at the same time endangered internal tranquillity by multiplying a species of inhabitants who had no interest in the soil. For if a slave can have a country in the world it must be any other in preference to that in which he is compelled to labour for a master.

Having raised the issues of effectiveness and fairness, Ramsay continues with an intellectual concession to his Southern readers:

Such is the force of habit and the pliancy of human nature that though degrading freemen to the condition of slaves would to many be more intolerable than death, yet Negroes who have been born and bred in habits of slavery, are so well satisfied with their condition that several have been known to reject proffered freedom and as far as circumstances authorize us to judge, emancipation does not appear to be the wish of the generality of them. The peasantry of few countries enjoy as much of the comforts of life as the slaves who belong to good masters. Interest concurs with the finer feelings of human nature to induce slave-holders to treat with humanity and kindness those who are subjected to their will and power. There is frequently more happiness in kitchens than parlours and life is often more pleasantly enjoyed by the slave than his master. The political evils of slavery do not so much arise from the distresses it occasions to slaves, as from its diminishing the incitements to industry and from its unhappy influence on the general state of society. Where it is common, a few grow rich and live in ease and luxury but the community is deprived of many of its resources for independent happiness, and depressed to a low station on the scale of national greatness. The aggregate industry of a country in which slaves and freemen are intermixed will always be less than where there is a number of freemen equal to both.[31]

But Ramsay then puts forward another argument:

Though the Southern Provinces possessed the most fruitful soil and the mildest climate yet they were far inferior to their neighbours in strength, population, industry and aggregate wealth. This inferiority increased or diminished with the number of slaves in each province contrasted with the number of freemen. The same observation held good between different parts of the same province. The sea coast which from necessity could be cultivated only by black men was deficient in many of the enjoyments of life and lay at the mercy of every bold invader, while the Western Country where cultivation was more generally carried on by freemen, though settled at a later period, sooner attained the means of self-defence and, relatively, a greater proportion of those comforts with which a cultivated country rewards its industrious inhabitants.

Ramsay's intent was not to rail against the South. Despite its disadvantages, Ramsay proffered a counter-argument to slavery based on his understanding of the Southern psyche: 'in the Southern Colonies, slavery nurtured a spirit of liberty among the free inhabitants' through its contribution to their prosperity. In the words of William Loughton Smith, Grand Master of the Grand Lodge of South Carolina, Ancient York Masons (1793-98), slavery was in 'the true political interests of this country':[32] 'All masters of slaves who enjoy personal liberty will be both proud and jealous of their freedom. It

---

[31] Ibid., p. 36.
[32] Quoted in Douglas R. Egerton, *Death or Liberty: African Americans and Revolutionary America* (Oxford: OUP, 2009), p. 160.

is, in their opinion, not only an enjoyment, but a kind of rank and privilege. In them, the haughtiness of domination combines with the spirit of liberty. Nothing could more effectually animate the opposition of a planter to the claims of Great Britain than a conviction that those claims in their extent degraded him to a degree of dependence on his fellow subjects equally humiliating with that which existed between his slaves and himself.'[33]

Ramsay creates a unity of approach with the South by describing how the colonies were 'enslaved' by the British, a term used by Henry Laurens. But rather than compare directly how the South treated its actual slaves with the British behaviour towards its American colonists, a comparison that could only offend the South, Ramsay does so indirectly and thereby perpetuates the myth of the contented slave.

Ramsay argues that British mercantilism placed America 'in a state of perfect uncompensated slavery' and that 'the state of society in the Colonies favoured a spirit of liberty and independence [and] their inhabitants were all of one rank'. This was fantasy and an artifice designed to unify the embryonic American nation. In the final analysis Ramsay was unwilling to challenge the consensus Southern view that slavery was immutable and morally defensible.

> The political creed of an American Colonist was short but substantial. He believed that God made all mankind originally equal: that he endowed them with the rights of life, property and as much liberty as was consistent with the rights of others. That he had bestowed on his vast family of the human race, the earth for their support and that all government was a political institution between men naturally equal, not for the aggrandizement of one, or a few, but for the general happiness of the whole community. Impressed with sentiments of this kind, they grew up, from their

---

[33] Cohen, Ramsay, *The History of the American Revolution*, p. 40.

earliest infancy with that confidence which is well calculated to inspire a love for liberty and a prepossession in favour of independence.[34]

To this place our fathers ... possessed of the principles of liberty in their purity, disdaining slavery, fled to enjoy those privileges, which they had an undoubted right to, but were deprived of, by the hands of violence and oppression, in their native country ... we never, with submission to Divine Providence, will be slaves to any power on earth.[35]

Ramsay could not condemn slavery directly without compromising the objective of uniting the emergent nation but he could raise questions about its economic efficacy, albeit accepting that any such challenge would be ineffective. Slavery was embedded within the structures on which Southern Society rested. Indeed, even the Civil War failed to alter the psychological and social prejudices of the Southern white population. And it would be another century before Southern culture altered and Montesquieu's dictum could be regarded as within sight, with slavery understood to be 'contrary to the fundamental principles of all societies'.[36]

Although it underlay wealth creation, the exploitation of slaves created a spectrum of concerns for the South. These were not only theoretical issues regarding the utility of slave labour, but practical matters. The most fundamental was security: the threat posed to the white population by slave insurgency.

Fear of a slave rebellion, especially an insurrection in conjunction with a Spanish attack, had been one of the reasons that the trustees had banned slavery from Georgia. The same fear was present in South Carolina and reinforced by experience. Southern politicians had recognised the risk in the seventeenth century and in 1698 passed an act for the 'Encouragement of the Importation of White Servants' to off-set the numbers of blacks in the

---

[34] Ibid.

[35] Ibid., p. 63.

[36] Montesquieu, *The Spirit of Laws*, volume 1, p. 285.

Carolina colony.[37] It was followed by legislation imposing import duties on slaves, albeit that this had a revenue-raising purpose as well as moderating the number of slaves entering South Carolina.

The Stono Rebellion of 1739, the largest slave rebellion in colonial America, prompted a hike in import duties to near-prohibitive levels and slave imports collapsed as a result. Nonetheless, the collective memory of rebellion faded and tariffs were cut and slave imports resumed a decade later. The same set of circumstances re-ran in the 1760s, with a temporary rise in duty instigated by safety concerns. But these were exceptions, not the rule. Colonial fears over security were trumped by the demand for slave labour, with imports running at an average of between 1,000 and 2,000 per year, and sometimes exceeding this by a large margin. Littlefield cites British naval office lists that record over 32,600 slaves entering South Carolina between 1717-67. And the South Carolina Treasury cites a figure of 70,800 between 1735-75, with the majority, some 86-88%, imported directly from Africa with the balance from the West Indies.[38]

Few Southerners disavowed slavery and there was no political undercurrent in favour of abolition either before, during or after Independence. Law and custom demanded that blacks be treated as chattel and with disdain. Financial self-interest allied to the preservation of property rights – a theme embraced by all political parties throughout the period – were the principal contributory factors, with slave owners disinclined to be dispossessed of what in many cases comprised half or more of their wealth.

Through their dominance of the legislature, slave owners had the means to sanction and intimidate those who threatened their interests. There are

---

[37] Thomas Cooper (ed.), *The Statutes at Large of South Carolina: Acts, 1685-1716* (Columbia, SC: South Carolina, 1837), volume 2, pp. 153-4.

[38] Daniel C. Littlefield, 'The Slave Trade to Colonial South Carolina: A Profile', *South Carolina Historical Magazine*, 91.2 (1990), 68-99, esp. 77; reprinted in *South Carolina Historical Magazine*, 101.2 (2000), 110-41.

many illustrations. Okoye refers to Jonathan Edwards Jr.'s warning to abolitionists to anticipate 'opposition and odium' and to the vilification of Colonel Richard Bland for seeking to extend legal protection to slaves.[39]

From the South's perspective slaves were 'as legitimate subjects of property as their horses and cattle'.[40] Indeed, Okoye's paper underscores the irony of 'patriotic' Americans making the case for Independence by comparing their status vis-à-vis Britain with that of their own slaves. He points to the South's insistence that black slavery was part of the natural order. From the South's perspective, either all men were not created equal, or blacks could not be regarded as men.

Moral relativism has sought to explain away slavery as a phenomenon of its time. But the brutality of slavery - physical and mental - was considered contrary to principled behaviour even in the early eighteenth century. Moral relativism does not explain slavery. Financial and white societal self-interest does.

GEORGE WASHINGTON

Morgan explores the development of an alternative Northern perspective on slavery through the example of George Washington, whose slaves were manumitted after his death in December 1799.[41] In his will written five months before, dated 9 July 1799, Washington stipulates that the 123 slaves held in his own right and the 33 inherited from his brother-in-law should be set free upon his death. Washington also makes provision for those of his slaves who were too elderly to work and for their children's education, and

---

[39] F. Nwabueze Okoye, 'Chattel Slavery as the Nightmare of the American Revolutionaries', *William and Mary Quarterly*, 3rd series, 37.1 (1980), 3-28.

[40] Ibid.

[41] Philip D. Morgan, '"To Get Quit of Negroes": George Washington and Slavery', *Journal of American Studies*, 39.3, (2005), 403-29.

prohibits the sale and transportation of dower slaves held in trust for his wife's heirs.

Morgan's argument is that although Washington's intellectual journey towards abolition began in earnest in his final two decades, there were indications even in the 1750s that his prejudices as a Virginia planter were not fixed. This is not convincing. The quoted examples from the 1740s and 1750s suggest that Washington's treatment of slaves was typical of a Virginia slave owner and that his use of black overseers in the 1760s at three of his five plantations was simply a financially advantageous method of controlling his workforce irrespective of the instruction that his white overseers 'take all necessary and proper care of the Negroes ... using them with proper humanity and discretion'.

Morgan also fails to explore satisfactorily the extent to which Washington's 'humanity' was motivated by money. That one black overseer performed 'as well as the white overseers and with more quietness than any of them' simply confirms that Washington, like other planters, sought to achieve the most cost effective means of managing his slaves. The provision of a minimally more humane environment was always likely to improve labour productivity in an environment where a bad taskmaster bred resistance. More to the point, Morgan acknowledges that Washington was obliged to deal with 47 slave runaways from his estates in the decades from 1760, and that slave flight was a constant problem. The disclosure undermines any notion that Washington's was a 'contented' slave workforce. Indeed, Morgan offers several examples of Washington's relatively callous approach to the purchase and sale of slaves.

Morgan's arguments only become more convincing when he charts Washington's move away from slavery in the 1770s. He makes the point that his shift from labour-intensive tobacco growing to mixed farming had as a consequence a requirement for fewer but more skilled labourers, and it is easy to concur with the point that 'whatever opposition to slavery was emerging in Washington at this point was almost entirely economic'.

Also rooted in practicality rather than morality was Washington's reaction in 1775 to the declaration of martial law by John Murray, 4th Earl of Dunmore, the royal governor of Virginia, and his offer of freedom to slaves who joined Virginia's loyalist forces. The offer raised the fear, albeit not the immediate prospect, of a slave revolt in Virginia. Washington reacted by seeking leave from Congress to counter the offer recruit free blacks into the patriotic forces; the plan was approved within a fortnight.

John Laurens's suggestion two years later that South Carolina slaves who volunteered for military service should be emancipated was also approved in principle, subject to South Carolina's legislative consent. Morgan suggests that Washington anticipated that South Carolina would withhold approval and, if it had consented, that there would be adverse repercussions. A positive decision would 'render slavery more irksome to those who remain in it [and] be productive of much discontent in those who are held in servitude'.[42] Washington's analysis was accurate and Laurens's scheme failed to be adopted.

Washington's stance on slavery was driven mainly by economics and his appreciation of the financial advantages versus disadvantages became increasingly negative as the war progressed. Fighting disrupted trade and pushed many estates into loss and debt; and although crops went unsold, operating costs stayed relatively fixed. Washington even reached a point where he considered selling his slaves - 'I every day long more and more to get clear' - but worried about picking the right time. Regardless, when the war ended and trading conditions normalised, Washington reverted to the status quo ante and in his settlement negotiations with the British insisted on the physical return of escaped slaves to their owners rather than compensation

---

[42] Ibid., 416, esp. fn. 21.

in lieu, something the British were loath to accept for men with whom they had fought.[43]

In the 1780s following the war's conclusion, Northern opinion turned more forcibly against slavery. Carried by a rising moral tide and noting his more abolitionist political audience in the North, Washington wrote in 1786 that 'there is not a man living who wishes more sincerely than I do, to see a plan adopted for this abolition of [slavery] but there is only one proper and effectual mode by which it can be accomplished, and that is by legislative authority'.[44]

Later the same year Washington commented that 'I never mean (*unless some particular circumstances should compel me to it*)[45] to possess another slave by purchase; it being among my first wishes to see some plan adopted by the legislature by which slavery in the country may be abolished by slow, sure and *imperceptible* degrees'.[46]

The key words in these letters are 'legislative authority', something that the South had shown would be highly improbable given the control of its legislatures by slave-owning vested interests. Regardless, the steps towards abolition would be 'slow' and 'imperceptible'.

---

[43] The evidence suggests that Britain's position on slavery at this time was both opportunistic and principled. General Henry Clinton's 'Philipsburg Proclamation' in June 1779, issued from his New York headquarters, announced that all slaves owned by patriots would be deemed to be free whether or not they were willing to take up arms for the crown. The proclamation was and should be viewed as an attempt to undermine the revolutionary opposition, especially in the South. It was relatively successful, with up to 100,000 slaves seeking to escape to join the British, some of whom did so; after the war around 3,000 were relocated to Canada. And when General Carleton was negotiating with Washington over the evacuation of New York, despite Washington's arguments to the contrary, Carleton took the view that that the British should keep faith with those slaves who had entered their lines to fight.

[44] Washington to Robert Morris, 12 April 1786.

[45] Author's italics.

[46] Washington to John Francis Mercer, 9 September 1786.

Even if Washington was moving genuinely towards an abolitionist stance – and this is far from certain – he was beset by conflicting influences. In common with Ramsay, Washington sought to ensure that the federal structure of the United States and its collective unity would not be compromised by talk of abolition, let alone action. As a planter he understood that slavery was entrenched and that only 'imperceptible' change could succeed. And as a slave owner he was conflicted personally. Slaves were property and it was against the natural order in America (and England) to unjustly deprive a man of his assets.

Like others in his position, Washington could take refuge and put forward a defence citing his slaves' 'ignorance and improvidence', regardless that he might wish for a 'destiny different from that in which they were born'.[47] But Washington's slaves were only freed after his death. Until then any plans that he may have had for manumission were entirely theoretical.

Morgan concludes that 'Washington freed his slaves for three reasons: profit, principle and posterity'; and of the three, profit was the dominant factor. But Washington was a politician as well as a planter and was conscious of the shift within the North in favour of emancipation. He may also have anticipated that abolitionism would over time become the dominant political viewpoint. Washington was aware of a growing moral stance against slavery, a position that had been adopted and expressed by colleagues. But he also noted the South's objections. The decision to free his slaves through his will was pragmatic and permitted Washington to leave a moral legacy in tune with Alexander Hamilton,[48] the Marquis de Lafayette, Benjamin Franklin and John Dickinson.

---

[47] Morgan, "'To Get Quit of Negroes'", 423, esp. fn. 31.
[48] Hamilton was, among other things, an officer of the New York Manumission Society.

Virginia writ large adopted a similarly practical approach to slavery. Virginia's legislature had declared in 1782 that slaves who had fought against the British would be granted freedom, and allowed slave owners to free their slaves of their own accord, but any idealism was tempered by concurrent legislation that forbade free blacks entry to the state and required freed slaves to leave within a year. Virginia's planters dealt with trade disruption and losses in the 1780s by reducing tobacco cultivation and shifting to mixed farming. The move caused a surplus of slave labour and it was this that led to a rise in the rate of manumission. The proportion of freed slaves in the state rose from around 1% of the black population in 1782 to some 7% in 1800. Across the upper Southern states as a whole the percentage was even higher at *c*.10%.[49] That this was motivated by financial self-interest rather than ethically driven is confirmed by the reversal that occurred after the introduction of Whitney's cotton gin in the 1790s. Whitney's gin made feasible a wholesale expansion in cotton production and restored many estates to profitability. The result was entirely foreseeable. There was a large increase in the demand for slave labour and, in its wake, Southern states, including Virginia, passed new laws making manumission virtually impossible.

Lacking the plantations that had entrenched slavery in the South and the social and legal structures built to enforce it, few Northern states saw the continuation of slavery as a political imperative. Unlike the South, the trend towards abolition was not arrested by vested interest nor viewed as contentious. By 1789, seven states and territories had outlawed slavery: Vermont in 1777; Pennsylvania in 1780; New Hampshire and Massachusetts in 1783; Rhode Island and Connecticut in 1784; and the Northwest Territory in

---

[49] Peter Kolchin, *American Slavery: 1619-1877* (New York, NY: Hill & Wang, 2003); cf. also, Alan Taylor, *Slavery and War in Virginia, 1772-1832, The Internal Enemy* (New York, NY: W.W. Norton, 2013).

1787.[50] The number rose to nine in 1800, with the addition of New York (1799) and the Indiana Territory (1800). Two decades later the unorganised territories from Michigan to Oregon above the Missouri Compromise line were free of slavery, as were Ohio, Indiana and Illinois.

In contrast, slavery expanded in the South and across the southern interior. By 1800 there were nine slave states and territories: New Jersey,[51] Maryland and Delaware in the north; Kentucky (1792), Tennessee (1796) and the Mississippi Territory in the west; and North Carolina, South Carolina and Georgia in the south. And by 1821, the number included Alabama, Missouri, Louisiana, Arkansas and even Florida.[52]

Florida was ceded it to the British in 1763 under the Treaty of Paris and returned to Spain in 1783 after the War of Independence. Slavery in Spain's colonies was based on Roman law where a slave's legal condition was mutable - capable of change. Slaves were entitled to legal protection and could obtain their freedom through a variety of means including self-purchase and through state or private manumission:

> Slaves are in the power of their masters and this power [rests on the law] for we know that among all nations the master has the power of life and death over his slaves and whatever property is acquired by a slave is acquired by his master... At the present time neither Roman citizens nor

---

[50] The dates are indicative rather than absolute. Pennsylvania, for example, enacted emancipation only gradually and it can be argued that slavery did not end completely until 1848. Massachusetts' 1780 constitution may have made slavery unconstitutional but the relevant passage was not worded expressly as an anti-slavery clause and several legal suits were required to settle the issue, the last being in 1783. In New England elsewhere emancipation was generally immediate. In New Jersey and New York it was more gradual.

[51] New Jersey banned the importation of slaves in 1788 and passed an abolitionist law in 1804, freeing children of slaves to become tied 'apprentices'.

[52] In 1821, there were twelve slave states and twelve free states; in 1837, thirteen on each side; and in 1861, fifteen slave states and nineteen free states.

any other persons who operate under Roman law are permitted to employ excessive or groundless [punishment] against their slaves.[53]

Spanish Florida offered a sanctuary for escaped slaves and despite the penalties for absconding and high risk of recapture, the possibility of obtaining refuge encouraged a stream of runaways. Sadly and ironically, when Florida became a US territory in 1821 Spanish law fell away and chattel slavery was introduced.

English law in the thirteen colonies and the American legal code that governed slavery after Independence treated slaves as moveable property, placing them on a par with cattle or furniture and giving minimal or no protection against their owners' behaviour, even when egregious. And even when freed, slaves had limited protection in the South. Georgia's legal code, for example, made almost no distinction between blacks who were slaves and the small number that were free, some 300 or so in the 1770s, less than 1% of the black population. Examples of discrimination include the inadmissibility in court of any testimony by a black person, whether a slave or free man, against that of a white; the requirement for free blacks to have a white guardian and the same legal domicile as that guardian; and if a black could not prove that he was free he would be deemed to be a slave.

Georgia's slave code allowed unaccompanied blacks to be lawfully stopped and searched by any white and in the event of refusal or resistance, a defence of 'lawful killing' was permissible. Education for blacks - 'taught to write or suffering them to be employed in writing' – was illegal under Georgia law and punishable by a fine of £15 sterling; and free blacks were prohibited from competing with white labour. And although the Georgia Assembly went further than its South Carolina counterpart and voted to arm slaves and reward with freedom those who killed or captured British soldiers, there is no evidence that this occurred in practise.

---

[53] faculty.cua.edu/pennington/law508/roman%20law/GaiusInstitutesEnglish.htm, accessed 12 September 2016.

Henry Laurens

Where Ramsay was an instinctive abolitionist who modified his stance to accommodate slavery, and Washington transitioned to become at best a wavering abolitionist whose slaves were freed only after his death, Henry Laurens has been depicted by historians as having transitioned from a leading slave trader to an outright abolitionist. Laurens's withdrawal from the slave trade and his correspondence with his son, John, is cited as evidence of his moral epiphany and the lack of abolitionist action explained away by the argument that he chose to 'disguise' his beliefs in order to avoid giving offence to his slave-owning peers and preserve his status in South Carolina society.

Smith in 'Henry Laurens: Christian Pietist' refers to Laurens's riposte to Leigh's accusations of hypocrisy in ceasing his involvement in the slave trade, concluding that 'of the "several reasons for retiring from that trade", it is plausible that one, and possibly the dominant one, originated from his pietistic interpretation of Scripture'.[54] Smith argues that for Laurens 'the Bible was more than a book expounding doctrines for life, [it] was part of life itself, to be woven into the fabric of his present existence'.[55]

Offering support for this view, in August 1776 in a letter to his son Laurens states that he abhors slavery, blames Britain for enslaving Africans, and resolves to free many of his own slaves.[56] The letter is considered a 'statement of intent' for abolitionism and has become centrepiece of the 'Southern abolitionist' argument. It is deployed to show that even South Carolinians recognised the evil of slavery and its incompatibility with the

---

[54] Samuel C. Smith, 'Henry Laurens: Christian Pietist', *South Carolina Historical Magazine*, 100.2 (1999), 143-70, esp. 167-8.

[55] Ibid.

[56] Henry Laurens to John Laurens, *Laurens Papers*, volume 11, 224-5.

ideals of the American Revolution.[57] But Smith's analysis and those of other Laurens's apologists are overly simplistic and fail to persuade.

There are several arguments that run counter to Laurens being an abolitionist. First and most obviously the sentiments are expressed in Laurens's letters to his son. He wrote in such terms because he loved his son and had an over-riding desire to avoid alienating him. John had been educated in Europe, supervised by his father for part of the time. Following his return to America he completed his legal studies and against his father's wishes enlisted in the Continental Army where he soldiered alongside Hamilton and de Lafayette, both of whom were prominent and persuasive abolitionists. Indeed, Laurens and Hamilton served together as joint aide-de-camps to Washington.

John Laurens had been in favour of emancipation for some time. His plan that the South's slaves might enlist against the British was designed to assist 'the defenders of liberty with a number of gallant soldiers' and, at the same time, to give aid to 'those who are unjustly deprived of the rights of mankind'.[58]

Alongside a desire not to offend his son, Laurens may have been caught up in the Enlightenment rhetoric of the time. There is an argument that Southern anti-slavery documents such as the *Continental Association* and the *Darien Resolution* indicate that there were those who believed that abolition was the possible price of independence and this drove them to denounce slavery. Such an argument falls at the first challenge. When it became clear that abolition would not be required in the South, Lachlan McIntosh, the probable author of the *Darien Resolution* and the leader of Darien's revolutionary committee, reversed his position.[59] And others did the same, Laurens among them.

---

[57] Peter A. Dorsey, 'To "Corroborate Our Own Claims": Public Positioning and the Slavery Metaphor in Revolutionary America', *American Quarterly*, 55.3 (2003), 353-86.

[58] Quoted in Shaffer, 'Between Two Worlds: David Ramsay and the Politics of Slavery', 182.

[59] Dorsey, 'To "Corroborate Our Own Claims"', 357-9.

A third argument is that Laurens recognised the moral illegitimacy of slavery on an intellectual and moral level but was unwilling to accept its practical consequences. The financial costs was enormous and the implications for Southern Society equally great. In this analysis, economic, social and political fundamentals outweighed morality and were too substantial to be overcome.

But perhaps the most powerful argument against Laurens having changed his attitude to slavery lies in his actions rather than his words. Laurens's response to a potential slave insurgencies in 1775 and afterwards offers evidence that his attitude remained harsh and black slaves were not to be treated humanely.

With British warships positioned off Charleston, several hundred slaves fled to Sullivan's Island at the entrance to the harbour hoping to be rescued by the British and enlist to obtain their freedom.[60] White South Carolinians were aghast at Britain's attempts to promote insurrection. Laurens described it as a 'wickedness'.[61] He was then president of South Carolina's council of safety and 'when some of the fugitives had joined British raiding parties, Laurens ... finding "the prospect ... horrible" twice ordered that they be seized and "if nothing else will do" killed'.[62] Dorsey notes that 'five resisting but probably unarmed African Americans were massacred on Sullivan's Island'. The key issue is not Laurens's reaction to the potential insurgency *per se* but the contrast with his conciliatory approach to white loyalist insurgency.

Laurens's letter to his son of 14 August 1776 is littered with inconsistencies and if taken at face value indicates that Laurens shared the self-justificatory delusion of Southern planters as a whole. Speaking of his estates,

---

[60] There was an irony in this having occurred at Sullivan's Island in that it had been the entry point for virtually all slaves transported into South Carolina.
[61] Henry Laurens to John Laurens, 14 August 1776, *Laurens Papers*, volume 11, 224.
[62] Dorsey, 'To "Corroborate Our Own Claims"', 356 & fn.s 14 & 15.

Laurens writes that 'my negroes there, all to a man, are strongly attached to me – so are all of mine in this country; hitherto not one of them has attempted to desert; on the contrary, those who are more exposed hold themselves always ready to fly from the enemy in case of sudden descent'. And even in this - seemingly his most abolitionist letter - and while writing 'you know, my dear son, I abhor slavery' - Laurens could nonetheless refer to the 'not less than twenty thousand pounds sterling [that] my negroes [would] produce if sold at public auction tomorrow'.[63]

The point must be this, despite Laurens having confirmed that he was 'devising means for manumitting many of [his slaves and] cutting off the entail of slavery', he did not free his slaves either in his life or after his death, although he reputedly did free those owned by his son after the latter death.[64] Even in the 1790s, nearly two decades later, Laurens still owned some 300 slaves.[65] As Ramsay reasoned, 'white pride and avarice are great obstacles in the way of black liberty', and as Laurens confirmed 'what will my children say if I deprive them of so much estate'.[66]

Money had always been the key driver for Laurens whose fortune was underpinned by slavery. As Kelly notes, 'whether or not to enter the slave trade – was the central moral issue of Henry Laurens's life, and any assessment of the man and his character must attempt to answer why he did it'.[67]

The growing moral revulsion in London towards slavery from the mid-century onward, especially among Methodists and Quakers, was not an

---

[63] Henry Laurens to John Laurens, 14 August 1776.

[64] Paul Finkelman, 'Thomas Jefferson and Antislavery: The Myth Goes On', *Virginia Magazine of History and Biography*, 102.2 (1994), 193-228, esp. 210; also Gregory D. Massey, 'Slavery and Liberty in the American Revolution: John Laurens's Black Regiment Proposal', *Early America Review*, Winter Spring, (2003).

[65] Gary B. Nash (ed.), *Encyclopedia of American History: Revolution and New Nation, 1761 to 1812* (New York, NY: Facts on File, 2010), revised edn., volume III.

[66] Dorothy Schneider & Carl J. Schneider, *Slavery in America* (New York, NY: Infobase, 2007), revised edn., p. 61.

[67] Joseph P. Kelly, 'Henry Laurens: The Southern Man of Conscience in History', *South Carolina Historical Magazine*, 107.2 (2006), 107.

issue in Charleston.⁶⁸ When Benjamin Smith introduced a bill into the South Carolina assembly in 1764 temporarily prohibiting the import of slaves, Laurens was in the minority of legislators that argued forcefully against it. And even in the 1770s and after his retirement, Laurens remained active in the trade, assisting other merchants with their slave cargoes despite having notionally exited the trade himself.

Kelly suggests that Laurens's views began to change in the 1760s and that he admitted this privately; why else would Leigh choose to seek to humiliate Laurens in the eyes of his peers by tarring him not as an abolitionist but as a hypocrite: 'the goodness of his heart persuades him one moment that a certain branch of his profession is odious, nay, repugnant to all sound doctrine. He reads the Revelations, which speak of divers articles of merchandize, and finding that slaves and the souls of men are also in the enumerated list, swears that St John meant, in his vision, the pernicious practice of the *African trade*; he therefore withdrew himself from the horrid and barbarous connection, retaining however to himself, a few of those jewels which he had heretofore amassed, some of the wages of this abominable trade'.⁶⁹

Laurens's response was to deny that his decision to retire from the slave trade was an act of conscience. He was, he declared, reducing his mercantile business, did not have a partner and had no interest in getting one, but he simultaneously argues that his personal motives 'should have remained a secret with a very few, among whom is Mr. Leigh'. In short, the implication is that Laurens's private thoughts *were* known to Leigh and he considered their exposure a breach of confidence, albeit that this implies that

---

⁶⁸ The embryonic abolitionist movement in Britain featured a number of prominent figures including Granville Sharp, whose actions in and before the Somerset case of 1772 resulted in Lord Mansfield's judgment on a narrow ruling on *habeas corpus* that English law did not recognise slavery within England. Cf., Norman S. Poser, *Lord Mansfield: Justice in the Age of Reason* (Montreal, Canada: McGill-Queen's University Press, 2013), pp. 286-300, esp. 296.

⁶⁹ Egerton Leigh, *The Man Unmasked*.

there *was* a moral aspect to his decision to exit the slave trade. Confusingly, Laurens then accuses Leigh of having 'invented a falsehood' and of publishing it 'knowing it to be false'.

The inconsistencies in Laurens's second pamphlet are obvious.[70] Leigh's charge of hypocrisy – of Laurens having taken a supposedly moral stance while retaining his fortune and his slaves - was valid and unanswerable. Kelly seeks to explain Laurens's position by arguing that he was in denial: 'he did not have the courage to follow [his conscience] to the logical conclusion: that the jewels he had amassed were the wages of sin [and] he could not reconcile his past actions to this impulse of justice'. There is a sense in which this may be correct; indeed, his 14 August letter provides some support for the argument. But when Laurens wrote that 'negroes were first enslaved by the English' and that 'acts of parliament have established the slave trade in favour of the home-residing English and almost totally prohibited the Americans from reaping any share of it', he was expressing a view that was fiction and not only wholly at odds with reality but also contrary to his culpability and position in the trade.

Laurens eventually adopted an almost schizophrenic position on slavery. But his desire to minimise his contribution to the trade to gain points with his son was incompatible with his status as one of South Carolina's wealthiest slave-owning merchants and planters. When Laurens wrote of George III as having 'waged cruel war against human nature itself, violating its most sacred rights of life & liberty in the persons of a distant people who never offended him, captivating and carrying them into slavery in another hemisphere', he could more accurately have been describing himself.

---

[70] Cf. Henry Laurens, *Extracts from the Proceedings of the High Court of Vice-Admiralty, in Charlestown, South Carolina, upon six . . . informations adjudged by ... E. Leigh: . . . and some general observations on American Custom-House officers, and courts of Vice-Admiralty* (Charleston, 1768); Egerton Leigh, *The Man Unmasked* (Charleston, 1768); *Extracts . . . second edition, with an appendix (containing strictures upon ... a pamphlet entitled,* The Man Un- masked, *published by E. Leigh ...*) (Charleston, 1769).

Prince Hall Freemasonry

British and Irish involvement in African-American freemasonry is no more than a short footnote to this chapter.[71] In the eighteenth century and for part of the nineteenth, even when emancipated, blacks were largely excluded from freemasonry in America. This was the case even in quasi-liberal states, including Massachusetts, albeit that there were some black members of St Andrew's lodge, the principal Antients' lodge in Boston, and elsewhere.

The history of African Lodge, No. 459, America's first black masonic lodge, indeed, its first black institution, records that in 1775, Prince Hall (c.1738-1807), and fourteen other African-Americans, having been excluded from freemasonry in Boston, applied and were accepted for initiation into Lodge No. 441 (Irish Constitution), attached to the 38th Foot, an infantry regiment based at Castle William in Boston.[72] When the regiment was ordered to withdraw from Boston in 1776, Hall received a 'permit' from No. 441 that allowed the fifteen to convene a lodge as freemasons, process and bury their dead with masonic honours but not to undertake initiations or other ritual.

African Lodge was established accordingly in July 1776 but following the war failed to gain formal masonic recognition from other Boston lodges.[73] Frustrated, Hall petitioned the Grand Lodge of England (Moderns),

---

[71] Although there was no prohibition against blacks in Freemasonry, the masonic obligation required that its candidates be 'free-born'. The obligation had a mediaeval origin: apprentices were not accepted into a guild unless they were free from serfdom or bondage, in other words, an obligation to work for someone else. In practice the obligation was used to restrict blacks from becoming freemasons, whether or not they were free men.

[72] Irish records indicate that the warrant was issued to the 38th Foot on 4 July 1765 and that the lodge may have had around 50 members in the 1780s.

[73] Cf. phoenixmasonry.org/joseph_warren_offers_warrant_to_prince_hall.htm, for an alternative view; accessed 12 September 2014.

writing from the 'Sign of the Golden Fleece, Boston' to request a warrant.[74] His letter was received on 30 June 1784 and the lodge constitution granted on 29 September 1784, with African Lodge given warrant number 459. The appeal to London was inspired by John Marrant, the lodge chaplain, a radical Methodist priest who had been ordained in London and returned there in 1790.[75]

There was regular communication between African Lodge and London including, in 1785, a letter from Hall to the Duke of Cumberland, the grand master, thanking him for the warrant.[76] In 1787 and 1788, letters to the deputy grand master, Rowland Holt, updated London on the lodge's progress, setting out its initiations, expulsions and the death of certain members, and requesting an acknowledgement of their donation to the grand charity.[77]

A copy of African Lodge's 'General Regulations', dated 5 January 1789, was later received by grand lodge, as were letters to the deputy grand master and grand secretary, William White.[78] Impressed, London appointed Hall a provincial grand master in January 1791.

Correspondence with London continued, Hall writing on 10 November 1791 to request confirmation that a donation for charity had been received

---

[74] UGLE: GBR 1991 HC 28/A/1-2. The second of the two letters is addressed to a W. Moodey of Brotherly Love lodge, No. 55, London, and thanks Moodey for his kindness in receiving Bros. Reed and Menes on their recent visit to the city. It comments that African Lodge has still not received a warrant, only a permit for a procession on St John's Day and permission to bury their dead according to masonic custom. It continues, noting that the lodge was 'pressed upon' to apply to France for a warrant but declined, and now requests that Moodey act as their advocate in submitting their petition to Grand Lodge. Lodge No. 55, now the Howard Lodge of Brotherly Love, No. 56, was constituted in 1789 at Arundel in West Sussex.

[75] Cf. Peter P. Hinks, 'John Marrant and the Meaning of Early Black Freemasonry', *William and Mary Quarterly*, Third Series, 64.1 (2007), 105-16.

[76] UGLE: GBR 1991 HC 28/A/3a-b.

[77] UGLE: GBR 1991 HC 28/A/6-7.

[78] UGLE: GBR 1991 HC 28/A/1-12.

and asking for advice on how best to send money in the future.[79] In March 1797, Hall constituted a lodge in Philadelphia to work under No. 459's charter and in June a second lodge at Providence Rhode Island was formed on a similar basis.

African Lodge continued to pay dues to the Grand Lodge of England until 1797 and was in correspondence with London until at least 1798.[80] Indeed, Lodge No. 459 remained on the list of recognised lodges until 1813, when the union between Antients and Moderns resulted in the wholesale erasure of lodges with which London had lost contact.

African Lodge may not have been aware that it was no longer recognised by London after that date. In 1824 a letter was sent to the United Grand Lodge of England petitioning for renewal of the lodge's Royal Arch charter.[81] The letter notes that although fees had not been sent to London since the death of their founder members the chapter had recovered and it was intimated that monies would now be forwarded, plus the fee for a new charter. The petitioners included Sampson H. Moody, Peter Howard, Cornelius Abraham De Randamie and six other companions.

In 1808, a year after Hall's death, the lodges at Boston, Philadelphia and Rhode Island jointly formed African Grand Lodge which in 1847 was renamed Prince Hall Grand Lodge. The grand lodges of most Northern states recognise Prince Hall Grand Lodge and Prince Hall freemasonry as a legitimate part of freemasonry and are thus in amity; it is notable that a number of Southern grand lodges have yet to follow suit.[82]

---

[79] UGLE: GBR 1991 HC 28/A/10.
[80] UGLE: GBR 1991 HC 28/A/12, 24 May 1798.
[81] UGLE: GBR 1991 HC 28/A/13.
[82] Cf., for example, *New York Times*, 3 July 2009, p. A 15; and *The Guardian*, 3 July 2009: www.theguardian.com/world/2009/jul/03/atlanta-georgia-freemasons-race, accessed 28 September 2014.

Reflections

When America's colonists looked across the Atlantic to England in the eighteenth century and to London in particular, they saw the epitome of civilized society. London was not merely the capital of the British Empire and the largest metropolis in Europe, let alone America, with a population that until the 1740s dwarfed the thirteen colonies, it was also a political, financial, social and intellectual hub. London embodied the Enlightenment, was the source of refined taste and conversation, and was a centre of global influence. Those seeking to make the right connections, to sway political policy, to trade, and to raise and make money, came to London. The city was a global hub for finance, law, commerce and science; and it was at the core of British military and naval power. Many travelled there personally; those who could not employed lobbyists and agents who represented a multitude of competing interests, each contending to exert influence.

London represented the best and the worst that the British Empire had to offer. And for its elites and visitors, amid the multitude of entertainments, clubs and societies with which the capital was populated, one organisation stood supreme: the Antient and Honourable Fraternity of Free and Accepted Masons. The organisation was headed by a parade of celebrity aristocratic grand masters and its respected or merely notorious grand officers included parliamentarians, leading magistrates, senior crown officials and members of the learned and professional associations.

Associated with the Newtonian Enlightenment and Lockean principles, freemasonry laid claim to a past that dated to time immemorial and exuded an aura of exclusivity. Yet it was accessible to both the gentry and upper middling, and synonymous with convivial dining and drinking and social and business connectivity. With the advantage for some decades of an unblemished reputation, freemasonry was emulated among the wealthier colonists across the British Empire, and especially in America.

The lodges at Charleston and Savannah were established within a year of each other. That in Savannah was working in 1734 with its warrant issued in London a year later; that in Charleston followed the same timeline. But despite a common date of origin, each began somewhat differently. Charleston's Solomon's Lodge and South Carolina freemasonry more broadly was for some three decades a cloned version of London's elite lodges. The merchants, planters, officials and lawyers who made up its members would not have been out of place at London's exclusive Rummer or Horn lodges, and certainly not at commercially-oriented lodges such as the Ship behind the Royal Exchange or George Rooke's Golden Spikes. Solomon's Lodge contained among the most eminent in Charleston's community and the lodge functioned as it did in England, as a meeting place for members of the political, commercial and military elites.

The appointment of well-connected provincial grand masters including Hammerton and Leigh in South Carolina, and Lacy in Georgia, encouraged colonists to view the lodge almost as an outpost of London society. And with this came the sense of social exceptionality that in the 1740s and 1750s became a defining characteristics of English freemasonry. The naiveté of identifying with English mores would be exposed in the mid-1760s as political and economic tensions divided America from Britain and set colonial loyalist against American patriot, but this was not on the horizon a decade earlier.

That freemasonry in Savannah in the 1730s developed differently to that in Charleston was driven by the failure of Georgia's economy. Rather than being built in the image of an exclusive London lodge, the lodge at Savannah was viewed as 'tippling society' whose members were accused of fomenting division. The lodge fell into abeyance in the 1740s and resurfaced only when trustee government was replaced by direct crown rule and slavery legalised. Georgia's economy rebounded thereafter and the wealth that followed allowed and encouraged Georgia freemasonry to replicate that in South Carolina.

Before and after the war with Britain, many of those at the apex of white male Southern Society were freemasons, albeit with differing political sympathies pre and post. In the case of Georgia, the appropriate word is probably 'most' rather than 'many', given how freemasons dominated state politics.

Underpinned by slavery, the lodges at Charleston and Savannah, and elsewhere in the Deep South, were the clubs of choice for the South's elites. And freemasonry as an organisation became synonymous with political power and economic advantage, a circumstance that would remain the case into the nineteenth century.

Appendices

Appendix One
The Colonization and Commerce of South Carolina

Appendix Two
Moderns & Antients — An Irish Legacy

Appendix Three
Selected Lodge Membership Data

Appendix Four
Georgia's Grand Officers, Antients and Moderns (1780)

Appendix One

The Colonization and Commerce of South Carolina

France and Spain vied for territory in the Americas. Eastern Canada was settled by the French in the sixteenth century and Florida and Mexico by the Spanish. Both competed to gain a foothold on the Atlantic coast south of what would become Virginia. A French expedition under Jean Ribault landed in 1562 at Parris Island, present-day Port Royal in South Carolina, but without resupply from France the colony survived less than twelve months. Some four years later Spain established its own outpost, Santa Elena, at the same location. The site was occupied for almost a decade until ever more successful attacks by the first nations forced its evacuation. The following year, 1577, the Spanish returned and rebuilt and extended Santa Elena's defences; the local tribes were suppressed and some, notably the Cusabo, converted to Catholicism. Over the decade that followed the settlement expanded to reach an estimated population of around 400 soldiers and settlers.

Francis Drake's naval assaults on the Spanish Caribbean in the 1580s followed by an attack on St Augustine, Spain's principal base in Florida, precipitated a change in policy. Notwithstanding almost twenty years of occupation, Santa Elena was abandoned in 1587 and Spanish forces consolidated at St Augustine. But the move was tactical rather than strategic and Spain retained territorial ambitions for America. In later years Spain re-established military outposts north and west of Florida, and naval patrols along the Atlantic seaboard continued throughout the seventeenth century and into the eighteenth.

England's initial attempts at colonising America pre-dated the 1606 charter awarded to London's Virginia Company. Some three decades earlier in 1578, Elizabeth had awarded a patent to Sir Humphrey Gilbert, a military adventurer and court favourite,[1] granting him possession of the continent's 'heathen and barbarous lands, countries and territories not ... possessed by any Christian prince nor inhabited by Christian people'.[2] Gilbert intended to exploit the charter fully and formed a joint stock company to finance his expeditions. But although able to claim Newfoundland in Elizabeth's name he was less successful in establishing settlements to the south.

Gilbert died at sea while returning from Nova Scotia and his patent was reissued to Sir Walter Raleigh, Gilbert's half-brother through his mother.[3] Raleigh, another Court favourite, saw an opportunity to establish a privateering base from which to raid Spain's South American treasure galleons. His business model proved attractive to investors and funds were raised with relative ease; within a year, the money was in place for an initial reconnaissance mission to be undertaken under the joint command of Philip Amadas and Arthur Barlowe.

The expedition sailed in late 1584 taking a course via the Canary Islands and the West Indies, where it re-provisioned, then north along the Atlantic coast of present-day North Carolina to Roanoke Island on the outer banks. Barlowe's subsequent account of the voyage and of the hospitality he received was recorded in correspondence with Raleigh.[4] The description of the coast and interior could not have been more favourable: 'many goodly woods full of deer, conies, hares and fowl, even in the midst of summer in

---

[1] Rory Rapple, 'Gilbert, Sir Humphrey (1537–1583)', *ODNB* (online edn., Jan 2012).

[2] Letters Patent to Sir Humfrey Gilbert, 11 June 1578: avalon.law.yale.edu/16th_century/humfrey.asp, accessed 23 February 2014.

[3] avalon.law.yale.edu/16th_century/Ralegh.asp, accessed 23 February 2014. Cf. also, Mark Nicholls, Penry Williams, 'Ralegh, Sir Walter (1554–1618)', *ODNB* (online edn., Jan 2008).

[4] Arthur Barlowe, *The First Voyage to Roanoke, 1584*. Published in Richard Hakluyt, *Principal Navigations, Voyages, Traffiques and Discoveries of the English* (London: 1589) and reprinted as *Old South Leaflets*, 92 (1898).

incredible abundance… the soil is the most plentiful, sweet, fruitful and wholesome'.[5]

Barlowe's contact with the first nations had been equally encouraging: 'we were entertained with all love and kindness and with much bounty after their manner as [they] could possibly devise. We found the people most gentle, loving and faithful, void of all guile and treason… after the manner of the golden age… a more kind and loving people there cannot be found in the world, as far as we have hitherto had trial'.[6]

Encouraged by Barlowe's account, Raleigh procured funds for a follow-up expedition and within twelve months a force of six vessels and six hundred men set sail under the command of Raleigh's cousin, the naval commander Sir Richard Grenville.[7] Grenville was familiar with the Americas having invested in two of Gilbert's voyages; perhaps equally importantly, he also co-owned the *Castle of Comfort*, a 200-ton privateer.[8]

The expedition's temporary base at Roanoke was a promising location from which to attack Spain's galleons whose route out of Latin America ran north along the Florida coast before turning east to the Azores. While Grenville took to sea seeking Spanish prey, military command ashore was given to Ralph Lane, an army officer tasked by Grenville with reconnoitring the coast to locate a permanent base for the fleet. War between England and Spain was imminent and a defensible deep-water harbour would provide a useful refuge for privateers harrying Spain's American and Caribbean colonies as well as a potential naval base. In the event Lane failed. Running short of supplies and having received no further instructions from Grenville, Lane accepted an offer of return passage to England in mid-1586 when Drake's *Golden Hind* docked at Roanoke to re-provision. Grenville returned a few

---

[5] Ibid.

[6] Ibid.

[7] David Loades, 'Grenville, Sir Richard (1542-1591)', *ODNB* (online edn., Jan 2008).

[8] Ibid.

weeks later to find the base deserted. Leaving a small garrison of fifteen men behind, Grenville returned to privateering then sailed for England and home.

Despite the expedition's inauspicious end, Raleigh remained conscious of the value of an American naval base and of the wealth and prestige that would flow from a permanent settlement. A third mission was organised in 1587, with Raleigh intent on establishing a self-sufficient colony on the Chesapeake Bay. Once again funding was forthcoming and Raleigh organised a vessel, provisions and attracted some 150 colonists. Command was given to John White, a friend who had sailed with Grenville two years earlier.[9]

White's instructions were to collect Grenville's garrison then sail north and land at Chesapeake, but on their arrival at Roanoke they found the base deserted. It was the beginning of a series of problems. White's captain, Simão Fernandez, was more interested in privateering than sailing north and insisted that White and the colonists disembark. Just over a week later, White's assistant, George Howe, was murdered on an inland fishing trip. Help was sought from their local allies, the Croaton, who advised White that rival tribes, the Aquascogoc, Secota and Dasamonquepeio, were responsible for Howe's death and for attacking Grenville's garrison. White launched an attack on what he believed to be a Dasamonquepeio settlement. It was a disaster. Unable to distinguish between the different tribes, the colonists sacked a Croaton village killing women and children. The Croaton were furious; they ceased contact and refused to provide any further assistance. Unable to obtain food, the expedition was forced to rely almost entirely on the provisions they had brought with them. They also came under attack from the first nations. Faced with few alternatives, White was persuaded to return to London to organize the settlement's resupply.

The timing was wretched. A Spanish Armada was preparing to sail against England and the defensive preparations that preceded the attempted invasion and the naval battles that followed sequestered almost all available

---

[9] Karim M. Tiro, 'White, John (*fl.* 1577–1593)', *ODNB*.

vessels. White eventually procured two small ships but their captains insisted on privateering on route. The decision was ruinous. The vessels were captured and their cargoes seized, and White was forced to turn back: 'they robbed us of all our victuals, powder, weapons and provision, saving a small quantity of biscuit to serve us scarce for England'.[10]

Raising funds for a second relief mission to Roanoke took another year. When the *Hopewell*, *John Evangelist* and *Little John* reached Roanoke in 1590 they found the colony uninhabited. Despite a six-week search, no trace of any survivors was found and with the weather turning, White's captains encouraged him to sail for England. Although subsequent expeditions were mounted in an attempt to find out what had happened to the colony there were few clues and the settlers were presumed dead.

It would be another four decades before the prospect of English settlement in Carolina was resurrected with the grant in 1629 of a patent to Sir Robert Heath, Charles I's attorney general.[11] Heath was familiar with North America, a member of the council for New England and of the council of the Virginia Company, where he owned land.[12] His patent for Carolina and the Bahamas mirrored that granted to Raleigh by Elizabeth, with Heath charged with 'enlarging the Christian religion [of] our Empire & increasing the trade & commerce of this our kingdom... in the parts of America... neither inhabited by ours or the subjects of any other Christian king, prince or state but... by certain barbarous men who have not any knowledge of the Divine Deity'.[13]

---

[10] Quoted in David B. Quinn et al, *New American World* (New York, NY: Arno Press, 1979), volume 3, p. 324.

[11] Paul E. Kopperman, 'Heath, Sir Robert (1575–1649)', *ODNB* (online edn., Jan 2008).

[12] Charges of unprofessional conduct were levied against the Virginia Company in a report co-authored by Heath; the Virginia charter was withdrawn in 1624 and the colony thereafter returned to the crown.

[13] Sir Robert Heath's Patent: 5 Charles I, 30 October 1629: avalon.law.yale.edu/17th_century/heath.asp, accessed 23 February 2014.

Heath's attempts to colonise Carolina failed, as did those of Lord Berkeley to whom the patent was assigned. But despite their failure, Carolina was settled some three decades later, albeit from Virginia rather than from England, when the Virginia assembly approved a new settlement on the Albemarle Sound at the confluence of the Roanoke and Chowan rivers in 1653.[14] The township attracted other settlers, including a small Quaker community, and more land was purchased from the first nations adding to the scale of the settlement. Nevertheless, although Albemarle was arguably the first permanent English colony established in Carolina, it was more an extension of Virginia than the first step in the foundation of a new province.

The colonisation of Carolina in its own right began in the 1660s. With Sir Robert Heath's patent deemed unrealised and invalid, Charles II awarded a replacement in 1663 to eight political allies: Edward, Earl of Clarendon; George, Duke of Albemarle; William, Earl of Craven; John, Lord Berkeley; Anthony, Lord Ashley; Sir George Carteret; Sir John Colleton; and Sir William Berkeley. The Carolina Charter made its beneficiaries 'true and absolute Lords and Proprietors' of the province with joint legal title to an expanse of territory that stretched south from the Virginia border to Florida, and west from the Atlantic to the Pacific.[15] It incorporated the same entitlements and political imperatives of earlier charters, challenged rival French and Spanish claims, and ignored fully the indigenous American people.

The Lords Proprietors were commissioned with the 'enlargement of [England's] empire and dominions' and obliged 'by their [own] industry and charge to transport and make an ample colony'. In return they received

---

[14] The Albemarle Settlement was not included in the 1663 charter granted to the Lord Proprietors but was incorporated into an amended charter issued two years later in 1665.

[15] Charter of Carolina, 24 March 1663, revised 30 June 1665: avalon.law.yale.edu/17th_century/nc01.asp, accessed 24 February 2014. The original land grant ran south from Virginia's southern border at 36 degrees north, to 31 degrees north, incorporating the current state of Georgia. The southern boundary was relocated in 1665 to 29 degrees north so as to include the Albemarle settlements.

near-absolute control over the colony's land and resources and expected to profit accordingly. But rather than deploy indentured labour and finance transport and accommodation themselves, the Lords Proprietors sought to minimise their outlay and lessen the risk by seeking colonists willing to cover their own expeditionary expenses in return for land grants subject only to an annual fee or quit-rent.

The Proprietors negotiated their first arrangement with John Yeamans, the son of an affluent Bristol brewer and a prominent Barbados planter.[16] Yeamans was known to John Colleton, they were both leading figures on the island, and headed a group of investors willing to finance a settlement on the Lower Cape Fear. The Proprietors were elated; they secured a baronetcy for Yeamans and appointed him governor of the new colony. Yeamans' three-vessel expedition set out from Barbados in 1665. Two ships were lost at sea and with only one making land, the colony was under provisioned and without critical mass. Perhaps sensing impending failure, Yeamans remained at Cape Fear for barely two months before returning to Barbados. The settlement itself survived for just over a year before being abandoned in 1667.

Despite the failure, a second attempt was made in 1669. Three vessels sailed from England via Ireland and Barbados, where additional colonists embarked and the ships re-provisioned. As with the first expedition, the final leg proved the hardest. A storm carried one vessel to Virginia and forced a second aground in the Bahamas; only the largest, the *Carolina*, a 200-ton frigate, succeeded in making land in May 1670 near present-day Beaufort. But although the colonists were also to establish a temporary settlement, the hostility of the local tribes persuaded them to relocate. Alternative sites were scouted and the construction of a replacement began in the late summer, some 200 miles to the south and around two miles inland along the Ashley River.

---

[16] Robert M. Weir, 'Yeamans, Sir John, first baronet (1611–1674)', *ODNB* (online edn., Jan 2008).

The new settlement at Albemarle Point was located on a defensible bluff with good access to the interior but invisible to the Spanish naval vessels that patrolled the Atlantic coast. The colonists' second ship, the *Three Brothers*, arrived from Virginia a month later and the following year came the first of what would be many vessels carrying colonists from Barbados. The settlement was named Charles Town in honour of Charles II and a decade later in 1680 with the population of around 1,200 having outgrown Albemarle Point, the town relocated east to the deep water harbour at the mouth of the Ashley and Cooper rivers.[17] Following Independence, 'Charles Town' was shortened to 'Charleston', the name used (historically incorrectly) throughout this book.

The first wave of colonists was led by William Sayle, an elderly former governor of Bermuda who had been appointed *de facto* governor by Yeamans.[18] Yeamans himself arrived in Charleston from Barbados in 1671 and took office the following year. He brought with him two hundred African slaves to clear land for his plantation and secure the bounty the Proprietors awarded to slave owners. It became the first slave-worked plantation in the colony.[19]

Yeamans has been depicted as 'epitomising the enterprising Barbadians who played a large part in settling South Carolina',[20] but the description is only partly correct. He was self-centred and venal and more aptly characterised as a 'pirate ashore'.[21] The circumstances of his marriage to Margaret Berringer set the tone. Yeamans was widely believed to have conspired with her to poison her husband, Benjamin Berringer, Yeamans' former business

---

[17] Named for Anthony Ashley-Cooper, later 1st Earl of Shaftesbury (1621-1683), the Lords Proprietors' *de facto* leader. Cf. Tim Harris, 'Cooper, Anthony Ashley, first earl of Shaftesbury (1621–1683)', *ODNB* (online edn., Jan 2008).

[18] Cf. Virginia Bernhard, 'Sayle, William (d.1671)', *ODNB* (online edn., January 2008).

[19] A bounty of 100 acres was awarded for each slave.

[20] Weir, 'Yeamans, Sir John', *ODNB*.

[21] Ibid.

partner in Barbados. Although the death was investigated by the Barbados royal council and Yeamans cleared, their judgment may not have been entirely impartial. Yeamans was not simply one of the island's most prominent planters; he was also a fellow member of the council, a judge in the Court of Common Pleas and colonel of the island's militia. Yeamans' marriage to Berringer took place less than three months later. But regardless of his behaviour and reputation in Barbados, it was Yeamans' conduct as Carolina's governor that persuaded the Proprietors to reassess his suitability for the role.

Lord Ashley's remarks to Sir Peter Colleton,[22] Sir John's son, underline the point:

> Though I am willing to believe all that you say of Sir John [Yeamans] and to have as good an opinion of him as may be, yet I must deal freely with you and tell you I cannot foresee what advantage we shall receive from all those able parts you mention… Since he came in we hear of nothing but wants and supplies. We must build a house for the governor, and we must make provision for the entertainment of the council; so that, if to take the care of one, whatever becomes of the people – if to convert all things to his present private profit be the mark of able parts, Sir John is without doubt a very judicious man. Notwithstanding all this, my dissatisfaction in him ceases as soon as he ceases to discompose their affairs; but you must give me leave to profess to you that unless these things can be cured and I find that care being taken of the plantation, I shall not have patience quietly to sit still and look on whilst the colony is destroyed; and should it fail by his perverse and indirect management, the indignation of having a design of so fair hopes and so great consequence on which I had set my mind ruined by his covetousness nor ambition will make me require satisfaction

---

[22] Sir Peter Colleton, 2nd Bt. (1633-1694), was the eldest son of Sir John Colleton and deputy governor of Barbados and president of the royal council from 1672 until 1677; he became a Lord Proprietor on his father's death and was entrusted with recruiting settlers from Barbados where he was one of the leading planters.

in the remotest part of the world, for in this, which is my darling, and wherein I am also entrusted by others, I cannot suffer myself and them to be injured by anybody without great resentment.[23]

Yeamans' interests as governor were neither those of the colony nor those of the Lords Proprietors but entirely his own. His profiteering from food shortages alienated both the Lords Proprietors and his fellow settlers and his commission as governor was revoked in 1664.[24]

Freemen and their families comprised around a quarter of the early settlers; the balance was made up of servants and indentured labourers.[25] More than half of those who settled Carolina in the three decades to 1700 came from Barbados, with a majority of the remainder from elsewhere in the Caribbean and continental America, especially Massachusetts and Virginia, with a minority from the home nations and continental Europe. The influences shaping the colony in its formative years were thus those of the Caribbean sugar colonies. The islands provided a blueprint for what would become a *rentier* social structure that emulated Barbados's economic model. It created an elite of inter-connected planters, merchants and lawyers, with wealth and political influence concentrated in a cousinage of inter-married families.[26]

---

[23] Shaftesbury to Peter Colleton, *27 November 1672*, in Benjamin Martyn & Andrew Kippis, *The Life of the first Earl of Shaftesbury* (London: Richard Bentley, 1836), volume II, p. 98-100.

[24] Weir, 'Yeamans, Sir John', *ODNB*.

[25] Indentured workers contracted for an average of four to five years' service in return for passage and keep. At the end of the contract, they would usually receive a capital sum and be released to work on their own account. A minority were impressed into indenture but the majority contracted voluntarily.

[26] Cf., Karen Northrop Barzilay, *Fifty Gentlemen Total Strangers: A Portrait of the First Continental Congress* (PhD Dissertation to the Graduate Faculty of The College of William and Mary, VA: Ann Arbor, 2009), p. 40, esp. fn. 12. (UMI # 33532901.) Also cf. P.J. Marshall, *The Oxford History of the British Empire: The Eighteenth Century* (Oxford, OUP, 1998), volume 2, p. 297.

Slavery was essential to the plantation system and slave exploitation became ingrained within South Carolina's economic and social culture. The result was a distorted allocation of resources towards the colony's plantations and a political bias in favour of the social and legislative structures necessary to protect them. The right to own slaves as chattel or property was also embedded in the *Fundamental Constitutions of Carolina*,[27] a decision that suggests the input of the Colleton family.

The *Constitutions* was an amalgam of medievalism and Enlightenment that had been drafted mainly by John Locke,[28] Ashley's secretary and later an opponent of slavery.[29] It was adopted by the Lords Proprietors in 1669. Although never ratified by the Carolina Assembly and dismissed by many historians as impractical and quasi-feudal, the *Fundamental Constitutions* did more than set out a framework for governance. It also emphasised the vast extent of the land available to incomers, something especially attractive to settlers from the Caribbean's crowded islands and to adventurers and migrants from Europe. But perhaps the most marked feature was the commitment to support religious toleration.

With the exception of Catholicism, the Lords Proprietors intended that the colony should be a religious haven. Clause 100 stated that the only constraint for recognition would be the three-fold declaration 'that there is a God', 'that God is publicly to be worshipped' and 'that it is lawful and the duty of every man ... to bear witness to truth ... whether it be by laying hands on or kissing the bible, as in the Church of England, or by holding up the hand, or any other sensible way'. Subsequent clauses provided additional assurances to religious migrants: 'no person of any other church

---

[27] *The Fundamental Constitutions of Carolina*, 1 March 1669: avalon.law.yale.edu/17th_century/nc05.asp accessed 23 February 2014.

[28] J.R. Milton, 'Locke, John (1632–1704)', *ODNB* (online edn., May 2008).

[29] Locke's view was that 'slavery is so vile and miserable an estate of man, and so directly opposite to the generous temper and courage of our nation, that it is hardly to be conceived that an Englishman, much less a Gentleman, should plead for it'. Cf., Locke, *First Treatise of Government* (1690).

or profession shall disturb or molest any religious assembly' and 'no person whatsoever shall disturb, molest or persecute another for his speculative opinions in religion or his way of worship'.[30]

The practical consequence was a rapid proliferation of religious refugees and places of worship. St Philip's, an Episcopalian church, opened in Charleston in 1681; a Baptist church followed in 1682; a Presbyterian church was established on Edisto in 1685; and a Huguenot church in 1686. Congregationalist and Presbyterian churches were built in the 1680s and 1690s, as was a Quaker meeting house. And by the mid-eighteenth century, Charleston's Jewish community which previously was sufficiently numerous to justify a purpose-built synagogue, *Kahal Kadosk Beth Elohim*.

Electoral enfranchisement was also offered. Despite the dominant position of the Lords Proprietors, the franchise in Carolina would be open to all men of age who held at least fifty acres,[31] albeit that office holders would require a more substantial landholding: 'the sheriff... and the justices shall be inhabitants and have each of them five hundred acres apiece freehold within the precinct for which they serve';[32] 'in the precinct court no man shall be a juryman under fifty acres of freehold, in the county court or at the assizes no man shall be a grand-juryman under three hundred acres of freehold [and] in the Proprietors' courts no man shall be a juryman under five hundred acres'.[33] In the same vein, 'no man shall be chosen a member of parliament who has less than five hundred acres of freehold within the precinct for which he is chosen'.[34]

Carolina's migrants benefited from other advantages. First, an ability to obtain full legal rights: 'whatsoever alien shall, in this form, before any precinct register, subscribe these fundamental constitutions, shall be thereby

---

[30] Clause 109.

[31] *The Fundamental Constitutions of Carolina*, Clause 85.

[32] Clause 61.

[33] Clause 68.

[34] Clause 72.

naturalized'.[35] Second, judicial equality: 'no cause, whether civil or criminal, of any freeman, shall be tried in any court of judicature without a jury of his peers'.[36] And third, the right to own and control his own slaves: 'every freeman of Carolina shall have absolute power and authority over his negro slaves'.[37]

The workforce in the Caribbean colonies had originally been a mix of indentured labour and convicts, among them many Irish sentenced to transportation to the islands. The term of contract or sentence was fixed, with an indenture typically running from five to seven years after which the labourer would be free to work independently, assuming that he had survived. But indentured labour was costly, with planters funding the transatlantic passage and expense of housing, food and clothing. In addition, at the end of the indenture each labourer was entitled to a land grant or a cash settlement in lieu. Planters consequently sought less expensive options.

An alternative was introduced in the mid-seventeenth century by Dutch and Portuguese traders. They had shipped African slaves to Brazil since the early 1500s, underpinning sugar cultivation and mining in that colony. Barbados was encouraged to follow suit and did. The number of slaves rose exponentially from 200, less than 5% of the island's population, in the early 1640s, to around 40,000 in 1670, some two-thirds of the total number of inhabitants. Three decades later in 1700, the number of black slaves accounted for over three-quarters of Barbados's population.[38] The economic advantages were clear. Not only were African slaves cheaper than indentured labour, they also had better immunity to disease and were generally more skilled. A further benefit was that their children could be added to the la-

---

[35] Clause 118.
[36] Clause 111.
[37] Clause 110.
[38] Gary A. Puckrein, *Little England: A Plantation Society and Anglo-Barbadian Politics, 1627-1700* (New York, NY: NYUP, 1984; Moore, 'The Largest Exporters of Deerskins from Charles Town', 144-50.

bour force at minimal cost. A child's legal status was determined by that of the mother, something that encouraged the sexual exploitation of female slaves.

Slavery was adopted across the Caribbean as a function of economic self-interest. Faux philosophical rationales based on racial superiority and religion came later. The profits that accrued to planters, slave traders, ship owners and merchants, and the intangible but equally important sensation of power and control, outweighed ethical arguments raised against the practice. Within a few decades of South Carolina's initial settlement in the 1670s, Barbados's economic and social model had been adopted by the colony with few objections.[39]

In the latter half of the seventeenth century and throughout the eighteenth, the colonial planter became a symbol of financial success. The wealth amassed in Barbados and other Caribbean islands, a function of Europe's insatiable demand for sugar, rum and molasses, and in South Carolina, a result of rice and indigo production, was immense, as was its corollary, political influence. The Caribbean's planters and merchants acquired large estates in England and became a powerful interest group with well-paid lobbyists and the support of over twenty seats in parliament.[40]

But if Barbados and other Caribbean colonies were so attractive, what motivated so many to leave and settle Carolina. Among the several factors that drove the exodus was the physical constraint imposed by the relatively small acreage suitable for agricultural production. Other influences included the displacement of indentured and freed white labour by slaves, and the demise through buy-out of smaller landowners. Primogeniture provided another reason for younger sons to acquire land elsewhere. And a series of natural disasters in the Caribbean in the mid-1670s, including a lengthy

---

[39] Edgar, *South Carolina: A History*, pp. 36-9.
[40] Cf., for example, Christopher L. Brown, 'British Slavery and British Politics' in Edward E. Baptist & Stephanie M.H. Camp (eds.), *New Studies in the History of American Slavery* (Athens, GA: University of Georgia Press, 2006).

drought and destructive hurricanes, persuaded planters to diversify their landholdings to reduce their risk. In short, when the Lords Proprietors opened Carolina to colonisation, the Caribbean's scions and servants alike viewed the coastal plain as an opportunity to recreate the Caribbean plantation model on a broader scale and more secure basis.

Given its relatively small population, the number of settlers relocating from the Caribbean to Carolina declined over time as a percentage of total migrants and by the turn of the century an increasing proportion came from elsewhere in North America with a minority directly from the home nations. The largest proportion was Scottish and Ulster-Irish at around 40%, with Welsh migrants accounting for around 10% and continental European migrants, mainly Protestants fleeing persecution in France and the German states, a further 10%.[41] The balance was predominantly English. Many were enticed by advertisements, pamphlets and newspaper articles which praised the benign climate, natural resources and abundant food in Carolina. Pamphlets were also printed in French and German, targeting Huguenot and Palatine migrants.

One of the earliest tracts was written by Thomas Ashe, an Indian trader. He described the seasons as 'regularly disposed according to nature's laws, the summer not so torrid, hot and burning as that of their southern, nor the winter so rigorously sharp and cold as that of their northern neighbours'.[42] Like Barlowe before him, Ashe also praised the 'great stocks of tame fowl', the plentiful fishing and the multitude of crops 'which flourish in a perpetual and constant verdure'. And he reminded potential settlers that generous land grants were available: the Lords Proprietors 'give unto all masters and mistresses of families, to their children, men-servants and maid-servants if

---

[41] Edgar, *South Carolina. A History*, p. 50.

[42] Thomas Ashe, *Carolina, or a Description of the present state of that country* (London, 1682), reprinted in Bartholomew R. Carroll, *Historical Collections of South Carolina* (New York, NY: Harper & Bros., 1836), volume I.

above sixteen years of age fifty... acres of land to be held forever annually paying a penny an acre... to commence two years after it is surveyed'.[43]

Most pamphlets focused on the Low Country rather than the less accessible up-country and omitted mention of the many diseases including malaria and yellow fever, and the possibility of attack from Native Americans, let alone the French and Spanish. Nonetheless, the broad thrust of such advertorials was accurate. The Carolina colony had several long and navigable rivers, excellent coastal access, abundant game and fertile soil. Adding to the mix, England's mercantilist policies offered bounties that promoted trade with the mother country and rewarded certain agricultural exports. Within a generation the colony had become an economic success story with trade in animal skins and wood products providing the funds to co-finance a massive expansion of land clearance and rice and later indigo plantations. The prosperity that followed was inseparable from the colony's reliance on slave labour, a policy that was uniformly regarded as agricultural good practice.

In the colony's early years captured Native Americans had been forced into slavery and worked alongside blacks and white indentured labour. But this practice was relatively short-lived, lasting little more than a few decades. There were two main reasons. First, the economic benefits of first nations' slavery were outweighed by those that accrued from trading, something that was compromised if such enslavement was sustained. And second, the indigenous population was small and in decline. Estimates vary but the number of Native Americans in Carolina in the late seventeenth century may have been as few as the low tens of thousands. They comprised a host of competing and co-operating communities: the Saluda, Savannah, Yuchi and Muscogee (or Creek) living mainly along the Savannah River; the Cherokee, a key source of deerskins, north-west and up-country; the Cusabo, Kiawah, Wappoo and Yemassee, principally on the coastal plain; and the Sioux to the north and west. The tribes moved as the seasons dictated and often warred with one another over access to hunting territory, but the greatest impact

---

[43] Ibid.

on the indigenous population was disease, a consequence of the interaction with white traders and settlers as the colonial frontier expanded westward.

The indigenous population had declined drastically and repeatedly as European soldiers and traders brought diseases from which the first nations had zero or limited immunity. The Spanish in Florida and traders and settlers from Virginia and Carolina carried tuberculosis, measles, smallpox, chickenpox and syphilis hundreds of miles inland as they built new trading relationships. John Lawson,[44] the naturalist and surveyor who explored Carolina in the early 1700s, was one of many who were aware of the potentially lethal effect of first contact: 'the small pox has been fatal to them... most certain, it had never visited America before the discovery thereof by the Christians..., small pox and rum have made such a destruction amongst them that on good grounds I do not believe there is not the sixth savage living within two hundred miles of our settlements as there were fifty years ago'.[45] Within two or three generations white settlement and trade led to the decimation of the indigenous peoples. In the South, the Creek population is thought to have numbered some 200,000 prior to the arrival of Europeans; afterwards it is believed to have declined to less than 20,000.

Despite the decline in population, the colonists' interaction with the first nations underpinned early transatlantic trade. Carolina's exports in the late seventeenth century were a combination of naval stores and deerskins. The output and value of naval stores - pine, pitch, tar and turpentine - was driven by demand from the Royal Navy and the naval bounty paid by the British government. And deerskins provided the colonists with an even higher value opportunity which by the early eighteenth century dominated export traffic.

Between 1700 and 1715, deerskin exports averaged around 55,000 pelts annually, rising to a peak of more than 120,000 in 1706. The trade

---

[44] David R. Ransome, 'Lawson, John (d.1711)', *ODNB*.

[45] John Lawson, *A New Voyage to Carolina* (London: published privately, 1709).

supported a vast number of frontiersmen, agents, brokers and more than a hundred merchants in Charleston, the final leg of an inter-connected network that extended several thousand miles over rivers and trails across America's continental interior.[46] Deerskins were sourced principally from the Creek and Cherokee tribes and paid for by bartering firearms, tools, glass and other simple manufactured goods, as well as rum. Although there were periods when export volumes ran at lower levels, notably during the Yemassee War and 1720s when relations with the Creek and Cherokee deteriorated, deerskins and animal pelts remained South Carolina's second most valuable export after rice until the 1750s. And even then, the shift in emphasis was not triggered by a decline in demand from Europe but by the expansion in revenues earned from indigo cultivation and competition from traders in Georgia and later Florida who disrupted South Carolina's prior monopoly.

European demand for deerskins was sufficiently strong to identify the business as a potential source of provincial government revenue within a decade of the trade's inception and in 1703 Carolina imposed an export levy on both leathers and skins. In 1722 the duty was increased to 6d for Indian-dressed skins weighing 1lb or more, and 3d for those weighing less. South Carolina's public treasurer's records for the period 1735 to 1775 indicate that the tax was levied on some 660 exporters ranging from leading merchants and factors such as Benjamin Stead, James Crokatt, George Austin and Henry Laurens, individual ship's captains working for overseas syndicates and on their own account. The total market was vast. And although deerskins and other animal hides were shipped principally to England, especially London, Bristol and Liverpool, they were also exported directly over thirty other destinations across Europe.

Deerskin and later rice exports provided a framework for South Carolina's prosperity but natural and other disasters periodically threatened

---

[46] Moore, Jr., 'The Largest Exporters of Deerskins from Charles Town, 1735-1775'.

to undermine it. The colony suffered a smallpox epidemic in 1698, an earthquake and fire in 1699, and a hurricane and flood in 1700. The destruction caused by hurricanes and property loss through fire would be a constant vulnerability but the colony's greater concerns were man-made: the risk of attack from the south and west by the Spanish and French, and from the indigenous tribes used as proxies.

The issue came to a head in the early decades of the eighteenth century when two successive conflicts convinced both the Carolinians and London that the Lords Proprietors were incapable of securing adequate defence to ensure the colony's survival. What was known as Queen Anne's War, the North American theatre of the War of Spanish Succession from 1702-1713, pitched Britain's American colonies against the French, Spanish and their allies among the first nations with townships, settlements and trading posts raided on a disjointed frontier extending north to south from Canada and New England to South Carolina, and west to east from the Mississippi to the Atlantic coast.

But more devastating for Carolina was the Yemassee War from 1715-1717. Carolina's settlers were pitted against an alliance of tribes[47] with settlements sacked and some four hundred colonists and traders killed in guerrilla attacks. Many colonists sought protection in Charleston where the influx threatened to overcome food stocks and housing. Hostilities lasted for nearly three years and ended not through military victory but because distrust and enmity between the various first nations began to outweigh their common anti-settler sentiments. The colonists aided the process with offers of gifts and promises of improved terms of trade, and obtained the necessary peace treaties.

Although relatively short, the political impact of the Yemassee War endured and in 1719 the dislocation and cost became a central argument in South Carolina's revolt against proprietorial government in favour of direct

---

[47] The tribal alliance included the Apalachee, Apalachicola, Catawba, Cheraw, Cherokee, Congaree, Muscogee, Waxhaw, Yemassee and Yuchi.

crown rule. The colonists were led by Arthur Middleton, a first generation Carolinian born to Barbados migrants, one of the colony's principal planters.[48] He had inherited 12,000 acres in South Carolina including *The Oaks*, a 1,650-acre plantation, alongside land in Barbados and England, and owned at least 120 slaves in South Carolina alone.[49] Middleton had been elected to the Commons House of Assembly in 1706 and served almost continuously until 1721 when he was appointed to the royal council; he was its president from 1721 until 1737. Middleton's attitude to office had much in common with that of Yeamans and he exploited his position to acquire thousands of acres of land as well as gaining personally from the disposition of public offices.[50]

In December 1719 Middleton presided over a convention in Charleston that resolved to petition George I for direct crown rule. Dissent over colonial governance was not new. In 1691 the colonists had argued successfully for the partition of the province and the appointment of a deputy governor to administer the northern half, an administrative division formalised in 1712 with the emergence of North Carolina. But the 1719 upheaval was less about administration than the pressing concern that the absentee Lords Proprietors had failed and would continue to fail to protect the colony. South Carolina was becoming a valuable trading partner for Britain's merchants and ship owners. Their financial self-interests were aligned with the colony's own merchants and planters, and the combination made for an effective transatlantic lobby. *De facto* crown rule was introduced to the colony in 1720 and the Lords Proprietors' former appointee, Governor Robert Johnson, returned to London. Negotiations over what compensation should be paid to the Proprietors nonetheless took close to a decade to conclude.

---

[48] Alexander Moore, 'Middleton, Arthur (1681–1737)', *ODNB* (online edn., May 2005).

[49] Edgar & Bailey, *Biographical Directory of the South Carolina House of Representatives*, pp. 454-5.

[50] Ibid.

The immediate corollary of the removal of the Lords Proprietors' remit was a rise in expenditure on the colony's defences and increased confidence which led directly to an expansion in the acreage under cultivation and higher land values. Middleton and his fellow planters gained accordingly. Their estates were extended and the greater output generated larger profits, much of which was reinvested in the colony. Middleton's personal land holding expanded by around half to some 18,000 acres across the Low Country, in addition to property he acquired in Charleston.[51] Middleton's eldest son, Henry, also a member of the South Carolina Commons and in 1774 president of the first continental congress, increased the family's estates still further via a combination of land purchases and the proceeds of three marriages. He would ultimately own twenty plantations totalling around 50,000 acres, and become one of the largest slave owners in the state with around 800 slaves.

Crown rule reinforced the growing commonality of interest between South Carolina's elites and their counterparts in England. On each side of the Atlantic personal and economic imperatives aligned with trade and profit the drivers. Economic success was as much a moral imperative as it was financial: 'a flourishing trade gives encouragement to the industrious,... increases the power of the nation [and] puts it in the power of every prudent and industrious man in it to enjoy more of the innocent pleasures of life'.[52] But as trade with America grew, mercantilism trumped economic logic. From the mid-eighteenth century onward, London would impose restrictive customs and trade regulations that hampered and constrained the colonies; the consequent imbalance in the terms and conditions of trade and the personal costs incurred would propel America towards Independence.

---

[51] Cf. Alexander Moore, 'Middleton, Arthur (1681–1737)', *ODNB* (online edn., May 2005).

[52] Arthur Dobbs, *An Essay on the Trade and Improvement of Ireland* (Dublin, Ireland: J. Smith & W. Bruce, 1729), p. 3.

The economic and political dominance of South Carolina's plantocracy was founded on rice, the colony's principal cash crop. From the 1720s, when improvements to the colony's defences were first implemented, to the 1770s and the revolutionary war, rice comprised between half and two-thirds of the province's exports by value. In terms of volume, rice exports doubled from a modest 220 tons in 1700 to more than 530 tons in 1710, and increased almost exponentially over the next three decades to more than 3,600 tons in 1720, 9,000 tons in 1730 and 15,000 tons in 1740, plateauing at 15-18,000 tons per annum in the 1750s.[53] The price of rice moved with global demand and supply but averaged between £6 and £8 per ton for most of the period, albeit that it fell to around half this level in the late 1740s. To put such numbers into perspective, the annual export of 15,500 tons of rice in the 1750s might earn gross revenues of around £110,000 in sterling. The potential net return to South Carolina's planters and merchants was of course less, a function of freight rates and insurance costs. A good crop almost always resulted in higher freight rates and a smaller crop in lower rates, as demand for tonnage rose or fell respectively.[54] Another factor was whether Britain was at war, which affected not only the availability of ships and sailors but also the cost of insurance.

Trying to estimate the financial returns to planters in current money is notoriously difficult and different figures are obtained depending on whether the data is adjusted for earnings or price inflation. If adjusted in line with taxed earnings, £10,000 gross revenues would be equivalent to around £10

---

[53] R.C. Nash, 'South Carolina and the Atlantic Economy in the Late Seventeenth and Eighteenth Centuries', *Economic History Review*, ns, 45.4 (1992), 677-702, esp. 680.

[54] Cf., esp., Kenneth Morgan, 'The Organization of the Colonial American Rice Trade', *William and Mary Quarterly*, 3rd series, 52.3 (1995), 433-52. Also, Peter A. Coclanis, 'Rice Prices in the 1720s and the Evolution of the South Carolina Economy', *Journal of Southern History*, 48.4 (1982), 531-44.

million; but using a price deflator reduces the figure to £2-3 million.[55] No figure is 'correct' however an earnings deflator provides an indication of 'income value' and could be considered a more appropriate reference point. Regardless, by either standard the monies represented a high level of income and the revenues were shared among a relatively small number of planters and merchants. The return on equity was such that an efficient planter was expected to double his capital within five years: a compound return of close to 20% per annum at a time when interest rates were 4%. The consequences were obvious: the demand for credit expanded and the demand for and price of cultivatable land and the slaves to work it rose substantially.

The counterpart to the colony's surging wealth was a sizeable uplift in domestic demand. South Carolina's expanding income created and sustained a substantial import trade in luxury and manufactured goods, and in wines and spirits. Merchants also engaged in trans-shipping both to the Caribbean and West Indian colonies and other British colonies in North America. The profits from the export, import and re-export trades financed the construction of new infrastructure. This was not simply the multitude of town houses and mansions that were constructed across Charleston and the surrounding Low Country. There was a strong commercial element, including docks, warehouses and shipyards around Charleston's harbour; taverns, retail and wholesale stores; the workshops that lined the city's main streets; and the many public buildings in the city. From the mid-1730s and for the balance of the eighteenth century, South Carolina would be regarded correctly as one of Britain's most important colonial trading counterparties and its profits financed a physical infrastructure to match.

South Carolina's population grew in tandem with its economy. The colony's relatively benign climate and productive land encouraged population growth, both organic and via a steady stream of migrants. The number of white settlers rose from the low hundreds in 1670 to 3-4,000 by the turn

---

[55] Cf. www.measuringworth.com. Also projects.exeter.ac.uk/RDavies/arian/current/howmuch.html, accessed 25 January 2014.

of the century.[56] It doubled over the next decade to an estimated 6-8,000 in 1710, and increased by another ten thousand in each of the next two decade.[57] To reach around 25-30,000 in 1750. The colony's total population was of course larger. Estimates of the slave population differ but the figure is unlikely to have been much below 2,500 in 1700 and was some 20,000 in 1720.[58] By 1750 it had risen to between 40,000 and 60,000,[59] although reports from contemporary commentators suggest that the number could have been even higher.

In 1726, Samuel Wragg, South Carolina's London agent, testified before the Board of Trade that the colony had some 40,000 slaves with a thousand more imported each year.[60] Richard Splatt, a Carolina merchant who testified on the same day, also attested that 'the province annually takes about 1,000'.[61] Although their accounts may have been exaggerated to emphasise the colony's economic importance and prospects, the innate profitability of slave labour gives credence to their statements. As Splatt noted, although 'they sell at about £30 or £35 sterling per head... a negro can make £10 per

---

[56] Colonial and Pre-Federal Statistics, *Estimated Population of American Colonies: 1610-1780*, Series Z 1-19.

[57] Ibid.

[58] Ibid.

[59] Nash, 'South Carolina and the Atlantic Economy in the Late Seventeenth and Eighteenth Centuries', 689, puts forward a different number.

[60] However, see K.H. Ledward (ed.), *Journal of the Board of Trade and Plantations* (London: IHR, 1928), volume 5, *May 1726*, pp. 251-70; also, Elizabeth Donnan, 'The Slave Trade into South Carolina before the Revolution', *American Historical Review*, 33.4 (1928), 804-28, esp. 805. As an aside, Samuel Wragg co-owned the *Ann*, the vessel on which Oglethorpe and the original Georgia colonists sailed for Georgia. Cf. Headlam, *America and the West Indies, November 1732, Calendar of State Papers Colonial, America and West Indies* (London: IHR, 1939), volume 39, 6 November 1732.

[61] Ledward, *Journal of the Board of Trade and Plantations*, volume 5, May 1726, pp. 251-70.

annum clear profit to his master'.⁶² South Carolina's population in 1770 is noted at just over 124,000, of which *c*.75,000 were black slaves; a decade later it was around 180,000, including *c*.100,000 slaves.⁶³

In part because of the strong demand from within the colony but also as a function of Charleston's position as a strategic port and trading hub, the city's slave markets expanded to become the largest in North America, with slaves sold into the domestic market as well as transhipped, most notably to Savannah following the end of Georgia's ban on slavery in 1751 and before it developed its own slave markets.

In the four decades from 1735 until 1775, over 1,100 slave cargoes were handled by Charleston, a total of around 100,000 slaves; other cargoes landed at Beaufort, Georgetown and Port Royal.⁶⁴ Of the 100,000 slaves that passed through Charleston's markets, around 60,000 were sold in the third quarter of the eighteenth century, a figure which underscores not only the colony's agricultural development but also the appalling conditions in which slaves lived and worked. Virginia, the continent's ranking slave colony in 1760 with 140,000 slaves in a total population of around 390,000,⁶⁵ imported a mere 19,000 slaves between 1750 and 1775. By this time and in contrast to South Carolina where slave mortality remained high, Virginia's slave labour force had become virtually self-sustaining, with slaves born into slavery meeting the bulk of demand.⁶⁶

The cash that flowed from South Carolina's plantations allowed Charleston to grow from a hamlet at the end of the seventeenth century to become the focal point of a multi-lateral trade with England, continental

---

⁶² Ibid.

⁶³ Colonial and Pre-Federal Statistics, *Estimated Population of American Colonies: 1610-1780*, Series Z 1-19.

⁶⁴ Customs data suggests less than twenty for the period as a whole.

⁶⁵ Colonial and Pre-Federal Statistics, *Estimated Population of American Colonies: 1610-1780*, Series Z 1-19.

⁶⁶ Higgins, 'Charles Town Merchants and Factors Dealing in the External Negro Trade 1735-1775', 205-17.

Europe, and the Caribbean colonies. Charleston became a commercial and financial hub. The city's wharves and jetties were supported by warehouses built to accommodate off-loaded cargoes and house those awaiting consignment on the hundreds of vessels that carried the province's exports and brought in its imports. Local ship-building facilities were established for the inland, coastal and Atlantic trade, and sister ports developed to the north and south at Georgetown and Beaufort.

A torrent of merchants and traders established businesses in the city and supported an extensive professional class and lower middling layer of retailers, artisans and craftsmen. Newspaper advertisements from the period indicate that over 100 craftsmen advertised regularly in the 1740s alongside more than 200 merchants as Charleston began to overspill its western boundaries and grow beyond the original fortifications.

The main commercial areas remained close to the Bay or on the principal thoroughfares of Church Street, Broad Street and Tradd Street, but new premises were also constructed further afield as residential and business districts expanded.

In the new town and in the old, the colony's growing affluence was displayed physically in urban architecture while in the countryside large Palladian mansions were built as centrepieces to plantations and estates. The more lavish properties were constructed and furnished in the latest English fashion on patterns pioneered by Lord Burlington's principal architect, William Kent, as fashionable in the Low Country as he was in Hanoverian England.[67] Burgeoning prosperity allowed South Carolina's elites to espouse other English habits, including an associational and philanthropic culture, and as wealth developed further, the focus turned to the arts and sciences, and a desire to enhance Charleston's status relative to other American cities.

---

[67] William Kent's pattern book provided a popular catalogue for colonial furnishing and decoration; Drayton Hall, built in the late 1730s, remains one of the best extant examples of the Palladian genre in Charleston.

Conscious that the colony was without a newspaper or printer, a bounty was raised to encourage both. Charleston was rewarded in 1732 when Benjamin Franklin despatched Thomas Whitemarsh from Philadelphia to edit and print the city's first newspaper, the *South Carolina Gazette*.[68] Whitemarsh died of yellow fever the following year, but Franklin persuaded another of his printers, Lewis Timothée, to relocate and take up the post.[69] Eighteenth-century society was also synonymous with an upsurge in fraternal associations. The same held true in Charleston. The city's St Andrew's Society was established in 1729, a St George's Society in 1733, a Jockey Club at Goose Green in 1734 and a French Club in or around 1735, the last later renamed the South Carolina Society and remodelled by its Huguenot members as a benevolent society.[70]

Charleston's rising social status was flagged further with the opening of a purpose built theatre in 1736, one of the first in North America. It was also the year that Solomon's Lodge would receive its charter. The lodge became a pivot on which Charleston's social and political establishment turned and its members a microcosm of South Carolina's elite high society.

---

[68] Tangentially, Thomas Whitemarsh, like Franklin, was a freemason, initiated in St John's lodge in Philadelphia in 1731.

[69] Franklin contracted with Timothée [anglicized to 'Timothy'] to publish and print the *South Carolina Gazette* for six years; he agreed to pay a third of the overhead and receive a one-third profit share. Timothy died in an accident in 1738 and his wife, Elizabeth, took over the press; the business was continued by her son, Peter.

[70] A comparatively high number of Charleston's wealthiest merchant and traders were second or third generation Huguenots. The ability to trade relatively freely and the widespread availability of land had encouraged migration to the colony, but so too had its professed religious tolerance. Their commercial success encouraged others to follow and by the 1730s South Carolina had the largest Huguenot population of any of the thirteen colonies. The first Huguenots to settle were forty-five refugees who arrived in 1680. They were followed by others following the horrors of Louis XIV's Dragonnades and his revocation of the Edict of Nantes.

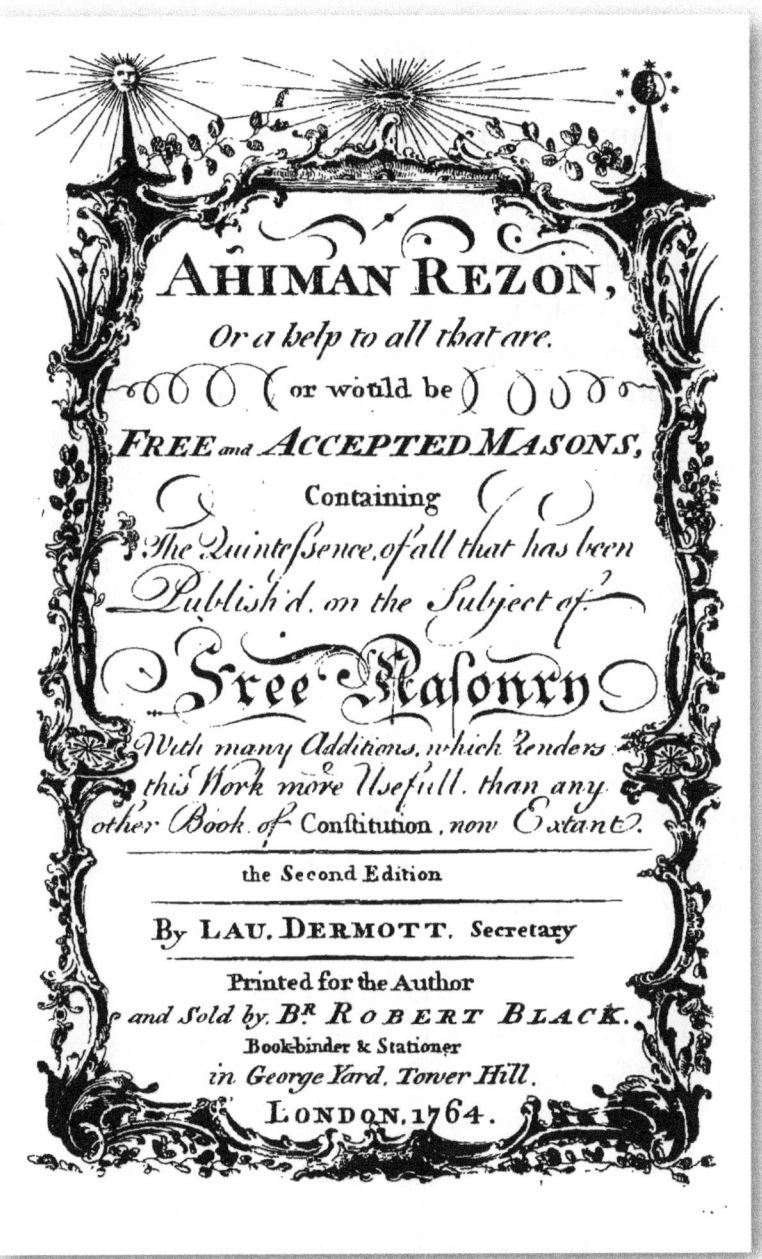

Frontispiece, *Ahiman Rezon*, 2nd edition (London, 1764)

Appendix Two

MODERNS AND ANTIENTS – AN IRISH LEGACY

In *The History of Freemasonry in South Carolina*, Mackey unintentionally introduces his readers to Antients freemasonry – that 'schismatic body' – by contrasting the popularity of Charleston's Antients' St John's Day celebrations with the more subdued activities of its Moderns. For Charleston's Moderns 'there was the usual dinner, but no procession to church, and ... no sermon', but for the Antients 'the procession was numerous and the splendid appearance which the brethren made was truly pleasing to the spectators. A most excellent sermon suitable to the occasion was preached before them ... after which they dined together at the lodge room in Lodge Alley'.

> In 1783, the Anniversary Communication was celebrated at the City Tavern, in Broad Street. The grand lodge had now again assumed its independent character, and in the summons of the grand secretary it is styled, 'The Grand Lodge of the Most Ancient and Honorable Society of Free and Accepted Masons of and for the State'. On this occasion there was the usual dinner, but no procession to church, and of course no sermon.
>
> 'In this year, the first notice occurs of the Ancient York Masons, a distinct body not recognizing the authority of the regular grand lodge. In 1783, their Lodges celebrated the Festival of St John the Baptist, in Charleston, and as this schismatic body subsequently played an important part in the history of Masonry in South Carolina, I suppose the reader will be interested in reading a full report of this their first public appearance. I quote it from *Miller's Gazette* of 25 of June, 1783.

The Ancient York Masons' Lodges of this city yesterday celebrated the Anniversary of St John the Baptist. The procession was numerous and the splendid appearance which the brethren made was truly pleasing to the spectators. A most excellent sermon suitable to the occasion was preached before them at St Philip's Church by the Rev. Mr. Stuart, after which they dined together at the Lodge room in Lodge Alley. The recollection that this meeting was one of the consequences of the blessings of peace did not a little contribute to the happiness of the day...

Commencing thus in 1783, they continue prominently before us in South Carolina until 1817, and the history of their grand lodge, which was established in 1787, must be treated *pari passu* with that of the regular Grand Lodge of South Carolina.[1]

Although the parallel should not be overstated, the political division between patriot and loyalist was also present in freemasonry. But the greater chasm between Antients and Moderns was social and it was this that drove the division between the two. Mutual antipathy was not limited to South Carolina but was present elsewhere in America and in England, where Antients freemasonry had originated among the London Irish in the 1740s. While the original Grand Lodge of England, pejoratively tagged the 'Moderns', had become an elitist body, Antients freemasonry was designed to be accessible to a broader cross-section of male society.

A Defence of Freemasonry, published in 1765 and written by Samuel Spencer, the Moderns' grand secretary, makes clear the Moderns' prejudices against

---

[1] Mackey, *History*, p. 53. His statement that Antients freemasonry was *pari passu* with the Moderns is disingenuous. The Antients had overtaken the Moderns in terms of both influence and numbers.

the Irish and English lower ranks within Antients freemasonry.[2] Spencer wrote *A Defence* as a rebuttal to Laurence Dermott's editorial in *Ahiman Rezon*[3] and as a promotional piece for the Moderns, but its style and content was self-defeating.

> With Regard to the Difference between *Ancient* and *Modern* Masons, there is certainly a great deal, the former being as remarkable for their *Tautology* and *Prolixity*, as the latter are for their *Brevity;* as the one like a *Methodist* Teacher, who attempts to preach extempore, will engross the whole Evening, in spinning out a *tedious* Lecture, while the other, like an *orthodox* Divine, delivers the Substance of the same Lecture (which fully answers the Purpose, and renders it much more agreeable) in less than an Hour. And I believe every sensible Mason will allow this to be the most material Difference, notwithstanding Mr. *Dermott's* Assertion to the contrary.
>
> He then tells us that a *Modern* Mason may with Safety communicate all his *Secrets* to an *Ancient*, but an *Ancient* cannot do so to a *Modern*, without further *Ceremonies*. It is true, an *English* Mason may safely communicate

---

[2] The definition of working class is an imprecise term in the eighteenth century. As Jeremy Black notes, 'There are problems with describing all those not in the social elite or the middling orders as the poor. That term was used in broader and narrower ways, but quite often quite restrictively for those on relief or dependent on charity. When the phrase 'labouring poor' began to catch on in the second half of the century, some commentators, such as Edmund Burke, attacked it as new-fangled cant. The vast mass of the population, both urban and rural, was in the category. The 'labouring poor' was a very varied group. Forms of status and security were attainable for some, although they were precarious. Commentators distinguished between the 'mob' and the 'people'. The former comprehended the bulk of the poor; while many of the latter had a more settled income and were artisans, their economic interests and social cohesion frequently expressed through membership of fraternities of workmen.' Jeremy Black, *Eighteenth-century Britain 1688–1783* (Basingstoke: Palgrave Macmillan, 2008), 2nd edition, p. 106.

[3] Laurence Dermott, *Ahiman Rezon* (London: published privately, 1756).

all his Secrets to either *Scotch* or *Irish* Masons, provided they have been made in Lodges *regularly* constituted by their respective Grand Masters, and so, *vice versa;* for as Masonry is universal, there is nothing in it, which one *regular* Mason ought to conceal from another; but the *English* Masons should be cautious with whom *they* converse, as there are many *irregular* Masons, i.e. made in *Lodges* under the Title of *Ancient*, or *York*, who some time ago pretended to be *constituted* or *authorized* by the Grand Master of *Ireland*, who (by the bye) I am credibly informed, refused to countenance them, as it would be highly absurd for one Grand Master to constitute *Lodges* in the Territories of *another*. However it is said that a certain *noble* Peer permits them occasionally to make use of his Name, though he never presides in any of their Assemblies.[4]

Spencer's *A Defence* denigrates the Antients as an institution and ridicules its members' social standing and impecunity. The pamphlet is offensive and counter-factual, especially where Spencer seeks to demonstrate that Anderson's *Constitutions* is historically accurate.[5]

---

[4] Sir William Stewart, 3rd Viscount Mountjoy and 1st Earl of Blessington (1709-1769). Stewart inherited the viscountcy in 1728 and was created Earl Blessington in 1745. He is mentioned as a freemason in 1731, a member of Viscount Montagu's Bear and Harrow lodge in Butcher Row. Stewart was grand master of Ireland from 1738 until 1740. He inherited titles and estates in Ireland and an English estate at Silchester, Hampshire, with town houses in Dublin and London. He was appointed Governor of Co. Tyrone (1748) and Governor of Carlisle Castle (1763). See Berman, *Schism*, pp. 6, 8, 14, 28-31, 38-41.

[5] James Anderson, *The Constitutions of the Freemasons* (London: John Senex & John Hooke, 1723); *The Ancient Constitutions of the Free and Accepted Masons* (London: B. Creake, 1731), 2nd edn.; *The new book of constitutions of the antient and honourable fraternity of free and accepted masons* (London: Caesar Ward and Richard Chandler for Anderson, 1738).

Anderson's history was designed to set a context for freemasonry in the same manner as the mediaeval *Old Charges*.[6] By positioning the Craft as dating from 'time immemorial', Anderson's faux narrative gave freemasonry an antiquarian aura and thus attraction. Dermott's dismissive labelling of the original Grand Lodge of England as 'Moderns' and his adoption of the title 'Antients' served the same purpose but with greater effect.

Other assertions included that the 'Grand Master of Ireland refused to countenance [the Antients]', and 'a certain noble peer permits them occasionally to make use of his name ... [but] he never presides in any of their assemblies'. They were also inaccurate. Irish Grand Lodge had ended its fraternal correspondence with the Moderns in 1758 when it entered a mutual recognition pact with the Antients, and William Stewart, 1st Earl of Blessington (1709-1769), whom Dermott describes as 'a father to the fraternity', would not have been expected to attend meetings of Antients Grand Lodge. The Antients had sought and gained his patronage. He was not expected to make a further contribution.

Blessington's appeal was the imprimatur that a well-regarded aristocrat provided. And he had particular resonance with the Irish. Blessington had a reputation for altruism and while grand master of Ireland in 1738-40 had led fund raising efforts in support of Dublin's poor and arranged food distribution to relieve the famine.[7] His actions became part of working-class Irish folklore and were remembered even three decades later.[8]

Recognition by Blessington and the Grand Lodge of Ireland, and later the Grand Lodge of Scotland, underpinned the Antients' status and afforded political protection. And it was effective. Even a century later, Blessington's

---

[6] The medieval *Old Charges* comprise the first written evidence of early English freemasonry. They detail the internal rules and regulations under which stone masonry was managed and set out an operating structure for the guild. They reflect the contemporary political and economic conditions prevalent at the time of writing and contain a faux history of freemasonry dating back to St Athelstan, St Alban and earlier. See Berman, *Schism*, Appendix II.

[7] See Berman, *Schism*, esp. pp. 39-41.

[8] *Gazetteer and New Daily Advertiser*, 23 September 1766.

Loyalists & Malcontents

William Stewart, 1st Earl of Blessington (1709-1769)
Grand Master of the Antients Grand Lodge, 1756-59
Grand Master of the Grand Lodge of Ireland, 1738-39
Stephen Slaughter, c.1744

decision was regarded with incredulity by the Moderns' apologists, Robert Gould, for example, writing that it was 'singular that Dermott secured the services as titular Grand Master [a] nobleman under whose presidency the Grand Lodge of Ireland conformed to the laws and regulations enacted by the Regular or Original Grand Lodge of England'.[9]

Advertisements for *A Defence* proclaimed that it contained 'a refutation of Mr Dermott's ridiculous account of that ancient society in his book entitled *Ahiman Rezon*',[10] but the pamphlet failed to dent the growth of Antients freemasonry, especially in America. The mixture of pseudo fact and disparagement instead validated the view that the Moderns' senior ranks were prejudiced.

Spencer's views are made clear at the end of the pamphlet when he unleashes an invective against the Irish and the less affluent. A condescending description of a three-hour lecture by 'a red hot Hibernian' is followed by a tirade about the initiation of a sedan chairman[11] who is too poor to disburse his lodge fee in full and pays half in cash and half with an IOU. The disdain is clear from the comment that such men are a 'disgrace to society' and that they possess 'scarcely a coat or shirt to their backs':

> Though there are several persons of character and ability among the Ancient Masons, the greater part of them are a set of illiterate and mean persons, such as chairmen, porters, walking poulterers, and the like, chiefly natives of Ireland, who finding it not convenient to stay in their own country, have fled hither to get an honest livelihood; they herd together at Hedge-Alehouses, and because they know the English Grand Lodge will not authorize their illicit and ignorant proceedings, and that the Grand Master of Ireland will not countenance them here, they have, with the assistance of some honest Yorkshire-Men, who have come to London on the same account, trumped up what they call Ancient or York

---

[9] Robert Freke Gould, *Gould's Freemasonry Throughout the World* (New York, NY: Charles Scribener's Sons, 1936), volume 2, p. 168.

[10] *Gazetteer and New Daily Advertiser*, 21 September 1765 et al.

[11] A 'chairman' was one of two porters who transported a sedan chair.

Masonry, and under the specious pretence of being the most Ancient, have drawn in several well-meaning and worthy persons, by whose assistance and application, a noble Peer has condescended to permit them to make use of his name, as their Grand Master, though (as I observed before) he seldom, if ever, presides in any of their Assemblies.

Their Initiation fee is, in general, small, viz. ten shillings, and I can safely declare, on the Word of a Mason (which expression I shall ever hold sacred) that I have known their Masters of lodges, many times, to take notes of hand, of the new Members, for half that fee, on account of their extreme poverty; notwithstanding Mr. Dermott's assertion, that their fee is never less than two guineas; and it is no uncommon thing for many of them to come to their Lodges, without a farthing in their pockets, and to borrow as much as will make up a sixpenny reckoning of three or four different Members. Nay, they go still farther, for if any of them happen to be penny less, as they walk the street, which (I presume) is often the case, they, without any ceremony, give the sign or signal of distress to the first Brother they chance to meet, who is obliged to answer, and assist them, or be deemed unworthy their vocation.

Their contributions to their charity are not voluntary, but obligatory, and every Member of a lodge is obliged to contribute monthly or weekly, a small sum, after the manner of a petty box-club, or the Ancient-Masons can have no charity for them.

The manner of their working the Lodge is as absurd, as it is prolix. The first time I ever went among them was out of curiosity, and a friend of mine introduced me, without paying any regard to that idle distinction between Ancient and Modern. My friend, and two or three more of the company were reputable tradesmen, the rest were chiefly such persons as before mentioned. I patiently sat near three hours, while a red hot Hibernian in the Chair, was delivering the first lecture...

Having sat a great while without opening my lips, except now and then to moisten them with a little porter, which is their constant and favourite liquor, I at last was witness to their form of initiating a Member, who was by profession a chairman [porter]. This man paid five shillings, and gave a note of hand to the Master for five more.

I could not help, though a stranger, expressing my abhorrence of such ridiculous, mean, and scandalous practices, but my mouth was soon stopped by the Master, who said, 'Upon my Soul now, but I believe he is a Modern!', then turning to me with an air of vast consequence, but seemingly much vexed, 'Sir, said he, the Devil burn me, but I believe you are a Modern-Mason, and that's as good as being no Mason at all!'. Having uttered this, they all cried out, with voices hoarse as thunder, for the space of five minutes, 'obligate him, obligate him'; which ceremony I was obliged to submit to, as I now began to think my life in danger, and glad was I, when I had got out of the house. But I have since that, gained admittance into several of their lodges, from the same motive of curiosity, and shall ever be ready to acquaint any regular Mason with their customs and ceremonies.

The manner of their funeral processions is a disgrace to society. I once saw one which went from Tower Hill to St Pancras; the corpse was borne all the way by sturdy chairmen, who now and then stopped, while others took their places; about 200 persons, clothed as Masons, attended, some in laced waistcoats, some in military uniforms, and others with scarcely a coat or shirt to their backs; who having sat in ale-houses adjacent to where the corpse lay, for three or four hours before, hooting and hollooing with the windows open, to the great disturbance of the neighbourhood, and the scandal of Masonry; many of them were at last so inebriated, that they required almost as much supporting as their deceased Brother; and countryman, which afforded much sport and diversion to several hundreds of spectators, who had assembled on that occasion.

A Defence concludes with an appeal 'To the Regular Masons of England':

Dear Brethren,
Having given you a true portrait of those deceivers, and false Brethren, I hope you will use your utmost endeavours to guard against all their Innovations, illicit, irregular and ridiculous Forms and Ceremonies,

holding fast the form of sound words, without wavering. Let not the Masters of lodges suffer any of their Brethren to become Members with those sham Ancients, as their Lodges, &c. are deemed irregular by our Laws, and all who assist at Makings in irregular Lodges, or attend Masons Funerals, clothed as such, without a special licence, are subject to the following censure of the Grand Lodge, viz., that they shall not be Grand-Officers, or officers of particular Lodges, nor admitted into Lodges, even as visitors. They shall likewise be rendered incapable of tyling, or attending on a Lodge, or partaking of the general charity, if they come to want it.

If any Person, whom these pretended Ancients have drawn in, finds that he is imposed on, and applies to a regular lodge to be initiated, I think there can be no harm in re-making him gratis, provided he is a person of character, and has paid the accustomed fee before, and will faithfully promise not to attend such irregular Meetings again. This opinion however, is submitted to the sense of the Grand Lodge.

Spencer's pamphlet is important because it emphasises that Antients freemasonry had extended associational culture from the aristocracy, gentry and upper middling to a far broader social base. Indeed, Antients freemasonry altered the eighteenth-century paradigm. From the five Irish-led lodges that constituted the Antients Grand Lodge in 1751, the number within its orbit increased to thirteen within twelve months; by 1753 there were thirty and the following year close to forty. Within three decades, the number was over 200, with around 75 Antients' lodges in London, over 80 in the provinces and nearly 50 overseas. And these figures exclude the daughter lodges of overseas provincial grand lodges and those Antients lodges that operated without a charter and went unrecorded by London.

Antients freemasonry may have been driven initially by the circumstances of London's Irish émigré community but it developed to accommodate the aspirational lower middling more broadly, especially their desire to access polite society and achieve social and financial betterment. By the end of the eighteenth century, around a third, perhaps more, of England's masonic lodges were loyal to the Antients but in America the figure probably exceeded three-quarters.

Alongside its Irish-influenced and more traditional masonic ritual, the main purpose of Antients' lodges was to provide a social space and mutually funded welfare. Ironically this was advertised in *A Defence*: 'contributions to their charity are not voluntary, but obligatory, and every Member of a lodge is obliged to contribute monthly or weekly, a small sum'.

Indeed, Antients freemasonry had a utility that went beyond fraternal socialisation. An argument used by Dermott to promote the organisation was that the Antients offered support to those in temporary financial difficulties. Quoting an unfortunately phrased letter from the Moderns' grand secretary to 'a certified petitioner from Ireland', Dermott refers to the Irishman being turned away: 'your being an Antient Mason, you are not entitled to any of our charity'.[12] Dermott also used the Moderns' treatment of the lodge at the Ben Johnson's Head[13] to underscore that the Antients, unlike the Moderns, provided a conduit for members to obtain masonic benevolence overseas: when members of the Ben Johnson's Head 'had been abroad [they had] received extraordinary benefits on account of Antient Masonry'. In short, the Antients' claimed not only greater masonic legitimacy but also greater utility.

Another example is in the Antients' use of membership certificates. They were provided on request but only to members who were current in membership and charitable dues. Such certificates acted as proto passports, allowing the bearer to be recognised and accepted by Antients' lodges elsewhere. They were a means to access a ready-made support network and an aid to itinerant workers and migrants hoping to find employment. Examples are found not only in England and Scotland but also in Ireland, the Caribbean and America. The minutes of lodge No. 20 at the Hampshire Hog in Goswell Street for 2 September 1754 record a Bro. Blunt's request for a membership

---

[12] Dermott, *Ahiman Rezon* (London, 1764), 2nd edn., p. xv.
[13] Grand Lodge *Minutes II*, 29 November 1754.

certificate 'as he is going to Jamaica'.[14] The certificate was granted - 'received honourably, as he has paid all his dues in our lodge'. And the following year when Samuel Galbraith, the senior warden, introduced Thomas Dowsett as a joining member, Dowsett standing, his 'being worthy of being a member', was attested by means of 'his certificate from No. 218, Ireland'.[15]

Antients freemasonry was carried to America by migrants, in particular expatriate Irish and Scots. This was especially so in the South, where the Scottish and Irish comprised some 40% of white incomers in the eighteenth-century. Dermott encouraged the process from London, singling out America's 'right worshipful and very worthy gentlemen' for flattery in the second edition of *Ahiman Rezon*.

A Philadelphia lodge was the first to seek a warrant from the Antients with a petition to form a provincial grand lodge. The charter was granted and minuted by the Antients at a meeting at the Five Bell's Tavern in London on 5 September 1759. Dermott as grand secretary was instructed to draw up a 'proper answer', and Joseph Read, of No. 2 lodge, appointed 'to convey the said answer to Philadelphia'.[16]

Bullock has commented on the rationale, noting that whereas 'Franklin's Moderns had brought together many of the province's most prominent men in a society that proclaimed their gentility, cultivation, and high social standing, the Ancients included many who lacked political power and social distinction. The new Ancient lodges proved the more popular and adaptable body. By the time Franklin returned from Europe for good in 1785, he could not enter a Pennsylvania lodge. The Grand Lodge he had headed no longer existed, and its past grand master could not even set foot in a lodge room without a ceremony of "healing" to convert him from

---

[14] Berman, *Schism*, pp. 60-4.

[15] Ibid.

[16] J.R. Dashwood (ed.), *Early Records of the Grand Lodge of England according to the Old Institutions* (London: Quatuor Coronati Lodge, No. 2076, 1958), volume XI of the *Quatuor Coronatorum Antigrapha* Masonic Reprints, p. 114.

an unacceptable Modern Mason into an Ancient brother'.[17] It is a demonstration of the Antients' supremacy in Pennsylvania and of the depth of the masonic schism that Benjamin Franklin's funeral in 1790 went unmarked by Philadelphia's freemasons. To take Bullock's words once again, Franklin was 'the wrong sort of Freemason'.

Pennsylvania's embrace of Antients freemasonry had its counterpart in other provinces, including Massachusetts, where an Antients' lodge was warranted in Boston in 1771, lodge No. 169;[18] and in South Carolina,[19] where Antients' lodge, No. 498, was chartered in 1761, a decade earlier.[20] Although Antients freemasonry in South Carolina overtook the Moderns in terms of members in the late 1770s, the Antients Grand Lodge of South Carolina was not established until 24 March 1787 and a division between Antients and Moderns remained until 1817 when a unified grand lodge was finally established.[21]

As an organisation that from its inception found itself in competition with the Moderns, Dermott recognised the importance of positive differentiation. Through his catechisms and editorial, he stressed the Antients'

---

[17] Steven C. Bullock, 'The Revolutionary Transformation of American Freemasonry, 1752-1792', *William and Mary Quarterly*, 3rd series, 47.3, (1990), 347-69.

[18] Mackey comments perhaps over-simplistically in his *History* that 'in 1752, the Grand Lodge of Scotland established a Lodge of Ancients in Massachusetts, which for a long time contended with the provincial grand lodge, which had been established in that Colony in 1733 by the constitutional Grand Lodge of England. In 1753, the Athol Grand Lodge, or, as it was also called, the Grand Lodge of Ancient York Masons, intruded on the jurisdiction of Pennsylvania, and eventually that Colony instituted a Grand Lodge of Ancients. In 1781, it also granted a warrant for the establishment of a Provincial Grand Lodge in New York'.

[19] The Provincial Grand Lodge of Pennsylvania states that they warranted three lodges in South Carolina between 1780 and 1786. However it is feasible that others may have been warranted earlier. Cf. Barratt and Sachse, *Freemasonry in Pennsylvania, 1727-1907*, volume II, p. 107.

[20] Lane, in *Masonic Records*, erroneously lists this as an English Constitution lodge.

[21] Cf., Mackey, *History*, pp. 95-109.

superior masonic legitimacy. His 'Philacteria for such gentleman as may be inclined to become Free-Masons' captured the essence of this approach and was instrumental in attracting and retaining members:

> First Question: Whether freemasonry, as practiced in antients lodges, is universal?
> Answer: Yes
>
> Second: Whether what is called modern masonry is universal?
> Answer: No
>
> Third: Whether there is any material difference between antient and modern?
> Answer: A great deal, because an antient mason can not only make himself known to his brother but in cases of necessity can discover his very thoughts to him, in the presence of a modern, without being able to distinguish that either of them are free masons.
>
> Fourth: Whether a modern mason may with safety communicate all his secrets to an antient mason?
> Answer: Yes
>
> Fifth: Whether an antient mason may with the like safety communicate all his secrets to a modern mason without further ceremony?
> Answer: No. For as a Science comprehends an Art (though an artist cannot comprehend a science) even so antient masonry contains everything valuable amongst the modern, as well as many other things that cannot be revealed without additional ceremonies...

Dermott reinforced the message through satire, joking that the Moderns had thought it 'expedient to abolish the old custom of studying geometry in the lodge and some of the young brethren made it appear that a good knife and fork in the hands of a dextrous brother (over the right materials) would give greater satisfaction and add more to the rotundity of the lodge ... from this improvement proceeded the laudable custom of charging to a public health to every third sentence that is spoke in the lodge'.[22]

He continued, arguing satirically that 'there was another old custom that gave umbrage to the young architects, that is, the wearing of aprons, which made the gentlemen look like so many mechanics, therefore it was proposed, that no brother (for the future) should wear an apron. This proposal was rejected by the oldest members, who declared that the aprons were all the signs of masonry then remaining amongst them and for that reason they would keep and wear them. It was then proposed, that (as they were resolved to wear aprons) they should be turned upside down, in order to avoid appearing mechanical. This proposal took place and answered the design, for that which was formerly the lower part, was now fastened round the abdomen, and the bib and strings hung downwards, dangling in such manner as might convince the spectators that there was not a working mason amongst them. Agreeable as this alteration might seem to the gentlemen, nevertheless it was attended with an ugly circumstance: for, in traversing the lodge, the brethren were subject to tread upon the strings, which often caused them to fall with great violence, so that it was thought necessary to invent several methods of walking, in order to avoid treading upon the strings'.[23]

The Antients' public image was strengthened by extensive news coverage, a testament to Dermott's effective press management, but the principal factor behind its growth was its embrace of a broad cross-section of male society. Moderns' lodges were elitist with high initiation fees, expensive dining and a unanimous vote required for membership, features that were effective at restricting entry to those of the same social class. In contrast, Antients' lodges were the preserve of the aspirational lower down the social ladder, farmers,

---

[22] Dermott, *Ahiman Rezon*, 2nd edn., pp xxix-xxxi.
[23] Ibid.

store and inn-keepers, apothecaries, barber surgeons, skilled artisans, small-scale merchants and up-coming professionals. Antients freemasonry included employers and employees in a wide range of professions and trades, men putting down the foundations of America's entrepreneurial society.

Antients freemasons were not poor. Bullock's analysis of Philadelphia's freemasons in the late eighteenth century suggests that where 84% of the city's Moderns were either merchants or professionals, some 87% of its Antients could also be considered relatively affluent.[24] Antients freemasons may have 'lacked the central qualifications of gentlemen' but 'they were not really part of the vulgar' but rather 'from the upper ranges of men outside the elite'. Bullock demonstrates that around half of Antients freemasons in Philadelphia ranked in the upper-third of the city's wealth-holders. There was a similar pattern in Boston,[25] and elsewhere,[26] where the 'essential dividing line [was] the social barrier between those who could claim honor and gentility and those who could not'.[27]

Bullock's thesis is correct but requires a caveat. In America, although both Antients and Moderns can be identified with social and financial status, and thus with political power, the Antients broader and more aspirational membership held the key to freemasonry's popularity, especially following Independence. Antients freemasonry was a symbol of the extension of economic and political power to middling America, and in this context it can be argued that its expansion was aligned with political change.

Many of those who shaped the early democratisation of American politics and led the revolutionary movement were freemasons, albeit that freemasonry

---

[24] Bullock, esp. 361.

[25] Ibid.

[26] See Berman, *Schism*, esp. chapters two & three. In London, the Antients' *Register of Members* records numerous middling occupations from attorneys, barber surgeons, merchants and gold and silversmiths, to jewelers, cabinet makers and watchmakers.

[27] Steven C. Bullock, *Revolutionary Brotherhood: Freemasonry and the Transformation of the American social order, 1730-1840* (Chapel Hill, NC: UNC Press, 1996), pp. 65-7.

per se was not at the root of such changes. In Boston, the Antients' St Andrew's lodge and provincial grand lodge contained prominent members of the Sons of Liberty and Selectmen,[28] including Joseph Warren, the first provincial grand master of Massachusetts;[29] Paul Revere, an Antients' grand officer from 1769, deputy grand master (1784, 1791-2) and later grand master (1794-97); William Palfrey, the Antients' grand secretary; Thomas Crafts, the grand treasurer; Edward Proctor, grand sword bearer; and William Molyneux, John Hancock, Caleb Hopkins and Thomas Urann, the latter both grand stewards.[30]

THE ANTIENTS IN SOUTH CAROLINA

Mackey's *History* is vague on the date of introduction of Antients freemasonry into South Carolina: 'at what precise date the Athol or Ancient York Masons invaded the masonic jurisdiction of South Carolina, I am unable to say. On this subject, the deficiency of records leaves us entirely in the dark, except with such dim and uncertain light as is furnished by conjecture'.[31] But he records that there were at least five such lodges in the state at the conclusion of the war, of which three had been constituted by the Grand Lodge of Pennsylvania and two by the Antients Grand Lodge in London.[32] Other sources give different figures.

Gould comments that the Antiens, 'the rival system', had eight lodges, warranted between 1760 and 1786. Of these one was chartered by the

---

[28] See Pauline Maier, *From Resistance to Revolution: Colonial Radicals and the Development of American Opposition to Britain, 1765-1776* (New York, NY: W.W. Norton, 1972), p. 307. Also Barratt and Sachse, *Freemasonry in Pennsylvania, 1727-1907*, volume I, xiii.

[29] Originally formed under the Scottish Constitution but later operating under the Antients' banner.

[30] See Jayne E. Timber, *A True Republican: The Life of Paul Revere* (Boston, MA: University of Massachusetts Press, 1998), pp. 67-9.

[31] Mackey, *History*, p. 61.

[32] Lodge No.s 38, 40 and 47 (Pennsylvania); and No.s 190 and 236 (London).

Grand Lodge of Scotland, and three and four respectively by Pennsylvania and the Antients Grand Lodge in England.[33]

The 1825 edition of *Ahiman Rezon* states that there were four Ancient York lodges, three of which held their warrants from Pennsylvania's grand lodge;[34] it continues, commenting that 'the York masons desirous to form a grand lodge of their own order, proposed terms of union to the existing grand lodge but as neither party was disposed to accept the conditions proposed by the other, the plan of union was abandoned. Lodge No. 236, which belonged to the grand lodge of ancient free masons of England, and not to the York masons, joining with the four York lodges, made the number necessary for the formation of an independent grand lodge. Assembled in grand masonic convention, these lodges resolved themselves into an independent grand lodge for South Carolina, on the first day of January, 1787. Their first grand master was the honourable William Drayton, then deputy grand master of East Florida'.[35] A month later, the Antients Grand Lodge for the State of South Carolina elected its grand officers; they were installed in office in March.

---

[33] Mackey, *History*, p. 261-2.

[34] *Ahiman Rezon* (Philadelphia, PA: Grand Lodge of Pennsylvania, 1825), p. 74.

[35] Ibid. p. 74. William Drayton (1732-1790), studied for the Bar at the Middle Temple alongside Peter Manigault. He established a law practice in Charleston and served as an assemblyman (1757-60, 1762-65), moving to East Florida in 1763 where he was appointed chief justice and to the royal council. A dispute with John Moultrie, the lieutenant-governor, led to his resignation, which was not accepted by London, and to his suspension for patriotic sympathies. Drayton's support for independence gifted him a positive reception on his return to Charleston where he was appointed to the bench and elected to the assembly. He embraced Antients freemasonry and at his death was grand master of the Ancient York Masons in South Carolina. His cousin, John Drayton (1766-1822), William Henry Drayton's son, was also an Antients' mason, junior grand warden in 1793 and grand master in 1800. He was governor of South Carolina from 1800-02 and again from 1808-10. As grand master, he led the state's masonic mourning for George Washington in February 1800.

Antients Grand Lodge for the State of South Carolina:
Grand Officers (1788)

Hon. William Drayton	Grand Master
Hon. Mordecai Gist	Deputy Grand Master
Edward Weyman, Esq.	Senior Grand Warden
Peter Smith, Esq.	Junior Grand Warden
Robert Knox, Esq.	Grand Treasurer
Alexander Alexander	Grand Secretary

A memorandum addressed to the Grand Lodges of England, Ireland and Scotland, and to those within America, was circulated following the installation:

> We, the Grand Lodge of Ancient York Masons for the State of South Carolina, and the masonic jurisdiction thereunto belonging, legally and constitutionally erected and organized, and in ample form assembled; beg leave, with all due respect, and in the true spirit of brotherly love, to announce to you our formation as such; to declare the purity of those motives which led to it; to assure you that, by this act, we mean not to dissolve, but to strengthen that union by which the ancient brethren throughout all nations are connected, and to request your countenance and correspondence.
>
> This act, brethren, is not without precedent, nor was the measure hastily or unadvisedly adopted; the truth of this assertion will appear from the facts stated in the preamble to those warrants we have granted the Lodges under our jurisdiction; a copy of which we have above prefixed, as containing a precise account of the foundation of this Grand Lodge.
>
> The necessity of the measure, and the motives which actuated the brethren to proceed in this important business, will appear obvious to the masonic world from a few plain facts. The Ancient Lodges in this State

were constituted under different authorities, and subject to different and very distinct jurisdictions; consequently the funds (the first natural object of which is the relief of such distress as comes immediately under the observation of the brethren) were necessarily subject to be diffused to distant regions, and thereby divided into such inconsiderable portions, that the charity was rendered of less effect than if those funds were more compact; add to this, that under the foregoing circumstances, and without a local head, it might become at least possible for the Lodges in this State to differ in sentiment, to deviate by degrees from the strict union of Freemasonry, and to vary from that conformity to ancient landmarks, and uniformity in working, which ought ever to be held sacred among the brethren.

To render the divine principle of charity more effectual, to cement harmony and brotherly love, to preserve union, conformity and uniformity among our Lodges, and to cultivate strict fellowship with all the Ancient Masonic bodies, within reach of our correspondence, were our motives for forming and establishing a Grand Lodge in this State, to 'guide, govern and direct' our local proceedings; and for the sincerity of those motives, we appeal to that Great Architect, who built up the human heart, and searches the inmost recesses of its fabric.

We entreat you to honor us with your friendly advice and fraternal assistance in the great work of Masonry, and we pray that the Supreme Builder and Ruler of Heaven and earth may graciously continue you, Right Worshipful brethren, in his holy keeping.[36]

Despite his partiality against the Antients and their 'innovations', Mackey concedes that 'the York Grand Lodge soon became very popular, and embraced a much larger number of the intelligent and influential citizens of the State within its fold than fell to the lot of its rival. Beginning in 1787 with five Lodges, it had in 1791, only four years after its establishment,

---

[36] Mackey, *History*, pp. 67-8.

thirty-five upon its registry. In fifty-five years of its existence the Grand Lodge of Free and Accepted Masons had accomplished just one-third of that amount of work'. He continues, commenting that 'it is clear that the Ancient York Masons had more enterprise and energy than their opponents ... [and] extended all over the country. In fact there were few [Moderns] lodges ... outside of the city, and, therefore, the most important part of Freemasonry in South Carolina is identified with the Ancient York Grand Lodge'.[37]

From the 1780s through to the second decade of the nineteenth century, South Carolina's Moderns and Antients 'ostracised the other' and vied for official recognition. Each grand lodge applied for and was granted an act of incorporation by the state legislature in 1791, but it was the Antients who would prevail. The Moderns 'granted very few warrants for the constitution of new Lodges' and their jurisdiction at the turn of the century was limited to some twelve lodges. The Antients had at least fifty-two lodges and their influence extended into the adjacent states and territories, with Antients lodges constituted in North Carolina, Georgia and Florida.

Unlike their rivals, the Antients' grand masters in South Carolina included a roll-call of war heroes: William Drayton (1787-1789), General Mordecai Gist (1790-1791) and Major Thomas Bowen (1792). In contrast, the Moderns were led by John Deas (1735-1790), who succeeded Egerton Leigh as provincial grand master in 1781 during the British occupation of Charleston. Deas had fought in the ranks in defence of Charleston in 1778 and in 1779 loaned South Carolina's new government almost £18,000, but

---

[37] Ibid., pp. 69-73.

when Charleston fell to the British in 1780 he swapped allegiance.[38] Although not exiled, Deas was fined 12% of his estates following Independence.[39]

Despite the circumstances of his installation, Deas remained in office after the war and as the antipathy between the Moderns and Antients deepened, he petitioned the Grand Lodge of England to recognise his title as grand master.

The first letter to reach London was dated 4 January 1788,[40] with a second sent five days later.[41] The content was the same in each case:

Petition of the Regular Constituted Lodges in the State of South Carolina...
That from divers causes the lodges in this state acknowledging the jurisdiction of the Grand Lodge of England have for a considerable time past been without a Grand Master to preside over them.

That in consequence thereof on the Festival of St John the Evangelist, we being congregated in Grand Lodge unanimously made the choice of

---

[38] For additional background information cf. Alain Bernheim, 'Lodges and Grand Lodges in South Carolina, 1788-1824', *AQC*, 125 (2012), 131-70.

[39] John's brother, David, had also been close to the crown and was twice nominated for a place on the royal council, the last being in 1770. He cooperated with the British and was similarly fined 12% of his estates, although a later petition for relief was successful. Both brothers were successful planters and merchants, slave traders and importers. In addition to an impressive town house near the centre of Charleston, John Deas owned the 3,000-acre *Thorogood* estate, inherited by his wife from her step-father, George Seaman, and rice and indigo plantations in Goose Creek, together with more than 200 slaves. Among other property, he also owned the 920-acre *Mount Pleasant* plantation on the Combahee River. Cf., Michael James Heitzler, *Goose Creek, South Carolina: A Definitive History 1670-2003* (Charleston, SC: The History Press, 2005), volume 1, pp. 257-8.

[40] UGLE: GBR 1991 HC 28/E/7.

[41] UGLE: GBR 1991 HC 28/E/8. Signed by Provincial Grand Officers John Troup, DPGM; Barnard Beckman, PSGW; John McCall, PJGW; John Sandford Dart, PGTr; James Ballantine, PGSec; and James Lynah, PGSwBr.

John Deas Esquire to be Grand Master of this state pro tempore and has been so since St John's day in the year 5781 [1781].

And we have to assure you that he is a hearty & zealous Mason, and who has served in all offices, as well in private lodges, as in the Grand Lodge of this state, who reveres the Craft and by his worth and character may reflect honour on the office of Grand Master of South Carolina.

May it therefore please your Worship to appoint John Deas, Esquire to be Grand Master of South Carolina.

And your Petitioners shall ever pray etc. etc.

A postscript to the letter notes the success of Antients freemasonry in South Carolina, observing that although they had originally operated under the Scottish Constitution, the Antients had 'declared independence' and formed their own Grand Lodge:

> we are sorry to observe that ... there has been introduced into this and the Northern States a kind of Schism in the Craft by a set of Masons who style themselves 'Free and Accepted Masons established in this State according to the Old Constitutions'.

The postscript informed London of a third masonic group working under the name of 'Knights & Princes of Free Accepted Perfect and Sublime Masons within the jurisdiction of the Grand Elect ineffable and sublime Lodge of Perfection'. And it ended by stressing the importance of receiving confirmation from London that Deas's position as grand master had met with their approval.

That the two letters were dated and dispatched within five days of each other indicates the importance attached to the correspondence. Indeed, in a move that may underline his concern, Deas wrote a third letter on 16 January 1788 reconfirming his willingness to accept the position of grand master of South Carolina, if permitted by London.[42] The implication is that Antients freemasonry was in the ascendance and that Deas's position as provincial grand master was under threat, as was Moderns freemasonry itself.

Having received no reply, the Moderns sent a follow-up letter. Dated 8 January 1790, it referred to the earlier correspondence, enclosed copies, and once more requested a response.[43] On this occasion a reply was forthcoming. The minutes of South Carolina's Moderns' grand lodge note that Deas wrote to the Grand Lodge of England on 7 June 1790 confirming receipt of their reply and asking for guidance as to what fees and reporting arrangements would be appropriate.[44]

The correspondence between Charleston and London suggests that there had been no masonic contact for some years. The letter of 9 January 1788 includes a request that the grand secretary of English Grand Lodge (to whom it was addressed) 'insert at the top of the petition the name, titles etc. of the Grand Master of England'. And a later paragraph asked for help as to 'how we should govern ourselves towards [the Antients]' and 'for a list of names of all the lodges in Europe, Asia, Africa and America who acknowledge the jurisdiction of the Grand Lodge of England'.

---

[42] UGLE: HC 28/E/10.

[43] UGLE: HC 28/E/11.

[44] UGLE: HC 28/E/13-14. As an aside, the minutes raise an issue regarding black freemasons in South Carolina. They record that John Troup, the deputy grand master, had received a letter from William Luyten, in which Luyten states his intention to establish 'a Lodge of Free Negroes'. The Grand Lodge of South Carolina took the proposal seriously and determined that for 'ridiculing, vilifying & making a mock of the Craft in the most insolent audacious, infamous and scandalous manner', Luyten and his associates would be excluded from freemasonry and copies of the relevant decision would be sent to all the lodges under their jurisdiction. Given his later actions, it is unlikely that Luyten's proposal was intended to be taken at face value. William Luytten (d.1800), was cabinet maker and loyalist merchant. He lived in Charleston and thereafter in Camden. Cf. E. Milby Burton, *Charleston Furniture, 1700-1825* (Columbia, SC: USC Press, 1997), pp. 103-4.

The absence of a response from London was not a result of Charleston's letters having failed to be delivered: they are held on file. It reflected either uncertainty in London as to how or whether to reply or was the result of incompetent bureaucracy.

London's communications with South Carolina had been meagre for years. The earliest correspondence on file is a letter sent by James Heseltine, the grand secretary, dated 4 September 1769.[45] Although he asks for information – 'I should be very happy to have an account of the state of masonry in your part of the world' – Heseltine actually wants to explain the fiasco of the failed attempt to incorporate the Grand Lodge of England by royal charter and asks that an explanatory letter be circulated to South Carolina's lodges to clarify London's position. A response from Solomon's Lodge dated 25 January 1770 confirms receipt and that the missive was being circulated as requested.[46] A second letter followed from Marine Lodge.[47]

The communication between London and Charleston afterwards was one-way, with Solomon's Lodge writing to London with information on the health of South Carolina freemasonry, providing a membership list, and details of lodges constituted in the province.[48] There is no extant correspondence from the mid-1770s until 1788.

Among the co-signatories to the 9 January 1788 letter from Charleston is Michael Kalteisen (1729-1807). Kalteisen had been master of Solomon's Lodge in Charleston in the 1770s and as Bernheim notes was on the 1774 membership list for lodge No. 190 (Antients), constituted that September.[49] But Kalteisen is best known as the founder of the German Friendly Society

---

[45] UGLE: HC 28/E/1.
[46] UGLE: HC 28/E/2.
[47] UGLE: HC 28/E/3.
[48] UGLE: HC 28/E/4-6.
[49] Alain Bernheim, 'Lodges and Grand Lodges in South Carolina', *Transactions of the Quatuor Coronati Lodge, No. 2076*, 125 (2012), 131-70. Cf. also, Lane's *Masonic Records*.

(1766), one of the oldest benevolent societies in the United States that is still active.[50]

Born in 1729 in Machtolsheim, a village in Württemberg, Germany, Kalteisen migrated to South Carolina in 1747 as an indentured servant.[51] He discharged his indenture in 1753 and acquired 50 acres of land in the German-speaking area of Dutch Fork, between the Broad and Saluda Rivers. Marriage brought another 150 acres and land grants added a further 2,000 acres spread across the colony's periphery.[52] Kalteisen was a migrant entrepreneur who developed a series of ventures from wood wholesaling to a province-wide messenger and transport service to inn-keeping. But although affluent, Kalteisen was largely excluded from conventional politics which were dominated by the planter and merchant elites. In response, he co-founded the Fellowship Society in 1762 which evolved into the Mechanics Party to represent the interests of Charleston's artisans and smaller merchants, although it became factionalised and two years later Kalteisen resigned.

In May 1775, shortly after news of the battles of Lexington and Concord reached South Carolina, Kalteisen co-founded a patriotic company to fight against the British: the German Fusiliers. Members of the German Friendly Society joined him and Kalteisen was one of three chosen as officers. He received a commission in the Continental Army in 1776 as Commissary, to which was added in 1778 that of Wagon Master General and, in 1782, Captain of Marines on the *South Carolina*, a frigate. Following the war, he was elected an assemblyman (1783–90) and to the 1788 constitutional convention in 1788; he later obtained several government offices, including command of Fort Johnson in Charleston Harbour, a position he occupied at his death.[53]

---

[50] Mary C. Ferrari, 'Charity, Folly and Politics: Charles Town's Social Clubs on the Eve of the Revolution', *South Carolina Historical Magazine*, 112.1/2 (2011), 50-83.

[51] Helene M. Riley, 'Michael Kalteisen and the Founding of the German Friendly Society in Charleston', *South Carolina Historical Magazine*, 100.1 (1999), 29-48.

[52] Ibid.

[53] Ibid., esp. 66-8.

Kalteisen's convictions regarding benevolence and morality were shared by other Antients' freemasons. Antients freemasonry had pioneered mutual benevolence and was recognised for its sociability and spirituality. But with the patriotic movement giving voice to more radical concepts, including broader democracy and republicanism, Antients freemasonry became imbued with a richer ethic. To be a 'good man and true' was now an almost sacred cause, ranking alongside decency, integrity and equality as core components of an existential post-revolutionary utopian ideal.

The 'Masonic Discourse delivered at Greenfield, Massachusetts'[54] and the 'Masonic Discourse at Haverhill, Massachusetts'[55] offer examples of the trend, something reinforced by what was seen as a concord between masonic and republican ideas.

> It is well known that our Order was at first composed of scientific and ingenious men who assembled to improve the arts and sciences and cultivate a pure and sublime system of morality. Knowledge at that time was restricted to a chosen few but when the invention of printing had opened the means of instruction to all ranks of people, then the generous cultivators of Masonry communicated with cheerfulness to the world those secrets of the arts and sciences which had been transmitted and improved from the foundation of the institutions then our Fraternity bent their principal attention to the cultivation of morality. And Masonry may now be defined as a moral institution, intended to promote individual and social happiness.[56]

---

[54] Delivered on 24 June 1802.

[55] Cf., *Two sermons on the death of Rev. Ezra Ripley, D.D* (Boston, MA: James Munroe & Co., 1841).

[56] From an address by De Witt Clinton, before Holland Lodge, the evening of his installation, 24 December 1793, reprinted in *The Craftsman*, 1866. Cf, also, Nancy Beadie, 'Encouraging Useful Knowledge…' in Benjamin Justice (ed.), *The Founding Fathers and "The Great Contest"*, pp. 94-6. Cf. www.masonicworld.com/education/articles/golden_sentences.htm, accessed 28 September 2014.

> Our institution asserts, in language not to be misunderstood, the natural equality of mankind. It declares that all brethren are upon a level, and it throws open its hospitable doors to all men of all nations. It admits of no rank, except the priority of merit, and its only aristocracy is the nobility of virtue.[57]

The social and political changes that helped mould post-revolutionary American society were reflected in Antients freemasonry. Unlike the Moderns, Antients freemasonry captured the prevailing zeitgeist of democracy, republicanism and Enlightenment idealism, and was perceived as promoting morality and virtue. This was epitomised in the person of George Washington, the nation's founding father, commander-in-chief, president and Enlightenment and Antients freemason.[58] And it was evident in the Deep South, demonstrated by the extent to which politicians were prominent freemasons.

A civic ceremony and procession in Charleston on 15 February 1800 marked the death of Washington on 14 December 1799, and a week later in the evening of 22 February, the Antients conducted a masonic funeral ceremony in memory of Washington. The Moderns were excluded from both events.

> On Saturday evening, the 22 of February, 1800, Masonic Funeral Honors, in memory of the late General George Washington, who was the friend and brother of the Ancient Craft, were performed in the new Lodge Room, in Charleston, by the Friendship Lodge, No. IX, Ancient York Masons. There were present, besides the members of the said Lodge, the Right Worshipful Grand Master, Lieutenant Governor Drayton; the Right Worshipful Deputy Grand Master, Colonel John Mitchell; the rest of the

---

[57] De Witt Clinton, 24 December 1793.
[58] George Washington was initiated an Antients freemason on 4 November 1752 at Fredericksburg, Virginia.

Grand Officers; the Officers of the private Lodges, who hold their meetings in town; and a numerous assemblage of visiting brethren.

The room was shrouded with black, strewed with tears, death's head's etc. In the centre was a dome, supported by five columns, dressed with crape and Masonic funeral decorations, resting upon a platform elevated a number of steps from the floor - the whole suitably lighted. Under the dome was placed a coffin, with the appropriate emblems; over the dome, a gilt urn, inscribed with the name of the deceased. Many other emblems and inscriptions were displayed, in a style adapted to the occasion.

The ceremonies were performed in a most solemn and impressive manner, and agreeably to Ancient form. Several excellent admonitions, and a Masonic funeral service, were delivered by the Worshipful Master. A band of music assisted, and anthems, and a solemn dirge, composed for the purpose, were performed. It is not easy to express the profound respect and veneration, the deep regret for departed worth and excellence, and, at the same time, the melancholy pleasure which filled every heart, and were displayed in every countenance.[59]

Antients freemasonry had become part of American's social and political fabric.

---

[59] Mackey, *History*, pp. 83-4.

Appendix Three

SELECTED LODGE MEMBERSHIP DATA

Solomon's Lodge, Charleston
Membership List (c.1770) [1]

Michael Kalteisen	*Master*
Thomas Harper	*Senior Warden*
William Graham	*Junior Warden*
Jacob Boomer	*Treasurer*
William Swallow	*Secretary*

John Miller	George Flagg
Darby Pendergrass	Samuel Bowers
William Holliday	Isaac de Costa
John Blott	John Ward
James Crawley	Thomas Barton
Philip Henry	Joseph Elliott
William Burrows	Barnard Beckman
John Blake	John Hatfield
William Littany	Edward Legge Sr.
John Miers	John Goldie
John Bradwell	Robert Beard
Benjamin Legare	John Badeley
Richard Cole	William Coats
Charles Roberts	William Wayne
James Strickland	Edward Legge Jr.
Samuel Gordon	William Rudhall
John Smith	William Cripps

---

[1] UGLE: GBR 1991 HC 28/E/5.

Grenadier's Lodge, No. 481, Georgia
Membership List, 21 February 1771 [2]

    Thomas Lee
    Oliver Bowen
    Edward Langworthy
    Jacon Oates
    John Drybrough
    John Morton
    William Time
    Sinclair Waters
    William Ray
    Gabriel Allan
    Samuel Elbert
    Joseph Habersham
    Francis Henry Harris
    John Habersham
    -   Chiffille
    James Anderson

---

[2] UGLE: GBR 1991 HC 28/G/16.

Appendix Four

GEORGIA'S GRAND OFFICERS (1780), ANTIENTS AND MODERNS

Grand Officers of the Grand Lodge of Ancient York Masons (1780)
- Antients-

Lt. Gov. John Drayton	Grand Master
John Mitchell	Deputy Grand Master
Benjamin Cudworth	Senior Grand Warden
Seth Paine	Junior Grand Warden
Lewis Cameron	Grand Treasurer
Alexander Alexander	Grand Secretary
Jervis H. Stevens	Grand Marshal
Alexander McCleish	Grand Pursuivant
Israel Meyers	Grand Tyler

Grand Officers of the Grand Lodge of Free and Accepted Masons (1780)
- Moderns -

Hon. John F. Grimke	Grand Master
James Lynah, MD	Deputy Grand Master
George Flagg, Esq.	Senior Grand Warden
Samuel Wilson, MD	Junior Grand Warden
Rev. Thomas Mills, DD	Grand Chaplain
-	Grand Treasurer
Brian Cape, Esq.	Grand Secretary
Mr. Lewis C. M. de Mortmain	Grand Sword Bearer
Robert Wilson, MD	Grand Steward
James Troup, Esq.	Grand Steward

Mr. Charles Kershaw	Grand Steward
Mr. Thomas Cape	Grand Steward
Mr. John Cape	Grand Steward
Mr. Paul Hill	Grand Tyler

Selected Bibliography

A multitude of books record and discuss the early history of the American colonies and of South Carolina and Georgia from both an American and British perspective. Detailed data and other information is also readily sourced online, including a range of sites offering electronic copies of primary documents from the period. The sources detailed below represent only a small fraction of relevant primary and secondary material.

Manuscripts

When I wrote *Foundations* in 2010 I commented that the digitisation and upload of primary data sources had opened up historical research in a way that would have been considered inconceivable less than a decade before. The revolution has continued and as I revise this note on the cusp on 2018 an avalanche of data has been made available for remote viewing and analysis. The advantages to the researcher are obvious; the downside is that considerable time can be expended sifting for relevance.

One of the most valuable data sources for this work has been digitised copies of eighteenth-century American and British newspapers within the *Burney* newspaper collection and on US websites, not all free to access. Other excellent resources include *British History Online*, a digital collection of primary and secondary material including the complete *Victoria County History of England* and the *Journals of the House of Commons* and *House of Lords*. The *Egmont (Sir John Percival) Papers* at the British Library in London provide a unique picture of colonial life in Georgia. They are online at the University of Georgia: http://fax.libs.uga.edu/egmont/. And there are several American websites analogous to *British History Online* such as *Facts on File* at www.fofweb.com and *Digital History* at www.digitalhistory.org.

The City of London, Middlesex and Westminster Sessions Papers and Quarterly Sessions Papers provide a record of eighteenth century London life. They are held in hard copy at the London Metropolitan Archives and are accessible online at *London Lives*: www.londonlives.org.

Biographical material can be sourced at the American National Biography Online: anb.org; the Oxford Dictionary of National Biography: www.oxforddnb.com; and the Royal Society's *Sackler Archive*, which includes information on past Fellows of the Royal Society. This can be accessed at www.royalsociety.org/library/collections/biographical-records.

Much of the archival material at the United Grand Lodge of England, Library & Archives in London, including the Minutes of the Grand Lodge of England, the Minutes of the Antients Grand Lodge of England, historic correspondence and other manuscripts, including lodge minute books and membership registers, are only accessible in person and by permission. However the early Minutes of the Grand Lodge of England and Antients Grand Lodge of England have now been digitised and can be downloaded from www.quatuorcoronti.com, the leading masonic research lodge.

Manuscript collections at the University Library of Cambridge, the repository for the Houghton Papers, and Oxford University's Bodleian Libraries, are accessible only in person.

British Parliamentary Papers, including the *Calendar of State Papers Colonial, America and West Indies*, *Calendar of Treasury Books and Papers*, *Treasury Books and Papers* and *Calendar of State Papers Domestic*; the *Survey of London*; the *House of Lords and House of Commons' Journals*; and the *Statutes of the Realm*, are available online at www.british-history.ac.uk.

Other relevant portals include the Institute of Historical Research at www.history.ac.uk, *The History of Parliament* at www.histparl.ac.uk, and the *House of Commons Parliamentary Papers* at www.parlipapers.chadwyck.co.uk.

I would also recommend:

Adams Family Papers	masshist.org/digitaladams
British Periodicals Online	britishperiodicals.chadwyck.co.uk
Connected Histories	connectedhistories.org
Early English Books Online (EEBO)	gale.cengage.co.uk
Eighteenth Century Collections Online (ECCO)	gale.cengage.co.uk
The National Archives	discovery.nationalarchives.gov.uk
Yale Law School	avalon.law.yale.edu

OTHER SELECTED PRIMARY SOURCES[3]

Anderson, James. *The Constitutions of the Freemasons*. London: John Senex & John Hooke, 1723.

- *The Ancient Constitutions of the Free and Accepted Masons*. Enlarged Second Edition. London: B. Creake, 1731.
- *The new book of constitutions of the antient and honourable fraternity of free and accepted masons*. London: Caesar Ward and Richard Chandler for Anderson, 1738.
- *The Constitutions of the Ancient and honourable fraternity of Free and Accepted Masons*. Revised and enlarged by John Entick. London: J. Scott, 1756.

Anonymous [prob. Samuel Spencer]. *A Defence of Freemasonry*. London: published privately, 1765.

Barlowe, Arthur. *The First Voyage to Roanoke, 1584*. Published in Richard Hakluyt, *Principal Navigations, Voyages, Traffiques and Discoveries of the English*. London: 1589.

Dashwood, J.R. *Early Records of the Grand Lodge of England according to the Old Institutions*, Quatuor Coronatum Antigrapha, Volume XI. London: QC, 1958.

- *The Minutes of the Grand Lodge of Freemasons of England 1740-58*, Masonic Reprints, vol. XII. London: QC, 1960.

Dermott, Lawrence. *Ahiman Rezon*. London, 1756. Also later editions published in London, Dublin and Philadelphia 1764, 1778, 1780, 1782, 1787, 1795, 1797 and 1825.

Dobbs, Arthur. *An Essay on the Trade and Improvement of Ireland*. Dublin, Ireland: J. Smith & W. Bruce, 1729.

Gwynn, Robin. *Huguenot Heritage*. Brighton: Sussex Academic Press, 2001.

Hales, Stephen. *A sermon preached before the trustees for establishing the colony of Georgia in America; ... on Thursday, March 21. 1734*. London, 1734.

Hansard, T.C. *Parliamentary Debates, 1803 to the Present Time*. London: Hansard, 1819.

Huguenot Society of London. *Registers of the French Conformed Churches at St Patrick and St Mary, Dublin*. Quarto Series, published on CD-ROM, 2004, Vol. VII.

---

[3] Soft copies of Anderson's Constitutions, Dermott's *Ahiman Rezon* and many (but not all) of the books and manuscripts cited below are available at ECCO, EEBO, and www.archive.org.

- *Registers of the French Nonconformist Churches, Dublin*. Vol. XIV.
- *Register of the French Church, Portarlington, Ireland*. Vol. XIX.
- *Registers of the French Church of Threadneedle Street, London, Part III*. Vol. XVI
- *Registers of the French Church of Threadneedle Street, London, Part IV*. Vol. XXIII.
- *Livres des Conversiones et des Reconnoissances faites a L'Eglise Francoise de la Savoye, 1684-1702*. Vol. XXII.
- *Register of the Church of Hungerford Market, later Castle Street, London*. Vol. XXXI.
- *Registers of the Church of Le Carre and Berwick Street*. Vol. XXV.
- *Register of the Church of Rider Court, London, 1700-1738*. Vol. XXX.
- *Register of the Church of St Martin Orgars with its History and that of Swallow Street*. Vol. XXXVII.
- *Registers of the Churches of The Tabernacle Glasshouse Street and Leicester Fields, London 1688-1783*. Vol. XXIX.
- *Registres des Eglises de la Chapelle Royale de Saint James, 1700-1756, et de Swallow Street, 1690-1709*. Vol. XXVIII.
- *Registres des Eglises de la Savoye de Spring Gardens et des Grecs 1684-1900*. Vol. XXVI.
- *Registres des Quatres Eglises du Petit Charenton de West Street de Pearl Street et de Crispin Street*. Vol. XXXII.
- *Registers of the Church of the Artillery, Spitalfields, 1691-1786*. Vol. XLII.
- *Registers of the French Churches of La Patente de Soho, Wheeler Street, Swan Street & Hoxton, also The Repetoire General*. Vol. XLV.
- *Naturalizations of Foreign Protestants in the American and West India Colonies Pursuant to Statute 13 George II, c.7*. Vol. XXIV.

Lane, John. *Masonic Records 1717-1894*. HRI Online Publications, 2011 at http://www.hrionline.ac.uk/lane/index.php

Laurens, Henry. *The Papers of Henry Laurens*. Columbia, SC: USC Press, 1968.
- *Extracts from the Proceedings of the High Court of Vice-Admiralty, in Charlestown, South Carolina, upon six ... informations adjudged by ... E. Leigh: ... and some general observations on American Custom-House officers, and courts of Vice-Admiralty*. Charleston, 1768).
- *Extracts ... second edition, with an appendix (containing strictures upon ... a pamphlet entitled, The Man Unmasked, published by E. Leigh...* Charleston, 1769.

Lee, Arthur. *Answer to the Considerations on Certain Political Transactions of the Province of South Carolina.* London: privately published, 1774.

Leigh, Egerton. *The Man Unmasked.* Charleston, 1768.

Martyn, Benjamin. *Reasons for establishing the colony of Georgia, with regard to the trade of Great Britain...* London: W. Meadows, 1733.

- *An Impartial Enquiry into the State and Utility of the Province of Georgia.* London: W. Meadows, 1741.

Montesquieu. *De L'Espirit des Loix.* Amsterdam: Chatelain, 1748.

Montgomery, Robert. *A discourse concerning the design'd establishment of a new colony to the south of Carolina, in the most delightful country of the universe.* London, 1717.

- *A description of the Golden Islands, with an account of the undertaking now on foot for making.* London: J. Morphew, 1720.

Purry, Jean Pierre. *A Memorial.* London, 1724.

Ramsay, David. *The History of the American Revolution.* Philadelphia, 1789.

Richmond, Charles. *A Duke and His Friends: The Life and Letters of the Second duke of Richmond.* London: Hutchinson & Co., 1911. Reprinted Husain Press, 2008.

Roberts, R.A. *A Calendar of Inner Temple Records. Vol. V: 1751-1800.* London, 1936.

Sachse, Julius F. *Washington's Masonic Correspondence as found among the Washington Papers in the Library of Congress.* Philadelphia, PA: New Era Printing, 1915.

Salley. A.S. (ed.). *Register of St Philip's Parish, Charles Town, South Carolina, 1720-58.* Charleston, S.C.: published privately, 1904.

- *Death Notices in the South Carolina Gazette, 1732-1775.* Columbia, SC: Historical Commission of South Carolina, 1917.

Songhurst, W.J. *The Minutes of the Grand Lodge of Freemasons of England 1723-1739.* Masonic Reprints, vol. X. London: QC, 1913.

Stephens, Thomas. *The Hard Case of the Distressed People of Georgia.* London, 1742.

Strype, John. *Survey of London.* London, 1720.

Talifer, Patrick and Anderson, Hugh, et al. *A True and Historical Narrative of the Colony of Georgia...* Charles Town, SC: privately published, 1741.

Trustees, Georgia. *An account, shewing the progress of the colony of Georgia in America from it's [sic] first establishment.* London, 1742.

Collections of the Georgia Historical Society. Savannah, 1840, et al, including

- *Proceedings of the Georgia Council of Safety, 1775-1777*. Savannah, GA: Georgia Historical Society, 1901.

SELECTED SECONDARY SOURCES

Barratt, Norris S. & Sachse, Julius S. *Freemasonry in Pennsylvania, 1727-1907*. Philadelphia, PA: Grand Lodge of Philadelphia. Vol's I (1908), II (1909) & III (1919).

Barzilay, Karen Northrop. *Fifty Gentlemen Total Strangers: A Portrait of the First Continental Congress*. PhD Dissertation to the Graduate Faculty of The College of William and Mary, VA: Ann Arbor, 2009.

Berman, Richard, *Foundations of Modern Freemasonry*. Brighton: Sussex Academic Press, 2011.
- *Foundations*, second revised edition, 2014. (See bibliography.)
- *Schism: the Battle that Forged Freemasonry*. Brighton: Sussex Academic Press, 2012. (Also see the bibliography.)

Blackburn, Robin. *The Making of New World Slavery*. New York, NY: Verso, 1997.

Bullock, Stephen. *Revolutionary Brotherhood: Freemasonry and the Transformation of the American Social Order, 1730-1840*. Chapel Hill, NC: UNC Press, Institute of Early American History and Culture, 1996. (Also see the bibliography.)

Carpenter, Audrey T. *John Theophilus Desaguliers. A Natural Philosopher, Engineer and Freemason in Newtonian England*. London: Bloomsbury, 2011.

Carroll, Bartholomew R. *Historical Collections of South Carolina*. New York, NY: Harper & Bros., 1836) vol. I.

Cashin, Edward J. *Colonial Augusta:"Key of the Indian Country"*. Macon, GA: Mercer University Press, 1986.

Chamberlayne, John. *Magnae Britanniae Notitia*. London: various editions.

Clarke, William Bordley. *Early and Historic Freemasonry of Georgia, 1733/4 – 1800*. Savannah, GA: published privately, 1924.

Clark, Peter. *British Clubs and Societies 1580-1800*. Oxford: OUP, 2000.

Cohen, Lester H. (ed.). David Ramsay, *The History of the American Revolution*. Indianapolis, IN: Liberty Fund, 2012.

Coulter, E. Merton & Sayle, Albert B. (eds.). *A List of the Early Settlers of Georgia*. Athens, GA: University of Georgia Press, 1983.

Dobson, David. *Scottish Emigration to Colonial America, 1607-1785*. Athens, GA: University of Georgia Press, 2004.

Dyer, Colin. *The Grand Stewards and Their Lodge*. London: Grand Steward's Lodge, 1985.

Eccleshall, George. *The Old King's Arms Lodge, 1725-2000*. London: published privately, 2001.

Edgar, Walter B. *South Carolina: A History*. Columbia, SC: USC Press, 1998.

- *Letter Book of Robert Pringle 1737-1745*. Columbia, SC: USC Press, 1972.

Edgar, Walter B. and Bailey, N. Louise (eds.). *Biographical Dictionary of the South Carolina House of Representatives, 1692-1775*. Columbia, SC: USC Press, 1977.

Gould, Robert Freke. *History of Freemasonry Throughout the World*. New York, NY: Charles Scribner's Sons, 1936, vol. 5. (reprint)

- *The History of Freemasonry: Its Antiquities, Symbols, Constitutions, Customs, Etc.* London: J. Beacham, 1885.

Harland-Jacobs, Jessica. *Builders of Empire: Freemasonry and British Imperialism, 1717-1927*. Chapel Hill, NC: UNC Press, 2007.

Heizler, Michael James. *Goose Creek, South Carolina: A Definitive History 1670-2003*. Charleston, SC: History Press, 2005.

Kolchin, Peter. *American Slavery: 1619-1877*. New York, NY: Hill & Wang, 2003.

Lane, Lauren E. Gender. *Labor, and Virtue in Eighteenth-Century Georgia*. University of Miami Scholarly Repository, Open Access Dissertations Electronic Theses and Dissertations. 4 May 2012.

Lemmings, David. *Professors of the Law: Barristers and English Legal Culture in the Eighteenth Century*. Oxford: OUP, 2000.

Library Committee of the Grand Lodge of Pennsylvania. *The History of the Grand Lodge of Pennsylvania*. Philadelphia, PA: Grand Lodge of Pennsylvania, 1877.

Mackey, Albert G. *History of Freemasonry in South Carolina*. Columbia, SC: South Carolinian Steam Press, 1861.

Marshall P.J. *The Oxford History of the British Empire: The Eighteenth Century*. Oxford, OUP, 1998.

Massey, Gregory D. *John Laurens and the American Revolution*. Columbia, SC: USC Press, 2000.

McCrady, Edward. *The History of South Carolina under the Royal Government, 1719-1776*. New York, NY: Macmillan, 1899.

McDonough, Daniel J. *Christopher Gadsden and Henry Laurens: The Parallel Lives of Two American Patriots*. Selinsgrove, PA: Susquehanna University Press, 2000.

Meigs, William M. *The Life of Jared Ingersoll*. Philadelphia, PA: J.B. Lippincott, 1897.

Morgan (ed.), Edmund S. *Prologue To Revolution: Sources And Documents On The Stamp Act Crisis, 1764-1766*. Chapel Hill, NC: UNC Press, 1959.

Poser, Norman S. *Lord Mansfield: Justice in the Age of Reason*. Montreal, Canada: McGill-Queen's University Press, 2013.

Pressly, Paul M. *On the Rim of the Caribbean: Colonial Georgia and the British Atlantic World*. Athens GA: University of Georgia Press, 2013.

Puckrein, Gary A. *Little England: A Plantation Society and Anglo-Barbadian Politics, 1627-1700*. New York, NY: NYUP, 1984.

Reese, R. (ed.). *The Clamorous Malcontents. Criticisms and Defences of the Colony of Georgia, 1741-1743*. Savannah, GA: Beehive Press, 1973.

Ross, Peter. *A Standard History of Freemasonry for the State of New York*. New York, NY: Lewis, 1899.

Sachse, Julius S. *Old Masonic Lodges of Pennsylvania, Moderns & Ancients, 1730-1800*. Philadelphia, PA: 1912.

Sedgwick, R. (ed.). *The History of Parliament: the House of Commons, 1715-1754*. Cambridge: CUP, 1970.

Smith, Julia Floyd. *Slavery and Rice Culture in Low Country Georgia, 1750-1860*. Knoxville, TN: University of Tennessee Press, 1985.

Smith, William Roy. *South Carolina as a Royal Province, 1719-1776*. New York: Macmillan, 1903.

Spalding, Phinizy (ed.). *Oglethorpe in Perspective. Georgia's Founder after Two Hundred Years*. Tuscaloose, AL: University of Alabama Press, 1989. (See bibliography.)

Taylor, Alan. *Slavery and War in Virginia, 1772-1832, The Internal Enemy*. New York, NY: W.W. Norton, 2013.

Underwood, James L. *The Constitution of South Carolina: the Relationship of the Legislative, Executive and Judicial Branches.* Columbia, SC: USC Press, 1989.

Wood, Betty. *Slavery in Colonial Georgia, 1730-1755.* Athens, GA: University of Georgia Press, 1984.

JOURNAL ARTICLES

There are literally hundreds of relevant journal articles and many more that are of tangential interest or complementary. Those cited in the footnotes provide a small tip of a far larger iceberg. *JSTOR* (jstor.org) is one of the better starting points for further research.

THE OLD
STABLES
PRESS

• Oxfordshire •

www.ingramcontent.com/pod-product-compliance
Lightning Source LLC
Chambersburg PA
CBHW031137160426
43193CB00008B/168